# ROOTS IN THE RHONDDA

## Patricia Luther Mellor

*This is a poignant family saga which follows the author's remarkable story from her roots in the Rhondda to her life today, oscillating between France and Wales, having gone global (to Pakistan) in between. This engaging story is lively and flows well throughout, highlighting the importance of education in her escape from poverty.*

Professor Eleri Jones, Dean of Research, Cardiff Metropolitan University

*This moving and extraordinary story of a family past and present crosses continents and oceans and covers over a hundred years in time. It takes us back to the early days of industrialisation and the sinking of mines in our valleys which led to the boom era of coal and all the vast changes that entailed. In so doing, it portrays the social history of the Rhondda and the uplifting spirit of its people. At the root of it all is the resilience of love, determination and courage that, despite hard and often sad times, produces an optimism that has given the extended Stevens family a story that deserves to be preserved.*

Kay Leakey, Senior Deputy Head (retired), Treorchy Comprehensive, Rhondda

*This fascinating tale charts the history of a number of generations of a working-class family from the Rhondda Valley. Their supportive and close-knit community in the village of Ynyshir meant that help was always at hand when times were hard. At the centre of village life was the church which afforded them another constant source of hope and strength in the struggle to survive. It is heart-warming to read how the family's firm Christian faith stood them in good stead as they strove to improve their lot. Their story serves as an splendid example to those who struggle to lift themselves out of the harsh circumstances into which they were born whilst still holding their place of birth and its people deep in their heart.*

Rev Paul Bigmore, Vicar of Saint Anne's Church, Ynyshir, Rhondda

# ROOTS IN THE RHONDDA

© *Patricia Luther Mellor* 2019

**ISBN: 9781699193006**

Front cover art work by Dinah Quesnel
Front cover photo of author as child
Back cover photos: author's own

Waye Forward Publishing, Cardiff

www.wayeforward.com

This memoir is dedicated to the memory of my dear parents, Annie May and Thomas Arthur Stevens, my late husband Archie Jonathan Luther and to my children Mark and Angie and my husband, Ray.

# ROOTS IN THE RHONDDA

*Patricia Luther Mellor*

# Acknowledgements

I wish to thank my daughter Angie for all her invaluable help during the writing of this memoir: for her constructive criticism and editing of my work and for helping me to find a means of publishing it. Her constant encouragement kept me from giving up when the road was long.

I am grateful also to my son Mark for inspiring me to get started on looking back on my family's antecedents, my own progress through life and his father's background.

I thank my husband Ray for his unstinting support, his patience in reading and re-reading my work, pointing out and eradicating all the inevitable slips and for his unfailing encouragement.

I am grateful to my friend Frank Farmery for his advice on creative writing at the outset which, I hope, has made my memoir more readable for the public. I am grateful to my friend Dinah Quesnel for her artistic depiction of the Rhondda which embellishes the front cover. My cousin Jane Buttery has helped me constantly with research into the Stevens family and has furnished many family photos and all the information to produce our Family Tree. My cousin Maureen Pountney has helped me enormously by filling in information about her father (and my uncle) Davie and our grandparents after they moved to Nuneaton. My nephew Reggie Luther has been invaluable in furnishing most of the details concerning the Luther family. My sister Ann has provided the names of all our favourite Welsh songs and hymns and, together with my sisters Morfydd and Mary and my brother Michael, reminded me of various anecdotes and incidents of our youth. I am grateful to them all for their help and support.

Finally, I am most grateful to Tim Watkins, Waye Forward Publishing. He has been my mentor and guide throughout the process of bringing my memoir to publication.

# Contents

# Prologue

The Rhondda into which I was born on 22nd October 1934 was a dark, dirty, dreary valley sunk into one of the deepest depressions of modern times. Despite the deprived environment of abject poverty of the coal-mining area where my parents struggled to bring me up, I always considered myself lucky to have been born with a "silver spoon in my mouth," albeit rich only in the love and security of my parents, Tom and Annie May Stevens. I was brought into the world without fuss by the local midwife just ten months after my parents had set up home in "rooms" in Gynor Place, Ynyshir. This tiny home was only a few streets away from William Street, where my mother grew up and where she was to return before too long to bring up her own family.

Several long interviews with my mother, Annie May, were recorded by my daughter, Angie, on 9th August 1983. At the time she was awaiting with eager anticipation the celebration of the 50th anniversary of her marriage to my father, Thomas Arthur. This was to take place on Boxing Day, 26th December of that same year, the same day that Angie, their eldest granddaughter, was to celebrate her twenty-first birthday. A family reunion was to be held when all their children and grand-children were to return to their roots in the Rhondda. Her heart full of love for her native valleys, Annie May read with intense feeling a poem about her beloved Rhondda entitled "Spirit of the Rhondda " which she had found recently in the Western Mail, a paper she read avidly every day.

# Spirit of the Rhondda
## *by Hughie Davies (extract)*

Perhaps you've never lived in
Rhondda,
Let me tell you of its life,
Of its people, mostly miners,
Of its spirit born of strife.

A hundred years have passed,
Since that lump of coal was found,
Along the Dinas mountainside,
Beneath the Rhondda ground.

The valley then was woodland,
Its streams were babbling brooks,
Trout and salmon abounded,
Aye and rabbits ran amok.

From Blaencwm down to Ponty,
The trees, the hills abound,
And squirrels scampered bough to
bough,
No need to come to ground.

No slag heaps disfigured these
stately brows,
No railway marked its seams,
It's one of nature's joys,
The stuff of poet's dreams.

But the giant born of Dinas,
Had a monstrous appetite,
And soon consumed the beauty,
As the daylight is by night.

We'll bring in Bristol's Jim,
And drag down North-Welsh Ted.
No matter that coal-mining,
Would pile up loads of dead.

The valley grew in numbers,
The race for wealth was on,
The rows of ugly houses,
That lined the breast along.

Chapels sprung up everywhere,
Pubs they lined the way,
Miners came in thirstily,
And drank the time away.

The rivers soon were poisoned,
The trout all died away,
And little boys with tin cans,
Would fish crachons in their play.

For this was growing Rhondda,
Growing uglier every day,
But the spirit born of struggle,
Came with us to stay.

It was shown in strikes and
lockouts,
Engaged in with the boss,
We fought for higher wages,
And all that meant in loss.

It was expressed in lovely music,
With choirs known through the
land,
And lusty youths would also join,
Their own prize silver band.

Bases, baritones and tenors,
Comedians of native wit,
Would make up a happy evening,
After toiling in the pit.

Yes, it's this glorious spirit,
Which has made us what we are,
To find its equal anywhere,
You would have to travel far.

And if, perchance, you find it,
It wouldn't be quite the same,
For that spirit was born in
Rhondda,
And from Rhondda it had its name.

These beautiful green valleys were amongst the most picturesque in Wales. The area was originally known as Ystradyfodwg - later to become known as the Rhondda Valleys. Before the advent of coal, they were described by Charles Cliffes as having "meadows of emerald greenness", and the air as being "aromatic with the scent of wild flowers and mountain plants."

The transformation of the valleys from an isolated, idyllic rural paradise depicted in the poem to a teeming ugly urban industrialised sprawl had been brought about during my grandparents' lifetime. Just four hill farms nestling in the green valleys had been swiftly swamped by the influx of workers from rural West Wales, South West England and other parts of the United Kingdom, swarming over their hills, cutting down the trees to provide pit props for the fast encroaching mines. The beauty and variety of the native trees were later replaced by vast plantations of fir trees covering the brows of the hills. However, the dirt, danger and destitute conditions suffered by this diverse workforce together forged this uplifting spirit of a close knit community which enabled the people to stand together and face all that fate had in store for them.

Annie May epitomised the spirit of the Rhondda as portrayed in Hughie Davies's poem. Head held high, despite the privations she endured during her lifetime, her determination to bring up her five children well and ensure that they all received the best possible education never faltered. Both she and Tom, himself a mine worker, made great sacrifices to achieve this goal but they never gave up the struggle.

Taking extracts from the aforementioned recorded interview, I will portray what life was like for my grandparents, parents and further generations living in the newly-industrialised Rhondda at the turn of the twentieth century.

# FAMILY TREE

B: date of birth   M: date of Marriage

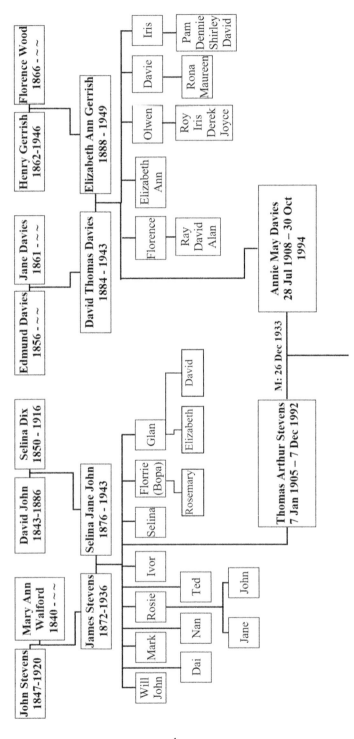

# FAMILY TREE

Cont…

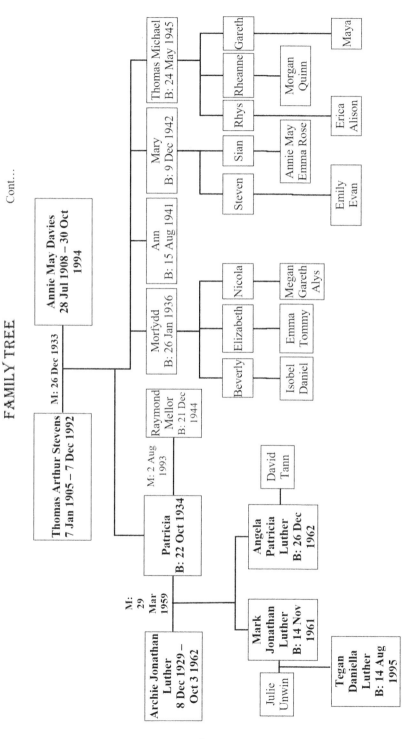

5

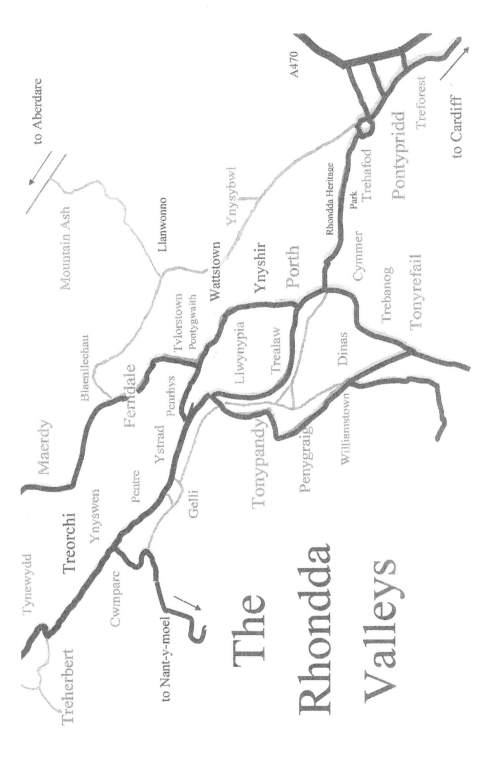

The Rhondda Valleys

# PART 1

## Spirit of the Rhondda

## My Inheritance

# Chapter 1
# Annie May's Story

The old horse, unaware of the tension all around, stood patiently between the shafts that fastened him to the ambulance cart. The icy wind, laden with coal dust, rattled down the street of terraced houses to the muffled sound of raised voices emanating from No 7. As the front door opened men's voices exploded into the stillness of the grey morning. The horse snorted restlessly tossing his head and the clattering of his hooves added to the din coming from the miner's cottage.

"Whoa Boy!" soothed his driver, gently stroking his mane to calm him down. The tall spare figure of Dr. Hurley emerged from the house, calm in the midst of the storm and turned towards the burley figure of the desperate miner.

"There's no argument", he said. "The child must be taken immediately to hospital!"

"I am defying you, doctor!" reiterated Dai Davies. "No daughter of mine will ever go to that hospital again!"

That child was Olwen, whose life, the family always maintained, was saved by the defiant stance of her father Dai Davies. She was the younger sister of Annie May, my mother, who was born into the Rhondda valley of the early twentieth century and whose reminiscences form the basis of much of the following narrative. It soon became evident that Dai Davies was idolised by Annie May, his eldest daughter. *"My father was a marvellous man"* was like a refrain running through the account of her life as we discussed her family and the changes that had transformed our valley and the impact that they had made on all our lives.

*'My father used to say that when I was born I was so small that I could have been put into a little milk jug – a really pint-sized baby!'* Annie May recalls.

The volume of noise that emanated from her puny frame foretold how sturdy and strong she would eventually become. My mother, Annie May Davies, was born on 28th July 1908, the eldest child of David Thomas Davies and Elizabeth Ann Gerrish.

Her father, Dai Davies, was a Welsh speaker whose family originated from rural west Wales and who came to the Rhondda for work in the mines. He grew up in a strict chapel family in the days when speaking Welsh could earn a child the school punishment of wearing a dunce's hat until another classmate was discovered speaking Welsh who would then inherit the shameful hat. He was a miner working in the local pit, *The Lady Lewis*, a stone's throw from his home in Ynyshir. This small heavily-industrialised village boasted a second working pit, *The Standard Colliery*, a little further up the valley towards the village of Wattstown.

The village of Ynyshir, (pronounced *Eneseer*) meaning *long island*, formed part of the urban sprawl between Porth, at the confluence of the two rivers Rhondda, and Maerdy at the top of the valley. This steep, narrow valley was called the Rhondda Fach, or *little Rhondda*, as opposed to the Rhondda Fawr, the *big Rhondda*, which was much wider and less steep than our valley. Rows of small stone terraced houses, distinguished from one another only by the numbers on the front doors and the comparative cleanliness of the doorsteps or the shine of the brass knockers and windows, soon lined the steep valleys as industrialisation grew. Ynyshir Road, the commercial centre of the village, stretched along the flattest part of the valley parallel with the newly extended railway tracks over which clanged and clattered the trucks carrying the coal down to Cardiff and Barry Docks for export all over the world.

Whilst miners and their families were crammed together in close proximity in tiny terraced houses along the floor and steep sides of the valley, colliery officials, overseers, safety men and hauliers were often housed in slightly larger houses situated on the end of the terraces as befitted their status. Overlooking the congested village, the colliery agents or commercial managers enjoyed fine views over their domains and comparative immunity from the all-pervading dust, grime and pollution emanating from the mines. Their elegant, spacious, detached houses, well isolated from those of the workers, dominated the sky line and were endowed with such fine names as Glenside, The Grove, Bryn Awel, Gorwell, etc. Other tall buildings were soon built to tower over the squat miners' cottages. Some of the largest buildings on the floor of the valley were the public houses. Three stories high, these new pubs, into which the miners flocked to slake their thirst with refreshing local beer, provided welcome respite from the hard toil in the stifling temperatures of the pits.

The pub was a male domain in the valleys. No respectable female would deign to pass its portals and drunkenness was much frowned upon in the chapel-oriented communities. Impressive stone chapels such as Bethel and Saron, almost as big as the pubs, exercised an immense influence over the populace. They were built on land leased from the collieries and funded by their congregations. The language of worship in these Methodist, Wesleyan, Congregationalist and Baptist chapels, was mostly Welsh. An alternative place to worship in Ynyshir was of course Saint Anne's in Church Terrace, the Anglican Church in Wales, constructed of rock-faced Pennant sandstone with Bath stone dressings in 1885, to serve the community.

Dai Davies was a well-known popular figure renowned for his fine tenor voice which earned him the nick name of "Dai Davies, Singer," from his workmates or "butties" as they were called in the locality. He was of medium height and strong build with broad shoulders and dark hair and eyes. Dai was a typical Welshman. One of his favourite pastimes was boxing and he acquired quite a reputation as a boxer, especially after it became known that he had sparred with the legendary Tommy Farr who famously travelled to America to challenge the great Jo Louis.

Annie May's mother, Elizabeth, or Lizzy as she was known, came from English stock. The Gerrishes were immigrants to the Rhondda from the West Country, coming at the time of the Industrial Revolution to make their living from the black gold of the coal mines. Lizzy's father, Henry Gerrish, brought his family to live in Ynyshir and they settled in Standard View not far from Station Road where Dai was living with his Welsh family. Lizzy was a small, neat, attractive young girl and she soon caught the eye of the charismatic young Dai. He took to teasing her using many soft sounding Welsh endearments – *cariad, bach, blodyn* (love, little one, flower) - that were incomprehensible to the English-speaking Lizzy. Nevertheless, despite the disparity in their native tongues, they were greatly attracted to one another and quickly fell head over heels in love. They were young and in love and soon found themselves in an awkward predicament. Lizzy was expecting a baby and there appeared to be no way that they could see that they could get married and bring up their baby together. They had no money and nowhere to live. There was certainly no room for them in the already overcrowded Gerrish household and it was highly unlikely that Dai's chapel-going family would take them in. Lizzy found it hard to become accepted by Dai's religious family who were loath to take this young "foreigner" into their midst. Nevertheless, Dai and Lizzie were in love and determined to make a life together.

When it became obvious that Dai would not give up his Lizzy under any circumstances, Dai's parents were forced to reconsider their stance towards the 'disgraced' couple. Eventually, Dai and Lizzy were married just a short time before the baby was due and moved into a temporary home with his parents and his sister, Annie, in Station Road, Ynyshir. This was not at all easy for the young bride and, as soon as they had managed to scrape a little furniture together, they moved with their new-born baby into a rented house at No 7 William Street, Ynyshir, just a stone's throw from Dai's family home.

As a baby and small child, Annie May was enveloped in a Welsh-speaking environment where only her mother spoke English to her. She understood Welsh and from a very early age attended Bethel, the Welsh Chapel of her father's family. The hymns and songs she heard as she grew were all in the Welsh language as were the songs her father sang to her. Dai taught Annie

May to sing almost as soon as she learned to speak. It was not surprising, therefore, that she began to acquire a large repertoire of songs in Welsh. However, since Lizzy spoke no Welsh, English naturally became the native tongue for their children, although Welsh remained the language of their culture, and especially of song.

Their home was in a typical row of stone-built miners' cottages with a Welsh slate roof. The street comprised two rows of fifty terraced houses facing each other built between the river and the railway line. The river was fast-flowing and black with pollution from the mines and had a long stone wall along it to protect the backs of the houses of William Street from flooding. It also helped to prevent adventurous youngsters from climbing down to play near the dangerous waters. No 7 was never in danger of flooding as its rear garden backed onto the lane opposite the back doors of Church Terrace which faced the railway line, while the river flowed behind the homes of William Street opposite us. At the junction of Station Road and Church Terrace stood Saint Anne's Church in Wales. Two big detached houses stood either side of it, flanking the road which ran over the humpbacked bridge spanning Ynyshir railway station. Ancient retired miners could often be seen at this vantage point chatting together as they took their ease on the wooden benches in the feeble sunshine before grasping their gnarled sticks with their blue-black scarred hands to creep slowly back home for tea.

There was no room to spread and so semi-detached houses were unknown in the area. The few detached houses belonged to the vicar, the doctor, the managers of the mines or the local gentry, usually mine owners themselves. The rest of the inhabitants lived packed together in rows of little terraced houses in a close-knit community. The stone for these houses was quarried from the hillsides where the houses were being built. Although there was little or no difference in the areas of Ynyshir, William Street was considered desirable as it was on the flat on the floor of the narrow valley and sported at its end the *Oval*, a large open playing field where football and cricket matches took place and from where small boys emerged as black as their fathers coming home from the mines. There was not a blade of grass to be seen on the field. In contrast, Heath Terrace, situated half way up the steep side of the valley, was considered a rough area and many were the fights that took place between the boys of Heath Terrace and William Street.

No 7 William Street was accessed through a front door leading from the pavement directly into a long narrow passage. A door to the right led into the front room or *parlour*. This room stayed empty until later on when, having lost his first wife and having entered into a disastrous second marriage, Lizzy's father, Henry Gerrish, came to occupy it. At the end of the passage, stairs led up to three bedrooms, two doubles and a spacious single. At the extreme right of the passage a further door led into the middle room which served as the family's living room. This was a comparatively large square room with a window giving onto the back yard of the house and a door leading to the *back kitchen*. This room acted both as a kitchen where meals were prepared, and as a bathroom. It also boasted a window looking onto the back yard where a large tin bath hung on a nail on the wall until it was needed.

All three rooms downstairs had open fires. In the middle and front rooms there were simple surrounds and mantelpieces and in the kitchen was a big black-leaded fire grate with hobs on each side and a large oven. A steaming kettle always sat ready on the hob to welcome any visitor with a cup of tea. Coal was, of course, used for both heating and cooking and came as part of the wages of the mineworker. It was delivered to the back door of the house and left in a huge pile in the back lane, or *gulley*, until the miner returned from work to shovel it all into his back yard where he had built a shed or a lean-to protecting it from the elements. Dirty as it was, at least the coal kept the house from being damp in winter and provided warmth for the family. Between the yard and the door to the *gulley* there was a small rectangular patch of garden. Here Dai would plant potatoes, carrots, cabbages and onions to supplement the family's diet and Lizzy could at last have her longed-for snowdrops, daffodils and tulips in spring and fragrant roses of several hues in summer to brighten her days. It was little enough, but they felt like kings in their very own tiny palace.

There was no running water inside the house but a single tap over a sink in the back yard provided this. The toilet, or *ty bach* (little house), was at the end of the yard, so they did not have too far to run when the weather was inclement. Most people had their toilets at the bottom of the garden, a longer dash from the house. Water for washing clothes and for bathing had to be carried from outside in a heavy iron boiler and heated on the open kitchen fire. This was an onerous and dangerous job and scalds were not an uncommon occurrence in the valleys. Lizzy and Dai kept their children well out of the way when performing these tasks. Miners did not have the luxury of pithead baths in those days so they would trudge home, as black as the coal itself after toiling in the pits, with only the flash of white teeth showing in the smile that greeted their loved ones. Soon they knew they would be easing their strained muscles in a hot bath before the bright crackling flames of the kitchen fire. Other members of the family looked forward to bath day once a week, usually at the weekend, when children too would bathe two at a time or one after another in front of the fire.

The last room of the house was the larder where all the food was stored. It was a long windowless room with a cold stone floor and shelves down one side. At the very end there was a large flat stone table on which milk and other perishable food was kept cool next to a big brown earthenware bread basin which was used both to store other food and also to mix such luxuries as the annual Christmas puddings. Life was very hard but Lizzy and Dai were over the moon with their house and little baby girl. They set about to save hard to create a cosy home for themselves and the little sisters and brothers they envisaged for their beloved Annie May

* * * * *

Dai Davies was a good collier and highly respected in the area, entertaining one and all with his fine tenor voice. Lizzy was content to bask in his reflected glory to all outside appearances, but in the home she came into her own. In those days, it was the man's task to go out to work to earn the money and provide for his family, and the woman's job to run the household and manage on however much or little her husband was able to provide. Lizzy was a thrifty and exceptionally good manager even though the wages were very meagre.

Fear and discontent was rampant all around them – fear of losing your job and the only means of earning your living, and discontent with the conditions of work and the way the mine owners ran the collieries. However, despite the depressing environment, life continued as they had hoped for the young couple. Since moving into the first real home of their own, their family began to swell. After Annie May came Florence, then Elizabeth Ann, then Olwen before they had their only son named after the proud father and called Davie. Finally, they had their youngest daughter, Iris.

Young Annie May was a happy and ebullient child who, as the eldest of a fast growing family, soon learned to help her mother with any little tasks within her capacity. She would pass the warm towel to her mother as she bathed her younger siblings or rock the cradle to help send them off to sleep. She adored her father and was definitely a "Daddy's girl." After working long hours in the pit, Dai threw himself into caring for his young daughters at home. He was a "hands-on" father long before it became the norm, so Lizzy could count on having a respite from her chores as soon as Dai entered the house. Sweeping up his daughters into his strong arms, he entertained them until bed time. He often changed them for bed and put them down to sleep. Then he would sing to them and teach them simple little songs before they finally dropped off to sleep to the strains of their favourite Welsh lullabies.

Taking after her father, Annie May proved to be exceptionally musical and Dai loved to display her talents to all and sundry. A shop counter would often provide a make-shift stage and the little toddler would be lifted up and asked to perform before an audience of appreciative neighbours and friends.

Annie May needed no persuasion. She sang sweetly and lapped up all the attention.

However life in the drab, grey, industrial valleys soon lost its rosy hue, even for a young couple in love delighting in their bonny brood. Many Rhondda women died during childbirth, which certainly in the early days would be in their own homes. Child mortality was high due to the appalling living conditions, poor diets, and the many diseases prevalent in those days when hard work, poverty and premature bereavement were the norm. The young family were not immune to this either.

Annie May and Elizabeth Ann both contracted whooping cough and then the dreaded scarlet fever. Annie May became ill first and was taken to Porth Cottage Hospital in the primitive old cabby ambulance - a covered cart drawn by a docile horse. The sick little girl responded swiftly to the treatment she received and soon became as happy as a queen in the hospital ward. At the drop of a hat, she was ready to sing for the doctors and nurses and was thrilled to bits to receive a penny as a reward for her efforts. On the other hand, a couple of weeks later her four-year old sister Elizabeth Ann was admitted to the hospital. Elizabeth Ann was an exceptionally pretty little child with fair skin, golden curls and big blue eyes. However, she cut a very sorry little figure on entering the hospital. She was pale and lifeless and burning up with fever. In stark contrast to the bright, cheerful disposition of her elder six-year-old sibling, poor little Elizabeth Ann did nothing but cry all the time. She was put into the bed next to her big sister but hard as she tried, Annie May was unable to get her to talk or to shake her out of her despondency. "Oh, Lizzy Ann, come and sing with me," Annie May cajoled.

"You'll get a penny too, then we can go and buy our favourite sweeties when we go back home together." But it was no good. She did nothing but cough, wheeze and cry all the time. Elizabeth Ann's health soon deteriorated greatly and she became critically ill. She was removed to a side ward where she had a tracheotomy and died soon afterwards. It was a terrible blow to the whole family but it was her father Dai Davies who was totally devastated. On hearing the news, he went straight to the hospital and removed Annie May before she could follow her little sister to the grave.

Henceforth, he and Lizzie nursed Annie May continuously at home until she made a full recovery. Nevertheless, Dai continued to pine for the little angel he had lost. He was a miner working in the dark low seams in the bowels of the earth. His job was very physically demanding and Lizzy was always careful to make sure that he was provided with a good nourishing lunch box to take with him to work. Normally, Dai had an excellent appetite and had no problem in devouring all that Lizzy had prepared for him, but now, more often than not his box returned untouched at the end of his shift.

"What's the matter, Dai?" Lizzy would ask, looking into his lunch box.

"Oh, haven't I eaten it? I must have forgotten about it" he would reply absent-mindedly.

"This won't do you know, Dai. You'll make yourself ill and then what will happen to us all?" Lizzy would gently scold him. He always promised to do his best to shake himself out of his deep depression but it took him many more months to recover his usual sunny disposition.

Soon after finally getting over that hurdle, the family was dealt another hard blow. The fourth daughter Olwen was struck down by a terrifying illness. In those days, measles, chicken pox, whooping cough, tuberculosis and diphtheria were rife and it was not uncommon for families to lose some of their little ones to these contagious diseases. Treatment and medication was not so advanced at that time. Their family doctor was Dr. Hurley, a much-respected Irishman who, though stern, was greatly liked by one and all. He used no means of transport to visit his patients, but his tall, spare, solitary figure was a common sight, striding along the steep narrow streets winding through the valley. It was a rare man to dare question his diagnosis or his decisions. Dr Hurley came to the house and after examining Olwen, pronounced that she had diphtheria and would have to be rushed to hospital without delay. The black cabby ambulance duly arrived at the door at the same time as Dai arrived back from the mine and the irresistible force met the immovable object. The doctor ordered the child to be placed in the ambulance but Dai absolutely refused to let the nurse take Olwen. "No fear! No other child of mine's going to that hospital from this house again!" he cried.

Annie May vividly remembers cowering behind her mother's skirts as the stand-off continued. The driver of the black covered cart got down from behind his horse which snorted softly as it shuffled between the shafts of the old cart. He then entered the house and climbed the dark stairs with the nurse to pick up their patient while Dai stood his ground and confronted the doctor.

"No, she's not going. I'm defying you, Doctor!" he reiterated. "No child of mine will go to that hospital ever again!"

Eventually, the nurse and driver were forced to leave without their little patient. In those days, few children from poor backgrounds survived this virulent disease and for days on end Olwen lay limply in the arms of her father, burning with fever. Dai nursed her tirelessly day and night, talking to her constantly, singing softly and encouraging her to fight on.

"Come now, cariad" he'd say. "Cwtch up (cuddle up) to Daddy and go to sleep. You'll feel better when you wake up. I'll sing you your favourite lullaby and you can sleep in Daddy's arms. I won't leave you. Don't be afraid, little one. You'll be better soon and be out running over the mountains with your sisters and your little butties before you know it. Daddy will keep you safe. Don't you worry." Then, singing softly, he would break into her favourite Welsh lullaby *Suo Gân*# as he gently mopped her fevered brow with a cool damp flannel.    At last the fever broke and the little girl and her devoted father were finally able to drop into a deep, healing sleep. Dai had never left his daughter's bedside until she was past the crisis and he stayed away from work as she slowly improved until she had fully recovered. The family gave thanks to God for this happy outcome, especially when they got to know later that the message sent to the hospital had been:

*"You have a very sick child coming to the hospital. She may not survive the journey!"*

\* \* \* \* \*


Throughout her youth, Annie May and her father would sing together at the drop of a hat and Annie May soon began to compete successfully in local Eisteddfodau and competitions. She won many ribbons and medals of which one of the most prized was the under-sixteen Semi-National of Wales at the tender age of eleven. Her eldest grandson Mark, himself the first professional singer in the family, still keeps these treasured mementos. Talking about her family and her love of singing, Annie May said:

*"My father was always happy when he was singing and, of course, he taught me and I was happy too. Unfortunately, I've got no voice now. It's gone these many years and I find it frustrating at times. I've got a grandson coming on that we hope will bring us all great happiness with his voice, and all my other grandchildren are doing well, and I hope we'll live a long time to hear about them and have great-grandchildren."*

Annie May had indeed lost her lovely soprano voice by over singing at an early age, but her musicality enabled her to harmonize in a lower register with any singers although she had never had a single music lesson in her life. Her wish was fulfilled in later life when she attended many opera performances where Mark took leading tenor roles in the New Theatre, Cardiff, home then of the Welsh National Opera and various other prestigious Opera Houses throughout Britain.  He had inherited his beautiful tenor voice from his grandfather Tom, and his great grandfather Dai Davies. Annie May was equally proud of the academic and sporting achievements of her other grandchildren and lived to hold her first great-grandchild, Isobel, in her arms at her christening.

---

# Suo Gân  a traditional Welsh lullaby written by an anonymous composer. It was first recorded in print around 1800 and the lyrics were notably captured by the Welsh folklorist Robert Bryan (1858–1920). The song's title simply means lullaby (suo = lull; cân = song).

As a child, Annie May was a bright, lively and cheerful little girl who thrived on responsibility. Her strong personality shines out in the few photographs we still have of her early years. The first shows a small bright-eyed infant, dressed like her two slightly bigger class-mates, in Welsh costume on St. David's Day. The three children are seated at a small round table, Annie May at centre stage with her hand resting on the teapot staring proudly at the camera flanked by her two contemporaries.

Annie May (centre) on St. David's Day

All Dai and Lizzy's children attended the chapel Sunday School regularly and took part most enthusiastically in the massed singing of the whole congregation. Over the years they learned to sing all the beautiful famous Welsh hymns in the mother tongue. Thus the love of Welsh culture was born in them at a very early age and it stayed with them all their lives. The three little sisters can be seen in the picture of Bethel's Sunday School dressed in their Sunday best, each with a ribbon tied in a bow on the left side of their heads. Little Davie, their young brother, dressed all in white, is in the front row. Their youngest sister Iris was not yet born. Every year the chapel held an Anniversary when the whole congregation attended and were entertained by the Sunday-School and everyone could join in singing their favourite Welsh hymns. The children vied with each other to sing solos, duets or recite poems in front of their proud parents. Needless to say, Annie May was more often than not the star turn of the show.

Bethel Chapel Sunday School - Florrie in R4 centre, Annie-May R3 3rd from L, Olwyn R2 3rd from R, Davie R1 3rd from L

In spite of the ugliness and the poverty of her surroundings, Annie May found something wonderful about the place.

*"We were all such friends,"* she remembered. *"If anyone was ill, they'd say 'Send for Mrs. So and So' and they'd bring any little tit-bit to share with you. Everybody helped one another. We were all a very happy lot. Although we didn't have much money, we had plenty of happiness."*

Annie May coped valiantly with all that was thrown at her. Her mother was a very house-proud woman and, not only were her children always well turned out, her house was always spotlessly clean despite the all-pervading coal dust. At a very early age, Annie May was roped in to help with housework. Her mother had strained herself by having six children in quick succession and through all the hard work necessary to keep her home and her children spic and span. Lizzy had her work cut out to cope with her growing family. Annie May soon learned to dust and polish the furniture, scrub the floors, then use sand and stone to scrub the front door step before hurling buckets of warm soapy water over the paving stones at the front of the house then scrubbing them clean with a hard sweeping brush. Lizzy ensured that the outside of 7 William Street was kept as clean and shining bright as the inside.

A very responsible child, Annie May could be trusted to run errands for her mother. The housewives used to make bread and cakes for their large families at home and then send them to the village bake house to be cooked. Annie May was tasked to take the bread there on her way to school and she was happy to do so. However, neighbours who were elderly or who had no competent school age children at home, would often wait on their doorsteps to waylay Annie May to ask if she would return to take their bread also. She could not refuse, as people all helped one another in the mining community of the day and she was often made late for school by doing her good turns. One day, she had to return three times to take the bread for different neighbours and, fast as she ran, she arrived very late for school.

"Where have you been, Annie May? This is not the time to come to School!" remonstrated her teacher.

*"Sorry miss, I had to take the bread to the bake house for Mam. Then Mrs. Jones and also Mrs. Evans asked me, so I had to run back twice,"* she explained.

Looking at the red-faced panting child, Miss Gwilym had no doubt that she was telling the truth but nevertheless she warned her,

"You must get here on time, Annie May, or you will be punished, you know. You will have to get up earlier to run your errands before school."

*"Yes Miss"* she replied meekly, silently resolving to go via the back gullies the next time. In that way she could miss the neighbours looking out for her on their doorsteps. When her mother was undergoing a difficult pregnancy or recovering from the birth of younger siblings, Annie May undertook to do the family shopping. Armed with the appropriate list, she would make several trips "over the road" to Ynyshir Road in the centre of the village. She visited the Co-op (pronounced locally as the Cop) for the groceries, 'Powel's' for green groceries and Jones the butchers for the weekly meat before she was able to play with her friends on a Saturday.

Taking her chores in her stride, Annie May really loved school and did well in her studies. She particularly loved to read and she fed her natural curiosity by devouring any books or magazines she could get her hands on. Apart from singing, she learned to recite and act in Welsh also. She particularly liked acting in school plays, taking part in the *Cyd Adrodd,* (in which groups of children act out a Welsh poem with great gusto, competing with other groups) and, of course, singing in choirs, smaller groups or solos. She took part fully in school life and thoroughly enjoyed it. However, Lizzy found that she needed her eldest daughter's help in the house more often than just after school and at weekends. To Annie May's dismay, she decided to keep her young daughter home from school every Friday to help with the housework. Although Annie May would have much preferred to spend the day in school with her classmates rather than at home scrubbing and polishing, she did not complain and threw herself into helping her mother with a good grace. On returning to school on Mondays, she always worked hard to make up for the lessons she had missed.

Nevertheless, life was not all doom and gloom for Annie May and her siblings. They would play happily together and had many friends. There being little or no traffic in the street they would play ball, hopscotch or skipping together on the road. They used their imaginations to devise other simple games and especially loved to dress up and perform for one another or for their parents when they could spare the time to watch them. The valleys provided a safe environment for children to play out unsupervised in those days. Everyone knew one another and children were ready to accept the authority of any of their neighbours. They were able to run free over the nearby hills and a favourite game was to make dens among the high ferns or to climb rocks. There was no need for gyms or such like. Children could expend all their pent up energy in the open air. Even sports competitions took place in the street, devoid of cars and watched by all the residents comfortably seated on chairs on their doorsteps. Rivalry could not have been fiercer even if they had been competing in today's Olympic Games. Annie May was a good runner and had no problem beating her female peers. However, she bit off more than she could chew when she took on the boys' champion, Dai Mason, whom she recalls was one of her first little boyfriends: *"You know, we were always looking at each other and laughing."*

Off they went sprinting down the street with Annie May straining to keep up with Dai. She would not give up although she was panting heavily and had turned a bright puce colour. The worried spectators urged her to give in but she refused and round they ran again with hardly an inch between them. At last the race was over and she was forced to admit defeat and fell into the arms of her anxious father. Seeing her bad colour and sheer determination, many had been afraid that she would drop down dead from her exertions just like the celebrated athlete Guto Nyth Bran who did just that having been given a congratulatory slap on the back after winning a famous race over the mountains. His story is commemorated on his grave stone lying in the churchyard of the twelfth century church, Eglwys Sant Gwynno of Llanwonno, which overlooks the Rhondda valley and is now a local tourist attraction.

Treats and especially shop-bought toys were practically unheard of in the valleys. Outings were few and far between. One such rare treat was vividly remembered by Annie May:

*"I remember it was on the Easter time and my mother couldn't take us out so she said to Dad 'You take the two girls out.' That was my sister Florrie*

*and me. We weren't very old. My mother always used to dress us nicely both in the same dresses. We looked like twins because there was only a year between us. So he took us to Cardiff. That was a treat! He took us into J. R. Jones, the restaurant, you know, upstairs. Of course we thought it was magnificent! We had nice food there and we thoroughly enjoyed ourselves. We could have anything with my father, whatever we wanted. We were delighted, my sister Florrie and me, sitting around this table with our Dad. There was a lady sitting at a nearby table and she came over. She sat down at our table and was talking to my father. We didn't wonder why she had joined us until she eventually said 'You are a widower, are you?' 'No,' he answered. 'My wife is at home.' She thought she had a good chance!"*

There was no such thing as two weeks' annual holiday for miners in those days. The miners were lucky to have a couple of days off in a year from the pit. *"Though times were hard, we were a jolly lot. We didn't have much money, but we had plenty of happiness. Of course there was no television and wireless when I was young. We used to spend all our days up on the mountainside, taking our picnics. The men had their couple of days off from the pit and we'd all go up as a family, droves of us, and we had a nice time. The men were laden with all the paraphernalia needed for the day. They carried kettles and built fires to make tea. We had Welsh cakes and hearty sandwiches made of thick slices of bread filled with fish paste, corned beef, hard-boiled egg or cheese and tomato. There wasn't the variety of food we have today. We all had good appetites and did justice to our substantial provisions in the fresh mountain air. There wasn't a crumb left to take back home. Of course we always ended up singing together and had a really good time."*

From the time that Churchill authorised the sending of troops to quell the Tonypandy riots during the miners' strike in November 1910, times were hard throughout the valleys. Wages were low and strikers had very little to live on during the long strike that lasted almost a full year. Eventually, the presence of troops ensured the defeat of the miners in 1911 and this was seen as a direct consequence of state intervention without any negotiation. This action was attributed, perhaps undeservedly, to Churchill whose unpopularity survives in South Wales to the present time. Young as I was, I well remember joining in enthusiastically to "boo" the renowned statesman whenever he appeared on the Pathe Newsreels during and after World War Two. In 2010, ninety-nine years after the riots, a Welsh local council made objections to a street being named after Churchill in the Vale of Glamorgan because of his sending troops into the Rhondda. Eventually, the desperate miners were forced to accept the 2s 3d per ton of coal, negotiated by William Abraham, M.P., before the strike.

During the First World War from 1914 to 1918, everyone pulled together to defeat the enemy. In the aftermath, however, relations between the state and the miners deteriorated once more. The ongoing confrontations between miners and mine-owners caused terrible hardships in the valleys, yet Lizzy's children were always clean and neatly dressed and rarely needed to queue for charity food in the infamous soup kitchens during the many strikes. Once when their mother was ill, the children had begged to join their friends in the church hall where they were thrilled to partake of the warm soup with everyone else.

"*Oh, please let us go,*" pleaded Annie May. "*All our friends are going and the soup's really lovely!*"

"Please, please, Mam" chorused the other little children.

"Very well, then," Lizzy conceded, "but you must go with Mrs Griffiths and behave yourselves. Watch your manners. You are in charge, Annie May, don't forget!"

Faces and hands clean and shining with anticipation, the children scampered off to meet their friends. As soon as she was better, Lizzy went to help serve out the soup in the nearby church hall. Her prowess as a cook enabled her to dish up very tasty as well as nourishing soups and she soon became a much appreciated member of the team. The loyal women worked hard and long to support their menfolk during the harsh struggle as the seemingly interminable strike dragged on. The men contributed vegetables from their gardens while their wives appeared to conjure up food from next to nothing. No one got fat on their efforts, but starvation was held at bay for many months, enabling the miners to hold out longer.

With wages being low and work insecure, Annie May and her siblings had little chance of staying in school and continuing their education.

"*I didn't have a lot of schooling but I wasn't dull by any means. I loved school. I was in everything – the Welsh dramas, singing, reciting, all sorts of things but my mother was going to have my little sister, Iris. Anyway, I was not quite 13 at the time. You were allowed to leave school at 13 years of age at the time. There were three children younger than me: Florrie, Olwen and Davie and then this new baby coming. So, we went up the school and asked if I could leave school to help look after the house. Of course there were no home helps and that sort of thing in those days. You just had to get on with it yourself. Anyway, they got permission for me to leave school before I was thirteen. I think I left at the beginning of the year before I was 13 in the July and Iris was born in April. My mother was in bed all the time so I went to bed one night and the next morning there was this tiny baby girl. She was called Iris. We all went in to see my mother and this lovely little baby. She wasn't very strong at that time but she got better and so did my mother.*

*In the meantime, I was the housekeeper and had to do all the work. My father was a marvellous man. He was working on the coal face underground but when he got home, he used to help me cleaning the upstairs and polishing the furniture. I did everything that was done in that house with the exception of the washing. We had a woman who came in to do that. I was not yet thirteen but I also did the cooking for the family. I was well schooled. My mother had us all doing jobs from the time we were ten. There was no question. We never said we didn't want to do it either."*

Willing and efficient as she was, Annie May was not a paragon of all the virtues either. Like all normal children she had her naughty little ways too. She had a very sweet tooth and a particular penchant for condensed milk. This came in small tins and was used to sweeten tea and desserts such as rice pudding. She loved to eat it by the spoonful when she got the chance. Her parents of course frowned upon this, but somehow Annie May had to come up with a solution.

*'I was a very greedy girl,'* she recalls. *'When my mother was out shopping or chatting to the neighbours, I was always left in charge of the younger children. Davie was a baby only able to crawl about and haul himself up by means of a chair. He had not learned to talk. This was my chance! I grabbed the newly opened tin of condensed milk left lying on a low shelf in the kitchen. Before I realised it, I had devoured practically the whole lot. Little Davie was clinging to my skirt, crying for a share. Swift as a flash, I scraped out the last remnants from the tin and fed him a spoonful, smearing his chubby face at the same time. I placed the spoon in his hand and he started to bang on the tin and the floor, as happy as a sand-boy. When my mother came in, she burst out laughing at the sight that met her eyes! Dad laughed too when the tale was recounted to him, so I had got away with it! It would have been no laughing matter if they had known who the real culprit was! I tried the same trick when I couldn't resist eating an extra banana, quickly placing the banana skin in Davie's hand, but was careful not to try it out too often.'*

# Chapter 2
# Life in London

Annie May having finally left school at the tender age of twelve to help her mother at home, set off for London soon after her fourteenth birthday to be a maid of all work for a young well-to-do couple, Mr. and Mrs. Phillips, who were expecting their first baby. It would be unthinkable today that such a young innocent child who had never ventured from home should be sent alone to a great metropolis to work in a foreign home far away from family and friends. Nevertheless, undismayed, her dark curls tied neatly back and yet full of trepidation at the thought of leaving her home and family, Annie May swallowed back her tears and launched herself into the unknown. She was to have her keep and to be paid thirty shillings a month, most of which would be sent regularly home to Wales to help with the family budget. She recalls:

*"I was fourteen years' old. There was no work, no money, no anything. There was a six months' strike and then you had to get back into the collieries. I don't remember if there was a shut-out that time. Anyway, lots of girls were going away to service, so I got The Echo. My mother didn't take it. So I looked in The Echo. I saw this advertisement so I wrote myself. Nobody told me to write. I could have stayed home, I suppose, like anyone else, but I wrote myself and it was to a Mrs. Phillips in Bayswater. It was a young married couple in Bayswater. Vivian, her husband was, and I wrote to her and she wrote back that she'd send my fare if I'd come. It was just her and her husband in the house and she was expecting a baby. She said she wanted someone to help in the house, so I went.*

*I always remember, my mother had a light-coloured flannel costume made for me and I had a blue hat with a cherry on the top and these curls down my back. That's how I went to London on the train. My mother took me to Cardiff. I cried all the way to Cardiff, not because I didn't want to go, but because I was leaving my mother. But I went. I will always remember. It was November. It was a pea soup fog. You couldn't see a hand in front of you. Mrs. Phillips was meeting me on Paddington Station. We got into a taxi and people had told me 'Be careful when you go to London. Don't speak to anyone because, you know, they'll take you away.' Oh God, I thought, I hope she's all right. She looked all right. Anyway, I went in this taxi and we went to Bayswater where they were living."*

Annie May settled well into her new life. Accustomed as she had been to the hard work helping her mother in the house and caring for younger siblings, she found the long hours and the work required of her easily within her capacity. Fortunately, the young couple who employed her took to her and treated her with respect in their home. They were delighted with her competence and her cheerful attitude to life.

*"They were a big family, Phillips the Poulterers, and Vivian was about the third son. The eldest son was the boss, but Vivian Phillips managed the Bayswater shop. We had our maisonette at the top over the shop. There was a lovely lounge. We had to go up a lot of steps to the lounge, then up the stairs again to the dining room. Their master bedroom was downstairs and my bedroom – a lovely bedroom I had – was downstairs too. Then the dining room, the bathroom and the kitchen were upstairs. The alarm went off at seven o'clock. I was up at seven every morning and was busy all day. At first, Mrs. Phillips showed me how to do things, but I was pretty good because I was used to it.*

*I used to eat by myself in the kitchen and they would eat in the dining room. I didn't do all the cooking at first. She would come and help me and show me what to do, but later on I did all the cooking – and all the work, washing, ironing, the lot. I was always called Annie May at home but Mrs. Phillips had a sister-in-law called Annie, so she called me May. I was always called Annie May by my mother, father, family and friends but afterwards lots of people called me May. It didn't make much difference, did it? They were very nice people, just like friends. They weren't like master and mistress but I used to have to call her 'Mum,' you know. 'Yes mum' or 'no mum' and so on."*

Annie May was allowed a certain amount of free time, including every other Sunday off. Mr. and Mrs. Phillips were kind to her and would often ask her to sing for them. It was not long before Annie May plucked up courage to ask them if they could help her find a chapel she could attend:

*"Of course, I used to sing at the time, so they used to get me singing. I wanted a chapel because I used to go to chapel in Wales. I went to the Welsh Wesleyan chapel always. That's where I was brought up, so I wanted an English Wesleyan chapel. That's what I told her. "We'll take, you, May," she said. "We'll find you a chapel."*

Mrs. Phillips was as good as her word. They found a chapel on the corner of Westbourne Grove and we went to a service there together. The minister was a very friendly Australian who was most welcoming, so Annie May was quite happy to join his chapel even though it was a Baptist chapel. "May will be fine here with us," he assured Mrs. Phillips.

From then on, Annie May was able to attend her chapel in London where she soon made friends. She also joined the Sunday School which she really loved, and she recalls one happy excursion which took place soon after she arrived:

*"It was a lovely Sunday School. Everyone was so friendly and one day, we all went on an outing to Southend-on-Sea. We were all singing together*

*in the bus, and then someone asked if I would sing a Welsh song. I sang Y Deryn Pur (The Gentle Dove.) It must have got back to the minister. The next Sunday, I was in my usual place up in the front row of the gallery with my friends, when the minister said, 'Annie will sing us a French song.' We were all rather confused until he corrected himself. 'Sorry, I mean a Welsh song, of course!' I was made in that chapel after that. I became quite well known and had many invitations out to tea etc. I really enjoyed chapel and threw myself wholeheartedly into the life of the chapel and made many friends."*

Several months later, Mrs. Phillips gave birth to a baby girl and wanted a Welsh name for her. She herself came from Macclesfield but it seemed that the family had Welsh connections further back. She asked Annie May to suggest a name for her, so the baby was named Gwyneth. Put on the spot, she recalls with a smile:

*"The only Welsh name I could think of was Gwyneth, so they called the baby Gwyneth."*

*Both mother and new born baby were ill after the birth, so two trained nurses were employed to care for the invalids. Annie May now had two extra to cater for and to look after in the house. However, she took it all in her stride and took this heaven-sent opportunity to find out what she could about nursing. When she had been asked in school what she wanted to be when she grew up, she would invariably tell her teacher, "I want to be a nurse."*

Both nurses were very nice to Annie May and chatted amicably with her as they all went about their various tasks. One nurse was from Saint Thomas's hospital and the other from a private nursing home. Neither minded answering Annie May's continuous flow of questions so she acquired some very useful information about the nursing profession.

*"Perhaps you will be able to train when you are older,"* they told her. *"You are very efficient in the house.*

Mrs. Phillips's sister and sister-in-law lived in Finchley Road. Both households were more well-to-do than that of Mr. & Mrs. Phillips. The family was often invited by one of them for Christmas. They each had two full-time maids and lived in very grand houses. The dining room, where the Christmas dinner was served, was very elegant and the table set out with the finest linen, exquisite crockery and heavy silver cutlery. The house was colourfully decorated throughout with a huge Christmas tree taking pride of place in the drawing room. All three maids also received presents from their appreciative employers. The gifts were beautifully wrapped and were of a much higher quality than those they would have received from their own families. The food was excellent too and Annie May partook of some delicacies she had never tasted before. It was her first taste of sherry trifle, a dessert she later became adept at making. In years to come, she would delight her children and grandchildren by repeating the one, to her, rather *risqué*, joke which emanated from her short time as a maid. She would recount that naïve country maids would be trained to be politely subservient by their rich employers. This would result sometimes in such hilarious *faux pas* as the maid, waiting at table and serving important guests, replying to the request for green peas thus:

'Yes, ma'am and no, ma'am, and ma'am if you please,
    Up the duck's arse you'll find the green peas.'

When little Gwyneth's health improved, Annie May would take her out for walks in her pram in Kensington Gardens or Hyde Park every afternoon. She was dressed in her afternoon uniform, a navy blue suit with a white trim, similar to those worn by the nannies out pushing the prams carrying the babies of their aristocratic employers. She was very fond of her charge who was happy and comfortable in her care. Annie May enjoyed chatting with other nannies, secretly comparing her baby to theirs. She had responsibility also for the family's dog, a little Pekinese, who was rather spoilt in her opinion. She was required to walk the dog every day too. However, she did not always take him to the parks as she was supposed to do. She often preferred to walk him towards some of the many big shops and department stores in the neighbourhood so she could window-shop as much she wished. Annie May loved to inspect the beautiful clothes displayed so tastefully in the windows and decide which would suit her best, though she did not have the money to purchase them. Some years later however, when still living and working in London, she saved up to buy a "costume" which she saw reduced in the shop window only to find out later that she had purchased a riding jacket and skirt!

Annie May was reasonably happy with her employers and an absolute treasure to them with the baby. She was well treated, had made lovely friends in her Chapel community and was able to return home to Wales for short visits every six months or so, but, even so, she was not fully content. Things were still difficult for her large family at home in Wales. She used to send her mother £1 out of her monthly pay of thirty shillings (£1.50) but she wanted to send more. Tentatively she asked Mrs. Phillips if she could have a rise. Unfortunately, although her employers would have liked to retain Annie May's services, they just did not have the means to pay her more.

"I'm sorry, May, we just can't pay you any more, though we'd like to keep you with us, of course. You have become just like one of the family. I thought that you were happy with us," said Mrs Phillips.

"Oh yes, of course I am!" she swiftly responded. "You are very kind and good to me and I love little Gwyneth. I know I would really miss her if I left but I would like to be my own mistress and earn enough to be able to send more money home to help Mam and Dad."

"If you need to try for more money, then you do so," said Mrs. Phillips reluctantly. Thus it was decided that they would try to manage without a maid after Annie May left and that they would help her to find a suitable job.

They knew an elegant lady who was a regular customer at Mr. Phillips's shop. She was a physiotherapist and needed a housekeeper. Annie May was offered a higher wage so, reluctantly, she gave in her notice and moved into the smart house in Baker Street to keep house there. However, after the friendly family atmosphere she had experienced in Bayswater, Annie May did not like it there. She only stayed a short time before finding a new job with a rich Jewish family. However, she was not happy with them either.

Her father, Dai Davies, came up to London to see his football team, Cardiff City, play at Wembley at that time. He soon realised that his daughter was unhappy in her job and immediately advised her to leave. She had come to realise that domestic service was not what she wanted out of life. Father and daughter were invited to tea in the Phillips's household where they all discussed what to do for the best.

*"If you are not happy in domestic service, May, perhaps you should try for a job in one of the smart London stores,"* suggested Mrs. Phillips.

Although, during her sorties on her time off, she had often admired the elegantly-dressed young shop assistants who worked in the famous London stores such as Harrods, from a little girl, Annie May had always wanted to become a nurse.

*"I just don't know, but I really think that I would like to become a nurse. I am good at looking after people, especially children, and I'm prepared to work hard."*

*"But you would need to be trained for nursing and you are still too young, you know,"* said Mr. Phillips.

*"Yes, but I am very responsible and can seem older than I really am and I'm sure that I would love the work and be good at it."*

The discussion went on for some time and Dai Davies fully supported his daughter in her desire to better herself, so when they looked around for an alternative career, it was decided that her experience suited her for entering the nursing profession. She would, of course, need references to apply for preliminary training as a nurse and Mrs. Phillips was only too happy to provide one. Annie May, however, was not only proud but also wanted to give herself the best possible chance of success, so rather than saying that she had been a maid, it was agreed that Mrs. Phillips would say that she had been employed as nursemaid for little Gwyneth.

\* \* \* \* \*

28

Thus armed with two glowing references and adding a year to her age, Annie May set about applying to the big London hospitals. Although she was under age, she managed to get accepted for a pre-nursing course in King's College Hospital. She really loved the work and studied hard and soon made friends with her fellow student nurses. She passed all the tests set and her practical work was excellent. All seemed set fair for her dream career. Then came disaster. She had to take a general paper to assess her level of education before she could be accepted on a course to study for her SRN qualification. Poor Annie May was faced with a paper which required her, among other things, to place Rome on a map of Europe and to write about her favourite author. Having left school at twelve, she had never heard of Rome, and Agatha Christie was the only author she had read profusely. She failed dismally and was called before the matron. The matron told her that she had achieved excellent results in her pre-nursing written and practical examinations which were all highly satisfactory.

*"Unfortunately,"* she explained, *"I am unable to offer you a place on an SRN course as your general education is not quite up to the standard required."* Annie May was devastated and could scarcely restrain her tears.

*"What can I do, Matron? I really love nursing. There's nothing else I want to do!"* Seeing that Annie May was about to burst into tears, the kindly matron tried to comfort her:

"Don't be upset, Annie May," she said. "I can offer you training to become an auxiliary nurse, so you will still be able to continue nursing."

*"Thank you, Matron,'* stammered Annie May as she hastily made her retreat.

Alone in her room, Annie May gave way to her feelings and cried as if her heart would break. Then, pulling herself together, she came to a decision. She would not stay on and watch girls whom she had beaten in the preliminary tests, go on to qualify as SRNs while she was relegated to training as an auxiliary. She vowed then that no child of hers would ever miss out on any opportunities in life through lack of education. She went to see matron and explained that she could not stay on under the circumstances and offered her resignation immediately. Matron was very understanding and helped her to choose an alternative hospital where she could continue to do further training. She never again sought to be accepted on an SRN course but gained wide nursing experience in several large London teaching hospitals, including the London Hospital for Tropical Diseases.

Annie May's stint in the Hospital for Tropical Diseases turned out to be a particularly happy and exciting time in her young life. She arrived there as a naïve young lady, keen to experience life to the full, ready to take all avenues open to her. She was still very small of stature – she never managed to stretch up to make the dizzy height of five feet. She had huge, dark, bright eyes and lovely, long, thick, brown hair with a slight wave in it. The small gap between her two front teeth, some said, augured well for her future. She carried herself confidently and had a bright outgoing personality. Her nose was slightly wide and she often bemoaned the fact in her youth. She would stand in front of the mirror and press her nostrils together to see what improvement she could achieve, telling herself:

*"I would be quite pretty if it wasn't for my nose!"*

However, this one unfortunate feature, as she saw it, never seemed to detract from her charm.

As a nurse, Annie May was quick, efficient and friendly. Nevertheless, there was one trait of her character that she was not so happy to acknowledge. She admitted to her grand-daughter, Angie:

*"They had a nickname for me in one hospital I worked in. They used to call me 'the bummer' because they thought I was a bit bossy. But we won't mention that. It's not that they didn't like me, but I did sometimes tend to take charge. I always got on with the other nurses, though.'"*

Nothing was too much trouble for her and she gained respect and friendship from patients, fellow nurses, doctors and other hospital staff alike. She fondly recalls:

*"I had a very happy time in London. I took every chance to see as much of the capital city as possible. I went to lots of places and saw all the shows. I saw Sybil Thorndike in Saint Joan – the Garrick Theatre was not far from Euston where I lived in the Tropical Diseases Hospital. They used to send complimentary tickets for the nurses so we'd go free. We were only earning £2 a month so we couldn't afford to go otherwise. I went out with other nurses from the hospital but I also had plenty of male friends to take me out, too. I saw the first all-black show in London. It was really spectacular. I saw "No, No Nanette," "Rosemary" and many other musicals. I went to the London Palladium and saw all the good artists.*

*I was taken to all the top restaurants – Hatchets of Park Lane, the Barshu in Soho, the Trocadero, Lyon's Corner House and lots of others. We took afternoon tea in smart hotels where they served dainty sandwiches with a wide variety of delicious pastries to choose from - "All the trimmings," as we would say. I hadn't been used to that but I did see it all. My eyes were opened as to how the other half lived, enjoying all the luxuries of life! I was very lucky in every way. I strolled in Kew Gardens, went boating on the lake in Windsor Park and on the Thames lots of times. I spent many a happy hour wandering through the famous London stores and got to know all the markets, too. I went to Portobello Road market that was open on Sundays too, not like the shops in Wales. I strolled round Covent Garden market, Berwick market and the Jewish market. Everywhere the stall-holders were friendly, always willing to display their wares to you personally. The trouble was that we didn't have much money to spend on clothes. I remember buying a 'costume' once for thirty bob (£1.50) in a sale but it turned out to be a riding outfit! Never mind, I wore it all the same."*

Sometimes, her patients were amongst those who offered to take her out to show her around or treat her to a meal or a musical etc. Having got to know them on the wards, Annie May often accepted these invitations. However, one such invitation did not turn out quite as expected. Just before he was discharged, one of the patients she had nursed for some time asked if she would like to go to see the new film that was showing at a nearby cinema. He was somewhat older than her but was a well-spoken gentleman and Annie May felt that it would be rude to refuse. She accepted the invitation and went to the cinema with him. To her amazement and disgust, no sooner had the lights been dimmed, she felt an arm around her shoulder and a hand on her knee. She immediately pushed him off and moved away as far as she could but the man continued to try to grope her. Annie May was horrified. She jumped up and rushed out of the cinema as fast as her legs would carry her. This was a very salutary lesson for her. She remembered the warnings given her by neighbours before she left Wales and vowed to make sure that no more predatory males would find it so easy to abuse her warm, trusting nature.

Towards the end of her course at the Hospital for Tropical Diseases, Annie May thought that she should try to get experience in a different sort of hospital. She discussed the matter with a young nurse with whom she had become friendly while working at the hospital. Together they decided to try their hands at psychiatric nursing, so she and her friend successfully interviewed for posts at a well-known London Psychiatric hospital. Once at their posts, they realised they were not cut out for this sort of nursing – they empathised too much with the pitiful patients for whom they cared. In later life, Annie May recounted how unfeeling and hardened some of her nursing colleagues were. True, they needed to be firm with violent patients who constituted a danger both to themselves and the staff. However, some nurses had little patience with those suffering from melancholia who went around weeping all day. These nurses were sometimes known to treat vulnerable patients in a cruel manner.

*"I thought I'd go into mental nursing at Hendon Grove. I was only there for a month and I knew it wasn't my cup of tea. I said that I wanted to leave but the head man in charge who was a doctor said, 'No, Nurse Davies, you haven't given it a proper try.' But I wasn't able to be hard with them, as you had to be at times. Some patients were violent and had to be restrained but you needed to be big and strong to deal with them and I was so small. I was too soft and felt for the poor, deranged patients. I remember one little lady in particular. She had a religious mania and insisted her food be given to*

31

*Lord Jesus. When her breakfast was brought, she would refuse to eat it and say, 'Give it to Lord Jesus.' Then the hardened nurses would force feed her a breakfast mixture of smoked haddock, porridge, tea, toast and marmalade. She struggled frantically and ended up with swollen and cut lips in the process. I couldn't do that. I would say, 'Come now, Miss Haslam. I have given some to Lord Jesus and now he wants you to eat your breakfast.' It took a little time to persuade her, but eventually she would eat her breakfast docilely."*

Unable to bear the suffering of the mentally disturbed patients any longer, Annie May and her friend tendered their resignations once again. Nevertheless, they were still told that they had not given it enough time to get used to the work and that they must stay on. However, the girls had made up their minds. They packed up their belongings and high-tailed it over the hospital wall, hoping that they would not be mistaken for escaping patients!

Annie May continued her nursing career working in the National Hospital for Diseases of the Heart, then at nineteen, she went to continue her training at Whipscross Hospital. It was 1926 the time of the week-long national strike. It brought the whole of the country to a standstill. Early in the week, Annie May was having lunch with her colleagues as usual, under the supervision of the Assistant Matron of the hospital. Talk started up about the current strike and the detrimental effect it was having on their lives. Above the raised voices, the Assistant Matron was heard to voice her opinion:

"It's those wretched miners that are responsible for all the problems that we Londoners are facing. If only they would go back to work, the strike would soon be over and things would get back to normal."

Annie May was absolutely furious at hearing the miners blamed for everything. Forgetting that she had not described her father as a miner when applying to be accepted on the nursing course, she blurted out,

*"Excuse me, Matron, my father is a miner and I know. I was in the 1921 strike when I was very young and it's not what you think at all. You don't know what their conditions of work are like. The owners still won't pay a living wage to men risking their lives to bring up coal to make them rich. The miners just have to strike. There is no other way!'*

Red as a beetroot, Annie May stood there trembling. A hush descended on the room. All eyes turned to the Assistant Matron.

"Oh! I'm sorry, Annie May. I didn't know that. I wouldn't have said anything had I known." Annie May sat down with a bump. She recalls:

*"Matron was very nice. She apologised immediately. I shouldn't really have said anything. I should have kept quiet but I couldn't help myself. I couldn't bear to see the miners put down unfairly. She could see that what she'd said had really upset me. She was very nice and understanding where*

*she could have been stern and harsh. She could have put me down in front of everyone but she was a fair and kind lady."*

The naïve girl from the Rhondda had matured into a smart, confident, self-educated, and experienced, though only semi-qualified, professional nurse. One thing was certain. No child of hers would ever be prevented from launching a professional career for lack of education. She vowed that any children she might have would go on to further and higher education, even university, though she knew of no-one from such a background as hers who had ever dreamed of achieving such dizzy heights. While Annie May continued to seek out nursing employment, her two younger sisters, Florrie and Olwen, remained in service all their working lives until they eventually married and settled in Bournemouth to bring up their families.

Younger brother, Davie, who had gone up to Nuneaton to work in the mines with his father, had left the pit after a mining accident. He was subsequently called up to serve in the army in the Burma campaign during World War II. After he was demobbed, Davey worked in the Stirling Metals Factory until 1950. Then he returned to mining at the Newdegate Colliery until ill health forced him to leave the pits for good in 1969. He finished his working career at the Dunlop factory in Coventry.

As for Iris, her youngest sister, Annie May was determined that Iris would have the chance in life she never had. She encouraged her to excel in her studies and sit the entrance examination for the prestigious Porth County Girls' School in the Rhondda. To her delight, Iris passed and duly took up her place in the best grammar school in the area. Annie May was as proud as Punch but her hopes were dashed when the adolescent girl later chose to accompany her parents to Nuneaton where well-paid factory work afforded her pretty clothes and money to spend. From then on, Iris remained in Nuneaton and was employed in various jobs before marrying to bring up her four children there. She was a dynamic and colourful personality and could turn her hand to almost anything. Thus, Annie May was the only one of the five Davies children destined to return to her roots in the Rhondda to marry and bring up her family in her native land.

Annie May continued to pursue her chosen career in London, returning regularly, as before, to her home in the Rhondda. Eventually, the strenuous work, entailing the lifting of heavy patients, told on her small frame. She strained herself and suffered an umbilical hernia. This necessitated a complete rest, so Annie May took the opportunity to return home to Wales on sick leave. She could not have imagined that a chance encounter during an exhilarating walk over the mountains overlooking her crowded valley would change the course of her life for the next sixty-six years.

# Chapter 3
# Tom's Story

While Annie May Davies was growing up in Ynyshir and subsequently in London, a young boy called Thomas Arthur Stevens, known as Tom, was born and bred in the neighbouring village of Wattstown. Although the eighth of eleven children, Tom was rather spoilt by his mother from a young age and turned out to be quite different from his siblings in many respects.

The villages of Ynyshir and Wattstown formed part of the coal-mining conglomeration of the Rhondda Valleys and were situated north of Porth, the confluence of the Rivers Rhondda. This confluence becomes the River Taff flowing on towards Pontypridd, the market town of the area, and from there to the Welsh capital, Cardiff (Caerdydd.) It is from this river that the nickname of the Welsh people is derived – *Taffies.* Prior to industrialisation, the wooded area cultivated by farmers from which Wattstown sprung was known locally either as Aberllechau or Cwtch. In the late 1870s the first deep mine originally known as Cwtch Colliery, renamed Standard Colliery and finally National Colliery, was sunk there. The pit was sunk by Edmund Hannay Watts of Northumberland who was also the owner of the colliery. The old Welsh village name was changed to Wattstown in the hope that it would draw immigrants from many diverse places into a close-knit community. Here too, rows of small stone terraced houses lined the valley floor dwarfed by the prolific chapels and pubs at every corner. Various non-conformist chapels looked after the spiritual health of their flocks while Anglicans worshipped in the Church in Wales, built in 1896 and dedicated to Saint Thomas. Aberllechau Road, the business hub of the village, stretched along the riverbanks parallel with the railway tracks

Tom was born on 7th January 1905, the eighth child of James Stevens and his wife Selina Jane John. He was named after his uncle Thomas John who was killed in the horrendous disaster in Wattstown Colliery in 1905. The family lived in a three-bed-roomed house at 29 Bailey Street. Just as the name of the village reflected the pit owner's name, the street was named after the brothers Crawshay and William Bailey who owned the land on which the National Colliery was built. The entrance to the colliery was situated at the top end of the street which stretched down to Wattstown Park at the lower end. Their home stood at the park end of the street where there was a space the size of a small house before the terrace continued as Lower Bailey Street. The family later managed to acquire this bit of land and constructed a garage on it with a wash house and storage room behind. This afforded much needed extra space for the growing Stevens family.

Tom's father James (Jim) came from West Harptree, Somerset working his way from Bristol by boat to seek work in the Welsh mines. The Englishmen who came to work in the Welsh valleys found the pretty Welsh girls much to their liking. Jim soon met and married Selina Jane, a young girl from a Welsh-speaking Treorchi family. Treorchi is in the Rhondda Fawr, the wider, more spacious of the two valleys, but the couple settled in Wattstown when Jim secured work in the National Colliery there.

Having set up home in Bailey Street, they produced a large family of seven boys and four girls all of whom survived into adulthood: William John (Will John), David James (Dai), Mark Henry (Mark), Mary Ann (Nan), Elizabeth Agnes Rosina (Rosie), Edwin George (Ted), Ivor Lewis (Ivor), Thomas Arthur (Tom), Selina, Florrie (Bopa) and Septimus Glanville (Glan.)

Father to so many children and tired after long, hard shifts underground, Jim proved to be rather forgetful at times. On one occasion, he was almost at the registry office when he realised he had totally forgotten the name he and his wife had chosen for their fourth daughter. As he was racking his brains, he caught site of an elderly family friend called Florrie who came up to congratulate him on the birth of his latest child, so he decided on the spot to name his daughter after her. The birth certificate read *Florrie* and so the new baby did not even have the full name of Florence on her birth certificate.

Tom's mother, Selina Jane, was industrious, sweet, loving, and always keen to care for her family as best she could. She worked hard and tirelessly to give each of her eleven children the best possible chance in life. Selina Jane knitted, sewed and patched her children's clothes, while husband Jim mended their shoes so that their children were always well turned out to go to school or chapel. They were always clean and tidy and there was no lack of books in the house if Selina Jane had anything to do with it.

Sweet and homely as she was, Selina Jane was a strong woman who was determined to educate her children to enable them to achieve their full potential. All the Stevens children attended the Aberllechau Primary School regularly. In addition to the onerous tasks of feeding, clothing and caring for her husband and their large brood, she undertook to go out to work, papering walls and bringing home extra washing to be done in the evenings after the children were tucked up in bed. This ensured she had enough money to keep her children in school, to have books in the house as well as to pay for music lessons for them, a priority in this family.

With such a large family to care for, Selina Jane used her boys' clothes and socks many times as hand-me-downs as the younger ones grew, and all were content with this situation except for young Tom. He was fussier than his elder brothers and took more pride in his appearance. The boys would happily grab any shirt or pair of socks from the general pile of clean laundry regardless of who had worn it last. Not so Tom! He hated to have to rummage in the huge pile of socks to try to find a matching pair and demanded that he could keep "his" shirts, socks and underclothes for himself. His mother seemed content to allow her eighth child this and other privileges denied to the others. As he was not too keen on *cawl* (a nourishing Welsh stew of numerous root vegetables, cooked with leeks and onions and as much mutton or lamb as could be afforded), his mother would occasionally treat him to some bacon and egg in secret. So, even as one of eleven children, he managed to get himself spoiled and this continued for the rest of his life.

Situated as he was in the centre of a large family, young Tom had to learn to survive amongst his boisterous siblings. He was bossed by the elder brothers and sisters and had to look after the younger ones at times in his turn. There were the inevitable squabbles, but on the whole they all got on quite well together and were brought up in a loving atmosphere. Tom spent many happy hours running free over the hills, swimming in the reservoir and playing football with his siblings and butties in the street and the nearby park. He was a serious and healthy little boy and was proud to recall that he never missed a day's school in his life. He was awarded a medal in recognition of this feat which his son, Michael, still treasures to this day. The accompanying certificate reads "Awarded to Thomas Arthur Stevens for good conduct and 100% attendance at Aberllechau Primary School July, 1915."

Tom joined the Cubs as a small boy and as a matter of course eventually graduated to the Scouts. He loved participating in this association and worked assiduously to acquire all his badges. When Tom was nine years' old, he was offered a chance to go on a camping expedition to Ogmore, a seaside village on the South Wales coast.

"Mr. Evans the scout master said I could go camping with the scouts to Ogmore in the Easter Holidays. Can I go, please, Mam?" he pleaded.

"How much will it cost?" was the first thing Selina Jane needed to know.

"Six pence," admitted Tom. "But we can pay a penny a week and there's still six weeks before Easter," added Tom hastily. His mother knew just how much his scouting meant to her eighth son, so she said gently:

"We'll have to see what Daddy will say about it." Tom was delighted, as he was confident that his mother would be able to persuade his father to let him go as it was Selina Jane who ran the finances of the household. Like all working miners, Jim brought home the weekly pay packet and threw it into the waiting lap of his wife. There his responsibility ended. It was up to his wife to see that there was enough to feed and clothe the family, pay the rent and all the other weekly outgoings and also that there was something left for the man of the house to enjoy a little smoke or drink with his butties occasionally.

As expected, the day came and Tom was off with his pals on the great adventure. They clambered into the waiting bus and began to sing their scout marching songs with great gusto. Leaving behind the congested valleys, they rolled on through the lush Vale of Glamorgan. They scanned the fields to see whether the cows were standing up or lying down to determine what kind of weather they were likely to have during their week's camping. Then they were at the coast and the bus echoed with *oohs* and *aahs* and cries of

"I can see the sea!"

"Where?"

"Over there!" as the excited boys strained to look out of the windows.

"Now boys, keep calm," said Mr. Evans, as the boys tumbled out of the bus.

"There's lots of work to do before we can sit around a camp fire to make our supper. First we must make camp and put up the tents, so we all have jobs to do."

He soon marshalled the boys into an efficient workforce. The tents were quickly erected and the sleeping bags neatly installed inside. Camp was made on a flat field high up overlooking the sea.

"Now, you must keep together and follow me down this path. We are going to search for drift wood on the beach to make our campfire."

Once on the beach, the boys scampered all over the place picking up pieces of wood, large and small. Back on the field, the flames were soon leaping up from a mountainous camp fire and the aroma of baked beans and sizzling sausages reminded the boys how hungry they were. They lined up to fill their mess tins, and then sat down at a safe distance around the fire to eat their fill before singing lustily their favourite songs. The pure sound of treble voices rang out in the still evening air as the boys sang together the famous scout song "Ging Gang Goolie" written by their founder, Robert Baden Powell. Sleepy after all the excitement and their recent exertions, they needed no persuasion to jump into bed under the tents with their pals. Soothed by the regular sound of the waves breaking on the shore, the high pitched chatter of excited young voices quickly died down as they dropped off to sleep one by one. Tom reaped great benefits from this most enjoyable of experiences. It inspired him to continue scouting as a boy and to encourage others to join the movement by training to become a scout master himself as a young man.

The Stevens family found times hard, especially when the children were young and there was only one breadwinner in the family. Like all children in South Wales at that time, they were destined to leave school at thirteen to go to work. Yet again Tom proved rather different from his other siblings. All his older brothers (except Dai who had a weak chest) were set to follow their father into the mines to work as colliers, hewing coal in the dark, low dangerous seams of The National Colliery, Wattstown. When young Tom left school at the end of the summer before his thirteenth birthday, he was most reluctant to join his older brothers working underground. However, work he had to, like all the others, so he voiced his concerns to his parents.

"I really don't want to work underground, Dad," he said. "It's pitch black down there and my stomach turns over when the cage clangs shut and drops suddenly down to the bottom."

"You'll get used to it, son," his father tried to console him.

"It's not just that. It's so noisy, filthy and boiling 'ot down there and there's no room to move. You have to crawl about on your 'ands and knees and then there's rats everywhere. You don't know if it's the rats or the trams squeaking and squealing. Ivor told me they ate his bread and apple last week when he put them down for a minute. I 'ated it down there when he took me down!"

"There's not much choice in the way of work in these parts, my boy," said his father solemnly. However, Tom stubbornly refused to back down.

"He doesn't have to go down the pit, you know, Jim," interjected his mother. "Not everyone works underground. There are plenty of jobs on the top, even if they are not so well paid on the whole. Tom could go in with our Dai tomorrow and see what's available."

So it was decided that Tom would ask the foreman what jobs were currently available on the top of the pit. The job he finally opted to take entailed various tasks at different times. These included emptying the journeys full of coal, sorting the shiny black anthracite from the small coal and the waste and washing the coal in the washery before it was weighed into tons and bagged to be delivered to homes or to huge industrial plants. Tom gradually became conversant with all these various jobs and was later called upon to oversee the men carrying them out on the top. For many years he refused to take promotion to the post of Colliery Official because, with a young, growing family, he needed to work overtime to provide adequately for their needs. Colliery officials received a regular salary and could not earn overtime money.

When reminiscing, Tom proudly told his children and grandchildren that he had often worked a staggering nine *turns* (shifts) in a week. The work was hard and unpleasant, but at least Tom worked in the fresh air and could enjoy God's light on his face. Thus it transpired that Tom never suffered from the miners' disease of silicosis, unlike some of his brothers and friends whose wheezing chests, intense coughs and respiratory problems due to the inhalation of coal dust, blighted and shortened their lives.

His elder brother, Ted, developed silicosis early in his life and had to give up work. He was paid compensation and a small disability pension. He then ran the household in the family home in Bailey Street and constructed a smallholding on the steep mountainside behind the house. The house itself had just a small garden which was accessed by means of some narrow, steep steps and towered over the meagre back yard. At the top, the garden opened out onto a large piece of land stretching over the mountainside which the brothers had fenced in to contain their smallholding. Ted grew all their vegetables and soft fruit and kept chickens and pigs, so they were quite self-sufficient. Even throughout the strict rationing during the Second World War, the family always managed to eat well. All the other brothers lent a hand at weekends and in their spare time after their mining shifts.

Thus it was that all the oldest boys followed their father Jim, down the pit while Tom worked on the surface of the same colliery. Dai also worked on top in the washeries as he had suffered lung problems from his youth. Only the youngest son Glan was spared from working in the pit. He started work in a grocery shop, called Terry Stores, in Ynyshir. Third son Mark, however, had been "farmed out" to his grandmother Selina John at about four years old and so always lived separately from the rest of the family. He ended up running a pub called *The Adare Hotel* in Penygraig in the Rhondda Fawr (the big Rhondda valley).

Eldest son William John won one of the very few scholarships to Porth Secondary Grammar School. He was given training in the colliery and subsequently became the Under-Manager of Wattstown Colliery, where all his brothers worked. The eldest girl, Mary Ann (Nan), also won a full scholarship. This scholarship, even more prestigious and very highly coveted, was to the Porth County Grammar School. At this time, it was a private school catering for the children of pit owners, managers and engineers as well as those of the local doctors, lawyers and successful businessmen. Before leaving, she passed her matriculation which gave her the qualification of uncertificated teacher, although she never actually entered this profession. After a fourteen-year courtship, she eventually married Edwin Llewellyn, but never left the family home. Her new husband came to live amongst the family, and to us nieces and nephews, he was indistinguishable from the other bachelor uncles of the Stevens clan. It was some time before we learned which one of the "boys" was Nan's husband! She took over the running of the huge household even before her mother died. Along with Nan, Uncle Ted appeared to be the "boss" over all his brothers and it was these two strong personalities who ruled the roost.

Even though Rosie also won a scholarship, the family could not afford to keep both girls in school. Rosie had to go to work in a butchery business belonging to a family named Davies in Aberdare in the nearby Cynon Valley to contribute her share to the family income. She was welcomed into the Davies household where she helped run the family business. Rosie was very efficient and fitted in well, forming a strong bond with Jack, one of the sons. Eventually, Rosie followed Jack Davies to Kent, to where he had *emigrated* with his family and they married in 1929. They had two children, Jane and John. Rosie turned out to be a good businesswoman. She set up a clothing and footwear business in Hersden, Kent in the 1930s. Through Nan, they sold clothes, bed linen etc. to the wider family and neighbours in South Wales over many years. Younger brother Glan later followed Rosie to Kent where he worked in the Chislet colliery offices and always helped his sister in the family business.

In her turn, Selina also won a scholarship and, being younger, the family could afford to support her in college to train as a teacher. She also lived with Rosie in Kent for some time before leaving to teach in London where she married Bill Evans and had a baby boy. Florrie remained at home to do most of the household duties until she married Dan Radcliffe, chief mining engineer of all the Rhondda pits. They had one daughter called Rosemary. Ivor, like Ted before him, had to give up mining after also contracting silicosis, and thereafter found work as a hospital engineer in Porth Cottage Hospital, the next village south along the valley from Ynyshir. When Florrie was later widowed, she moved from Treorchi to Porth so brother Ivor decided to make his home with her. It was a most convenient arrangement for everybody. Ivor acted as the man of the house and was well cared for by his sister in return. The hospital was only a stone's throw from their new home, as was Rosemary's Grammar School.

With six men bringing in wages and throwing them into the family pot, first into their mother Selina Jane's lap, later that of their eldest sister, Nan, the family became relatively well off. Many of them were musical, too. As they grew, they all took great pleasure in participating in musical get-togethers after the day's work was done. Musical instruments were purchased for any of the children who wished to learn as soon as contributions from youngsters' wages permitted, while the other members of the family joined in the singing. They bought a piano and Bopa became a competent player, both in classical and jazz. Glan took lessons and played the cello, Ted strummed the banjo and Ivor had a fine baritone voice.

Tom had a fine tenor voice. He also decided to learn to play the violin and bought himself an instrument as soon as he had earned enough money and became a really proficient violinist. He not only played to accompany musical evenings at home, but for many years was the leader of the second violin section of the Rhondda Symphony Orchestra. Brother Mark was also musically talented – a clarinettist. For a short period before Tom's marriage, he and Tom formed and played together in a small concert group. The love of music stayed with Tom for the rest of his life. It brought him and many others great joy and happiness. Music helped him and his family through many a difficult period in their life together in the future.

# Chapter 4
# Romance, Marriage and Adversity

Annie May had returned to Wales from London where she was nursing. She had come home for an umbilical hernia operation and was now recuperating on sick leave. One of her favourite pursuits when back in Wales was to go for long walks with her father and grandfather over the hills overlooking the busy valleys. It was so peaceful up there away from all the clang and clatter of the pits working twenty-four hours a day. It was on one such walk that Annie May first met Tom. She recounts:

*"I went out for a walk with my father and my grandfather who was living with us in 7 William Street. We went up the mountain where we always walked, right up to Llanwynno and over to Ynysybwl. There is a little pub there to this day, but it has been altered quite a bit. There's far more people going in there than there were. We didn't go into the pub as such in those days. But there was this little room with a piano in it. As soon as my father saw the piano, he was up on his feet and he said "Now come on, Annie May – harmonise with me." So, of course, always one to sing anything that was wanted, I stood in front of a little window looking out onto the mountain. I was a soprano then, and singing away with my father with my grandfather in the room with just another man there, too. That didn't stop us singing our hearts out.*

*I could see these two young men looking in and, after a few minutes, in they came. Tom was twenty-four at the time and the other young man, Ifan, was my age, a few years younger. They were friends and were in the local scout movement. In fact, Tom was the Assistant Scoutmaster when I met him. Anyway, they came in and went towards my father and grandfather, looking at me at the same time, and I was looking at them. After we finished singing, we all decided that we would walk back together. So my father and grandfather walked behind us and I walked in front with the two boys.*

*I didn't take much notice of either of them. Tom told me he was going to the Scout Jamboree on the Monday. He was going for a fortnight but this other young man was not. So he said to me, "Would you like to come to the pictures with me on Saturday night?" I didn't have anything better to do, so I went. Ifan was a shy young man and we went out together to the pictures and for walks for a couple of weeks and then Tom came home. I knew he always walked through Wattstown Park down to Ynyshir so I thought I'd pop up the Park on Sunday afternoon and I might see him. I popped up the Park and – well – there you are! He saw me and we had a chat. He knew I'd been going out with Ifan but it didn't make any difference and he asked if I would go to the pictures with him. So I did. Ifan was a very nice boy but I thought I'd give Tom a chance. From there it went on. I liked him. Of course, Tom and Ifan had been great friends, but I don't think they were great friends for very long after that. They got over it in the end.'*

As for Tom, that first meeting with Annie May on the mountaintop was vividly etched in his memory. Ifan and he were strolling over the hillsides when they approached the little stone pub in Ynysybwl.

"Let's go and have a beer," suggested Ifan.

"OK" rejoined Tom. "Last one inside buys the first round!" With that they both set off at breakneck speed over the rough ground. The sound of singing coming from a little window in the front of the old pub brought them both up sharp. They stopped to listen and as soon as they had got their breath back, they approached the window from whence emanated this exquisite sound. Standing at the window, was a pretty young girl singing her favourite Welsh folk song "Y Deryn Pur" *(The Gentle Bird)* in harmony with a rich tenor voice coming from within. Tom never forgot the impression this vision of loveliness had made on him.

"She was standing there with the sun shining on her beautiful dark hair, wearing a blue hat and singing as sweetly as a little bird," Tom was wont to tell us time and again in years to come. Awe struck, Tom whispered,

"What a lovely voice. It's as sweet and pure as a little bird!"

"She's quite a looker, too," rejoined Ifan. "Let's go and have a closer look." The two young men went into the bar and bought their drinks.

"Who are the people singing in the side room?" Tom asked the bartender.

"It's Dai Davies Singer from Ynyshir with his daughter just home from London. Dai comes here often with the old man and is always up for a song."

"Do you think they would mind if we went in to listen?" asked Tom. "We wouldn't disturb them."

"Not at all. Dai is very sociable and welcomes anybody who appreciates music. He'll have you both joining in the singing in no time!" the barman assured them.

Taking their drinks, the two young men knocked on the door and entered quietly. "Is it alright if we come in to listen?" asked Ifan.

"Of course! Come on in - welcome. Come and sing with us if you like." replied Dai. At first the two young men were too shy to join in with the singing but listened spellbound to the young soprano. However, it was not long before the friendly, lively atmosphere encouraged them to add their voices to swell the well known melodies.

"You've not got a bad voice yourself," Dai told the blushing Tom. "Tenor, are you?"

"I suppose so," spluttered Tom. "I play the violin mostly in the Rhondda Orchestra." Annie May looked with a little more interest at the young man. He was smart and good-looking with thick dark hair and a definite twinkle in his bright blue eyes. His companion was not bad looking either. It was turning out to be an unexpectedly pleasurable afternoon. In a flash it was time to make their way back home for Sunday lunch. By then, they were all in a very friendly mood, so they decided to walk back together.

Annie May, Tom and Ifan walked together in front, while her father and grandfather brought up the rear.

"I haven't seen you around these parts," ventured Tom. "Don't you ever go dancing to Porth Rink?"

"No. I live in London normally," replied Annie May. "I've come home on sick leave. I'm a nurse and I've strained myself, so I've come home for a rest. I might need an operation later on, I suppose."

Tom was even more impressed. This was no ordinary maid of the valleys. She had travelled far and had lived in the great metropolis of London.

"How long are you here for?" he asked. Surely he was not going to lose her so soon after making her acquaintance!

"I don't know yet. It will depend on how soon I get fit," replied Annie May.

Hoping to impress, Tom continued

"I'm Assistant Scout Master for the Ynyshir and Wattstown pack and I'm taking them up to the third World Scout Jamboree in Birkenhead next Monday."

"You'll enjoy that. I'm sure you'll have a great time. How long will you be away for?" asked Annie May.

"A fortnight," replied Tom despondently.

"I'm not going," cut in Ifan hurriedly. He had been feeling a bit left out while Tom had been hugging all the conversation. "Perhaps you would like to come to the pictures with me on Saturday, if you have nothing better to do," he ventured.

"Thanks. I'd love to," replied Annie May, smiling sweetly and with a naughty twinkle in her dark eyes as she noted Tom's discomfort. "What a shame you'll be away then, Tom," she said. "We could have all gone together."

Tom was cursing his luck but not to be outdone, he quickly responded,

"Never mind. I'll tell you all about it when I get back, that's if you've not returned to London by then. It'll be a great experience to take part in the Jamboree with scouts from all over the world."

"Yes and I'm sure you'll have a great time," said Annie May.

Indeed, it turned out to be a wonderful experience for Tom. The Third World Scout Jamboree organised by Robert Baden Powel took place in August 1929 in Arrowe Park, Birkenhead. It was to celebrate the Coming of Age of the scout movement, which had been founded twenty-one years earlier. On 2nd August, a Great Camp was set up over 450 acres to accommodate 30,000 scouts from 42 different nations. At the same time, the Girl Guides set up a hospital under canvas to treat such common ailments as cuts, burns, sprains and fractures. This hospital tent was well organised and the young girls turned out to be most efficient. Their excellent work changed the attitudes of the Heads of Boy Scout Movements from other countries towards Guiding.

When Tom returned and, having met up once more – and not entirely by chance on Annie May's part – in Wattstown Park, the two young people started to go out together regularly and gradually fell in love. At first, they were quite content to let things take their course and enjoy one another's company for the time being. They set out for long walks over the surrounding hills, went to the 'pictures', enjoyed music together and Annie May could often be seen riding pillion on Tom's motorbike. Occasionally, they went further afield – a trip to the big city of Cardiff or to the seaside at Barry or Porthcawl, either just the two of them or with groups of young friends.

Naturally there came a time when decisions had to be made about their future. There could be no question of a whirlwind romance and subsequent marriage for them due to the difficult financial circumstances in which they found themselves. They were both serious and sensible about things and soon realised that the times in which they lived were not conducive to setting up home together to start a family. None of Tom's older brothers had left home to venture into married life. Things were looking up for the large Stevens family while they all stuck together and brought their pay packets home to elder siblings Nan and Ted who did a good job of running the family home and smallholding. Once again, Tom was soon to prove different from his brothers.

\* \* \* \* \*

At first, Tom and Annie May told no one of their decision to try to make a life together. Tom called Annie May by a shortened form of her name as a sort of pet name for her, so hence forth the couple were known as Tom and May, except in May's nuclear family where she was always Annie May. After her hernia operation, which took place in Porth Cottage Hospital, May did not return to London. She was offered work as a nurse in Porth Hospital and decided to accept. This meant that she could go on seeing Tom and planning their future life together. Pay for nurses in small hospitals was quite poor as most of it went towards paying for their keep.

Tom had become a member of Wattstown Boys' Club as a teenager and had developed into an excellent billiards player. He would regularly win small amounts of prize money in the competitions. As he was living at home, Tom was expected to put his pay packet in with the rest of the family and so until he had broached the subject of his proposed marriage, he had to rely on his winnings from his billiards and his musical gigs to add to their savings. They carried on like this for some time but eventually came to the conclusion that it would take far too long to save enough unless something was done to improve things. They decided, therefore, to come clean and tell their respective families of their desire to get married. When Tom finally let the cat out of the bag in 29 Bailey Street, the cat was really amongst the pigeons!

"Why do you want to go and do such a silly thing, Tom?" shouted Ted.

"You're much better off home here with us," advised Ivor.

"I know that, but May and I love each other," said Tom, stubbornly. All his other siblings joined in the heated debate to try to dissuade him from such a foolish decision but Tom held firm. Hoping to gain an ally, he turned to his mother:

"You understand, don't you, Mam?" he asked, plaintively.

"Of course, love," she said. "But they're right, you know. Work is very scarce and you can't be sure to earn enough money to put food in your own mouth let alone keep a wife."

Selina Jane had been a wonderful mother. She gave all her children the security of a mother's unconditional love, but she had one slight flaw. She was rather possessive of her children, especially her sons, and wanted to keep them around her for life. Her eldest daughter Mary Ann, a very dominant and determined woman, was really the driving force of this philosophy, though. Thus many a girl's heart was broken by the Stevens boys who chose to break off their relationships and remain bachelors, spoilt by their mother and sisters at home. But, once again, Tom chose to be different. Although quite a favourite of his mother, things became rather difficult after he had admitted he wanted to get married. Finally, Tom was forced to leave home and take refuge with his brother Mark in the weeks and months leading up to the wedding. He went to live with his brother temporarily in the Adare Hotel, which Mark managed in Penygraig. The family made it quite clear to him that if he continued in his determination to marry Annie May, then he was *"out of the clan"* and would forthwith have to *"paddle his own canoe."*

Even Annie May's family was not keen for them to get married at that time. Another problem had arisen in the Davies household. Annie May's sister, Florrie, was in service in an elegant London house. She was seduced by the master of the house and dismissed from her job when she became pregnant.

She was given some money and sent to a hostel in which unmarried girls gave birth to their babies. As soon as the family found out that Florrie had given birth to a baby boy, Dai, the ever-loving and protective father, and Annie May went up to London and rescued them both before the baby could be put up for adoption. They brought them home and Dai and Lizzy decided to bring up the child, who was named Dewi (a Welsh version of 'David'), as their own, so that Florrie would not have to go through life with the stigma of having an illegitimate child. Sadly, however, shortly afterwards, although bonny and healthy, little Dewi fell victim to cot death which tended to occur more frequently in those days. Having realised that she herself could have been born out of wedlock, and having experienced Florrie's tragedy, Annie May vowed that such a fate would never befall her. She, herself, would still be a virgin when she finally married Tom at the age of twenty-five.

Well established as a nurse, Annie May had no trouble finding regular employment in her chosen profession. However, since married women were not allowed to work, she would have to give up nursing if she married, and Tom's pay would not be enough to keep them both, as work in the South Wales coalfields was most irregular and poorly paid. Her father advised her to think carefully before deciding to take the plunge while her mother warned:

"You are very silly to get married in these days, Annie May. There's not much work around and times are bad for everyone round here." Nevertheless, Tom and May were determined and nothing could change their minds. They racked their brains to try to find a way out of their seemingly impossible situation. Tom was now working in his brother's pub at weekends to earn extra money to swell their savings.

Having worked for almost three years in Porth Cottage Hospital, May decided to look for work in Bristol just across the Bristol Channel to boost her salary. The money she was earning in Porth was nothing compared with what she could earn in private nursing. May found a better-paid job working in the prestigious Boys' Public School, Clifton College, where she earned the princely sum of ten pounds a month. She worked in Bristol for a further two years while Tom remained working at the surface of Wattstown Colliery. Their courtship was to last almost five years altogether. They were not happy with the separation but were determined to do anything to make their savings grow to ensure a more secure start to their married life. Tom occasionally allowed himself the luxury of a trip across the channel to visit May in Bristol.

The South Wales Coalfield, like the other industrial areas in the North of England and Scotland, bore the brunt of the depression that occurred in the aftermath of the First Word War. After the collapse of the General Strike of 4 May 1926, conditions had worsened considerably for the miners. Mass unemployment and dire poverty were rife in the Rhondda. Angry with the dreadful conditions in which they were forced to work and the cut in wages

46

imposed by the mine owners, the miners were caught in a trap, afraid of losing their jobs and the means of eking out a living for themselves and their families. Desperate workers were humiliated by being made to queue up each day to be either taken on for work or rejected by the officials. This often resulted in miners being given just two or three days' work in a week which debarred them from qualifying for unemployment benefit or the "dole" as it was known in the area. This system engendered fierce anger amongst the miners who received less money for a few days' work than they would have received if they had been fully unemployed.

Due to the great hardship suffered in these deprived areas of Britain, several Hunger Marches to London took place during the 1920s. May's father, Dai Davies, joined in the South Wales Miners' March to London in 1927. Desperate to make their voices heard and to get their grievances redressed, they banded together to undertake the long, walk to meet up with fellow sufferers from the North of England and Scotland in the capital city. Desperately hungry as they all were, only the strongest and fittest could even contemplate undertaking such an exhausting marathon journey on foot. As they went, they sang to keep their spirits up along the route. Full of Welsh "hwyl," (emotion) Dai's strong tenor voice rang out to lead the singing and encourage his comrades on the march. The road was long, their feet were weary and hunger gnawed at their stomachs, but they pressed on. People along the way took pity on the marchers and gave the poor bedraggled miners hot drinks, food and shelter to sustain them on their weary march. However, the government of the day was deaf to their plight and the bosses remained firm, and so their great efforts gained them little indeed.

Unrest, tension and occasionally violence continued until it all culminated in the Great National Hunger March against the Means Test in 1932. Once again, Dai Davies was foremost amongst those who set out from the valleys on the long march to London. Inevitably, some of the men floundered along the way and were almost ready to throw in the towel.

"I just can't go on," moaned Evan Rees, "My boots are in 'oles and my right foot is bleedin'."

"You just sit down by there," said Dai, "You'll feel better after a little whiff. Look here – I've got some strong cardboard to put in your boots and a spare pair of socks you can have."

"But you'll need 'em yourself, Dai," Evan stammered.

"Oh no – my socks are thick and will last to London and back," replied Dai.

So they rested a while and a kind lady gave them hot drinks to refresh them. Then they rejoined their comrades on the march. Dai immediately burst into song, and, full of Welsh "hwyl," he helped keep up their spirits as their hearts swelled with emotion.

They sang in harmony as they marched along. Sometimes, it was the sad minor keys of well-known traditional folk-songs and hymns such as "Dafydd Y Garreg Wen" (David of the White Rock) or "Bugeillio'r gwenith Gwyn," a tale of unrequited love, whose haunting melody tugged at the heartstrings of the bystanders. At other times, it was the rising choruses of "Cwm Rhondda" (Bread of Heaven), "Calon Lan" (A Clean Heart) and such stirring battle hymns as "I Bob Un Sydd Ffyddlon" (For Everyone who has Faith) that roused the drooping spirits of the exhausted stragglers. Many bystanders were moved to admiration for the determined marchers and sympathisers offered them food and shelter all along the route. The marchers from South Wales, Scotland and the North of England converged on Hyde Park where they were greeted by a huge crowd of about 100,000 people. The march had sapped the energy of even the strongest by the time they had arrived in London. There the marchers were confronted by a force of 70,000 mounted police. Fearing public disorder, the pitiful band of 3,000 marchers was cruelly dispersed by the much superior police force, leaving seventy-five demonstrators badly injured and the miners facing yet another shattering defeat. Their petition, containing a million signatures demanding the abolition of the *means test,* was confiscated before it could reach Parliament. It was little wonder that Dai had advised his daughter to think hard about getting married in such grim circumstances.

In Bristol, May settled into a new job as private nurse in Clifton. She helped run the infirmary there and nursed boys who succumbed to the usual ailments of influenza, bronchitis etc. as well as bandaging up sports' injuries and treating minor accidents. She enjoyed the work and though she missed being near Tom, was able to make inroads into her "bottom drawer." During her time there, the school was honored by a visit of Queen Alexandra. While reviewing the nurses, all lined up in their smartest uniforms, the queen stopped by the little bright-eyed Welsh nurse and had a brief conversation with her. May was the envy of her fellow nurses who had not been so fortunate as to catch the eye of the visiting queen.

In her time off from her nursing duties, May toured the large department stores such as Bright's of Bristol to build her trousseau. The New Year Sales were a must for her and Tom who came up to help her choose household necessities such as crockery, cutlery and saucepans. Through Nan, they purchased blankets and bed linen as well as Tom's new suit for the wedding from Rosie's shop in Kent. They had decided on a white wedding in Saint Anne's Anglican Church in Ynyshir. May's younger sisters, Olwen and Iris, came up to Bristol to help her choose the wedding gown, veil and tiara that she would wear on her Big Day. This would ensure that there would be no possibility that Tom would catch a glimpse of it until he saw May coming towards him down the aisle in Saint Anne's. At the same time, the young girls chose the dresses that the bridesmaids were to wear on the day.

Though both families were now resigned to the fact that a wedding was inevitable, the young couple were not yet officially engaged. Some months before the planned wedding, May came home to Wales for a weekend break. May recalls:

*"We didn't tell anyone we were getting engaged. We went to Cardiff, bought the engagement ring and that glass toilet set I've got upstairs on my dressing table. He bought me that as a sort of engagement present, so I told my mother that we were engaged on the Sunday. We decided we'd get married on the Christmas time on Boxing Day. So I went back to Bristol to finish getting everything ready and returned home three weeks before the wedding. I was twenty-five in the July and got married at Christmas time and Tom was almost twenty-nine, as his birthday is on 7th January. Everything went off alright. We had a lovely white wedding in Saint Anne's Church, Ynyshir."*

The wedding was quite a smart affair. May was very beautiful in her elegant white gown, sparkling tiara and long lace veil and train. She carried a large bouquet and was attended by her sisters, Olwen and Iris, and Tom's niece, Ivy May, the daughter of his brother, Mark. Tom looked equally smart and handsome in his new dark wedding suit and as proud as punch to have his lovely bride on his arm. Their one-day honeymoon was spent walking along the cliffs overlooking the Bristol Channel in Penarth followed by an afternoon tea at the Angel Hotel in central Cardiff. On the train to Cardiff, however, Tom was slightly the worse for wear after having drunk one too many of the wedding toasts provided at the reception in Saint Anne's Church Hall. This left Annie May wondering for a moment whether she'd done the right thing in marrying him, but she quickly dismissed the thought as Tom made a rapid recovery in the fresh air over the cliffs.

The young couple could be justifiably proud of what almost five long years of saving and deferred gratification had brought. Tom had also reluctantly decided to sell his beloved motor-bike to swell the funds. Both their families had rallied round and had had time to save for quite substantial wedding presents. So, together with what they themselves had saved, they had everything necessary to start married life together. Tom's large family had clubbed together to provide the bedroom suite comprising of an oak wardrobe, dressing table, chest of drawers and bed while May's family gave them a dining table, and matching chairs. They bought the three-piece lounge suite and the sideboard themselves. They were thus able to fully furnish the rooms they were to rent in Gynor Place, Ynyshir, where they made their first home. This precious furniture went with them whenever they moved until they finally settled to bring up their family in 7 William Street, May's childhood home. In fact, the furniture was of such good quality and was so well cared for that some pieces survive to this day and are treasured by their children in memory of their secure happy childhood.

* * * * *

It was only to be expected that things would not prove easy for the newlyweds. They had married on Boxing Day 1933 bang in the middle of one of the worst depressions in British history. Now a married woman, the loss of her salary was sorely felt. Tom, like all workers dependant on the coal mines for a living, had to queue up with everyone else to plead for work each day. There was absolutely no security for them and May would be at her wits' end to make ends meet. It was then that his winnings on the billiard table and his evenings behind the bar in Mark's pub proved to be an absolute godsend. They were together, however, and never ceased to believe that better times would eventually come.

The young couple settled happily into the rooms they rented in Gynor Place where May was proud to cook, clean and make a home for her hard-working husband. She packed his lunch-box carefully with the choicest tit-bits as well as the usual energy-giving sandwiches. The first time that Tom opened the box that his new wife had packed for him, he was astonished to find that a clean white napkin had been included with the food. His butties had a field day teasing him about it!

"What you got there, Tommy bach?" asked old Evan Jenkins.

"Ee's brought 'is new white shirt in by mistake. Must 'ave thought ee was goin' to the choir concert, not to the pit!" cut in Selwyn.

"Oh, it's a tablecloth," added Ifan. "You goin' all posh on us now you're married then? You're not in the Ritz 'ere, you know."

Embarrassed, Tom tried to laugh it off.

"That's old London ways for you, mun. May'll soon get used to things 'ere." He then had to explain, as delicately as he could to May that it was not very suitable to take white napkins to work as they would immediately become soiled with coal-dust.

Despite the hardships they suffered, especially in the early years of their marriage, they never regretted their decision and thanked God for the family life they led together. Tom was always so proud of even the smallest achievements of his five children: "My chest is out" he was often wont to say. Their children were worth so much more to Tom and May than money. Always ready to help neighbours who were in an even worse predicament than they were themselves, they formed part of a close- knit community that stood together in the face of adversity. Indeed, towards the end of his life when only Ted survived out of all his siblings, Tom counted himself to be the lucky one, surrounded as he was by a loving, happily-settled family. His brother, on the other hand, alone in the empty family home, cut a sad and lonely figure with nothing but money in the bank. Though times were almost always financially difficult as Tom and May strove together to bring up their large family, their marriage was long and strong. They lived to become a real "Derby and Joan" couple, just missing out on celebrating their sixtieth wedding anniversary together.

# PART 2 :

## Life in the Rhondda

## (1934 – 1953)

# Chapter 5
# The Early Years

On 22nd October 1934, a little bundle of joy arrived in the new Stevens family to lighten the gloom just ten months after Tom and May were married. Their first child was to be called Michael or Patricia. I was born safely to a fit and competent young mother and a devoted father, struggling together to create a good life for their new-born daughter. Life was not all a bed of roses for the newlyweds however.

The Great Depression, usually attributed to the sudden devastating collapse of the US stock market on 29th October 1929, known as "Black Tuesday," lasted until the end of the 1930s. The steady decline in the world economy did not reach rock bottom until 1933, the very year in which Tom and May wed. This was not an auspicious beginning.

The aftermath of the First World War had caused a downturn in British exports such as coal throughout the 1920s. This was exacerbated in 1925 when Churchill restored the pound sterling to the gold standard which immediately slowed the economic recovery. Heavy industries, the bedrock of Britain's export trade (such as coalmining, shipbuilding and steel production) were concentrated in Northern England, South Wales and Central Scotland. These areas, therefore, bore the brunt of the recession where unemployment ran at a steady one million throughout the twenties. To offset the slowdown, export industry bosses tried to cut costs by lowering workers' wages, thus provoking the General Strike on 4 May 1926. When the strike was finally called off, the TUC had failed in its attempt to prevent wage reduction and worsening conditions for coalminers. Having fought on alone for several months, the miners were forced back to work with longer hours and lower wages.

Throughout the recession, the South Wales valleys endured mass unemployment and dire poverty. By the end of 1931, unemployment had reached almost three million in Britain. People were as desperate now as in the 1920s when a number of Hunger Marches to London had taken place, including the 1927 South Wales Miners' March in which my grandfather Dai Davies had participated. Now and again great unrest, tension and sometimes violence had broken out in Britain's most deprived areas. This had culminated in the "Great National Hunger March against the Means Test" in 1932 in which, once more, Dai Davies had been foremost amongst the miners who had marched from the valleys to Hyde Park in London only to face another bitter defeat.

To my doting young parents, I was the perfect little blue-eyed baby, despite the fact that I was as bald as a coot at birth. Soon, however, I grew pretty golden curls so my besotted parents entered me in a beautiful baby competition at one-year-old. They had quite overlooked the fact that I had not one single tooth in my head! So my wide gummy smile dashed the hopes of my proud parents. My two front teeth made their appearance at thirteen months, just too late for the beautiful baby competition. Nevertheless, to them I remained the most beautiful baby in the world as I continued to thrive, chuckling merrily in my cot or pram.

The joy in their hearts, however, did little to alleviate the struggle to make a living. It was only possible to bring home enough to keep starvation at bay. Many were the times when Daddy lined up alongside his fellow workers to be given just enough work to prevent him from being able to draw the meagre unemployment benefit. That meant that Mammy had to try to manage on less than if he had been on the "dole." Many a time, she would sit at the kitchen table counting the money over and over again, at a loss as to how to make it go round to cover all the necessary expenses.

Daddy had previously helped his brothers run the family smallholding, so he leased a patch of mountainside in Wattstown and established his own allotment. This was a large beautiful piece of land running over the hillside divided by a thin wire fence from a well-established, neighbouring allotment. This was tended by ninety-three-year old Fred Trow, who was always ready to give friendly advice and to exchange tips.

Daddy's allotment was neatly divided into sections where he planted potatoes and root vegetables – carrots, swedes, turnips, and parsnips in long straight lines with never a weed to be seen. Runner beans with their bright scarlet flowers climbed above the green vegetable section where cabbages, cauliflowers and Brussels sprouts flourished in their season. Clumps of juicy rhubarb spread their large dark green leaves over the ground next to the beds of lettuce, broad beans and sweet-tasting peas. Shiny blackcurrants and sharp, red and green gooseberries clustered on the bushes separating the green vegetables from the soft fruit beds of luscious strawberries, loganberries, and raspberries. At one end of the garden near the gate, a sparkling stream sprang out to gush down to a little pool which was covered with succulent watercress. At the other end stood Daddy's shed which held all his gardening tools, a little old table and a chair where he could sit down to rest after a hard spell of digging to enjoy a cool drink of fresh spring water while smoking his pipe. Fully content, he would peacefully survey his own Garden of Eden that his hard work had created. He was happy to think that his family would always have fresh vegetables and fruit to eat under all circumstances.

The couple had hardly settled into their pleasant rooms in Ynyshir when a small terraced house became available in Wattstown. Bryn Terrace was situated high on the hillside half-way between Bailey Street and the National Colliery where Daddy worked. This was more convenient because it was nearer to his work, his allotment and his family. Loading their precious furniture on to a horse and cart, they moved into the tiny rented house. Egged on by Nan, who was always fiercely determined to keep the Stevens clan together, Daddy's mother, Selina Jane had, at first, opposed Tom's marriage to Annie May.

Now living in closer contact, however, the two women got to know one another better and Selina Jane was soon won over by her new daughter-in-law's sweet and loving disposition. She realised what a good wife and mother Annie May was and became more and more fond of her. For her part, Mammy soon came to respect and love her mother-in-law dearly and a strong bond of affection developed between them. As money was short and Mammy was finding it hard to make ends meet, Selina Jane often gave her homemade cakes or pies or little bags of groceries to help out. The grandparents also appreciated being close to their new granddaughter and took the opportunity to spoil me. "Grampy" Stevens would bounce me on his knee and announce to all and sundry, "She's a real little Paddy is our Pat!" while Granny would knit the prettiest little bonnets and matinee coats and push me out in my pram to show me off.

Fifteen months later my sister, Morfydd, was born on 26 January 1936. During her second pregnancy, Mammy's health suddenly deteriorated and, by the time the baby was born, she was desperately ill with rheumatic fever and almost died. The baby, however, was fine – a lovely bouncing baby girl. Mammy did not find out until years later when her fourth daughter, Mary, was diagnosed with rhesus negative blood, that she, too, had the same blood type which had caused her to become so ill while carrying her second child. This time, the parents were hoping for a boy, so the only name they had in mind was Michael, yet again. Since Mammy was so ill, her kind Welsh-speaking next door neighbour, who was looking after her after the birth, proposed the charming Welsh name of Morfydd. Both parents were happy with this suggestion and so it was that the second daughter of the family came to have this pretty traditional Welsh name, often shortened to "Morfy."

Morfydd was a bonnie little baby with beautiful big brown eyes and a mop of shiny chestnut brown hair. The two babies were quite a contrast to one another as I had blue eyes and golden curls. Our mother was so happy when people stopped her in the street to admire her little ones. Since it took Mammy several months to recover from her illness, I was sent to my father's family in Bailey Street while baby Morfydd was looked after by my mother's Auntie Elsie for almost the first six months of her life. When Mammy recovered, life continued as before with the struggle to make ends meet, except that there was another mouth to feed, whilst we two babies were blissfully unaware of any problems. We grew up sturdy and full of life.

As the thirties progressed, things became steadily worse for those employed in the mining industry. The development of the motor industry in the Midlands meant that cities like Birmingham and Coventry were experiencing a boom. My grandfather Dai Davies decided that he might have to take his family away from the Rhondda and try his luck in the Midlands where jobs in the pits were to be had. His son Davie had followed him into the mines and was ready to up roots and leave for the Midlands with his parents. In 1936, things were at an all time low for Dai and Lizzy Davies and their family. Young Davie was now working in the pit alongside his father and because work was so short, two miners from the same family were not normally employed in the same pit. The older one lost his job. Dai was absolutely devastated when this was about to happen to him. A solution just had to be found. It was decided that twenty- year-old Davie would ride to Nuneaton on his bicycle to look for work. His parents and sister, Iris, were to follow.

On the way, Davie broke his long journey by staying overnight in a farm. The kind farmer's wife could not let him stay in the house as her husband was not at home, so he slept in a barn. On arriving in Nuneaton, he lodged with "Auntie" Ginny Jarman, as did many of the men from the Rhondda seeking work in the Midlands. Early in 1937 the rest of the family joined him and both father and son found work in Griff Clara colliery. Soon they took up residence in 227 College Street, Hill Top, where my grandparents spent the rest of their lives. Mammy was devastated at the thought of Iris giving up her place in Porth County Grammar School and begged her sister to stay with her in the Rhondda to finish her education. However, her mother, Lizzy, did not encourage Iris to stay. Naturally enough, the young teenager wanted to go where there was the possibility of a better life and money to earn in order to buy pretty clothes and make-up. Thus the family left their beloved Wales and moved to Nuneaton where they easily secured new jobs and became settled and more prosperous.

Before leaving for the Midlands, my grandparents had lived in No 7 William Street, Ynyshir, virtually all of their married life. When they left, my parents moved us in there into what had been my mother's childhood home. We saw little of our grandparents after that, though they did manage to make a few visits to us in Wales. Morfydd and I were old enough to remember our grandparents' visits, while Ann and Mary, born in the early forties, were just toddlers. On those occasions, our grandmother, whom we called "*Mam*", spent most of her time chatting cosily with Mammy and supervising the running of the house. When Morfydd and I had finished our chores, Mam would check that all was properly done. Stern and unyielding, she would stand, hand on hip, with her finger pointing accusingly at any mark that hadn't been removed well enough to satisfy her high standards. Woe betide the child who had left dust on the skirting boards! One day, little Mary toddled downstairs, smiling broadly, with all Mam's curlers sticking out drunkenly all over her tiny head. Mam quickly grabbed her precious curlers from her granddaughter, while the confused little child stood there not knowing whether to laugh or cry until Mammy burst out laughing and hugged her to show that all was well.

Our grandfather, on the other hand, consecrated most of his time and energy on us children. Even though I was so young, I can still remember "*Dad*," as we called him, playing with Morfydd and me and teaching us to sing. The first song I learnt with him was:

*How much is that doggie in the window?*
*The one with the waggely tail?*
*How much is that doggie in the window?*
*I do hope that doggie's for sale!*

The next song was one that became my party piece for many a year when I was young. I would dress up and dance around as I sang and acted the whole thing out.

*She was very very lovely, Tikka Tee Tikka Ta,*
*As bright as stars above me, Tikka Tee Tikka Ta.*
*She had a way of kissing that simply was divine*
*And oh, how I wish that she was mine, Tikka Tee Tikka Ta,*
*Tikka Tikka Tee, Tikka Tikka Ta, Tikka Tikka Tee, Tikka Tikka Ta.*

Morfydd in particular loved to sing with "Dad" and learned many songs at her grandfather's knee. Her party piece was the Teddy Bear's Picnic which she always sung with great gusto. Dad encouraged her and said that she already had the makings of a beautiful voice and would one day develop into a good singer. Unfortunately, he did not live to see how true his prediction turned out to be.

Mammy could not wait to give us a good start as far as education was concerned. She acquired brightly coloured books for us and set about teaching me to read. I was quick to learn and delighted her. In those days, children were allowed to start in the Infants' School at the tender age of three and I was speedily enrolled. Although most children were left crying or screaming when their mothers departed, I was a very docile child and showed no distress at all. At the end of the morning, I was brought home for lunch and was readied for my return to school for the afternoon session. I made no protestations, but was regularly unaccountably poorly, often with stomach ache. Mammy would wrap me up and put me down to sleep and gradually noticed that, after the school bell had stopped ringing, I seemed to have been miraculously cured. This went on for several days, with my mother even reduced to taking me to see the doctor. Our doctor, Dr. Orr, was unable to find anything wrong with me. He did, however, agree with my grandfather Stevens that I was a "real little paddy and would make the boys' hearts flutter" when I got older.

As my stomach aches persisted, Mammy began to smell a rat and eventually lost patience with her naughty daughter. She picked me up and threw me unceremoniously onto the settee, saying

"You have to go to school, Madam. There's nothing at all wrong with you. You've been putting it on all this time!" My eyes filled with tears and two big drops ran down my pink cheeks. My auntie Florrie happened to be visiting that day and was aghast at my mother's lack of patience with her sweet little niece.

"It's all right, Annie May" she spluttered. "I'll take her."

"Let me go to school with Bopa", I pleaded. "I'll be a good girl now," I promised, sobbing with remorse as I wiped away my tears.

"See you are then and don't try those shenanigans on me again, my girl," replied my stern mother.

So off I toddled under the protection of Bopa sucking a sweetie from my doting aunt and arriving in good time for afternoon school to the surprise of my teacher, who had come to the conclusion that I was a "mornings only" pupil. From that day onward I returned to afternoon school without further fuss.

Actually, I really liked school and made good progress from the beginning. I especially loved reading and pored over the beautifully coloured books provided for me. Even in the Infants' School we were soon divided into A and B classes and I was always put into the A class. It was generally said of me, "Pat's head is always in a book." When Morfydd joined me, she had quite a different attitude to school. She was lively, easily distracted and very sociable with the result that she preferred playing with her many friends rather than reading books. Therefore, her teachers sometimes had too high expectations of this bright-eyed pupil.

As we progressed through school, I, as the elder sister, was usually expected to look after Morfydd. It was I who had to go and fetch her coat if she forgot to bring it home from school, for example.

One day when we were playing on the mountainside together, an unfortunate accident occurred. As we roamed together, a stile into the next field barred our way. I was over it in a flash.

"Come on, Morfydd," I urged. She scrambled over and as she slid down on the other side, there was an ominous ripping sound.

"Oh, Morfydd, what have you done? You've torn your new dress. Mammy will be angry with you for spoiling it," I exclaimed.

"It's not my fault. I just fell against the stile and it ripped on a nail," she wailed.

"Well, you shouldn't have tried to climb over it, then", I rejoined. "You're too small."

"But you told me to climb over it," insisted Morfydd.

"Oh well, it's done now. Let's try to wash some of the dirt off it before we go home," I suggested.

Our efforts to remedy the problem only made things worse. So, hand in hand, two bedraggled little sisters slunk home together, dreading the moment when we would have to face our irate mother.

"What on earth have you been up to? I told you to try to keep your new dresses clean and now you've gone and ripped yours, Morfydd," she scolded. "How did you do it?"

Morfydd immediately burst into floods of tears.

"It wasn't my fault," she wailed. "Pat told me to climb over the stile and my dress got caught on a nail and ripped."

"It was just an accident," I tried to explain but I was cut short.

"You should have looked after your sister properly then this wouldn't have happened," retorted Mammy as she administered a sharp slap on my arm. How unfair! Morfydd had torn her dress but I had got the blame!

When we started having simple homework, mine was swiftly done but sometimes when Morfydd struggled with hers, I was expected to help her before we were both allowed to go out to play. When my parents had acquired 7 William Street from my grandparents Davies, Mammy had also inherited her maternal grandfather, Henry Gerrish, who inhabited the front room as a bedsit. "*Granshire*," as he was known, was a permanent fixture in our home. Granshire was a great personality. A redheaded Englishman, he was well integrated into the local community. He never appeared to be considered as a burden by his granddaughter. In fact, he was very useful to her, particularly after the three younger children were born, looking after the little ones whilst she tackled the housework. He became even more useful to us small children as our protector, as we came to know that if we ran behind his armchair, we would escape the wrath of my mother in the wake of small misdemeanours. We would remain safe in our sanctuary until Mammy had cooled down. He had many pithy little sayings that stuck in our minds. When we were forgetful and had to go back for something, he would say:

"*Your head will never save your legs*" and when we left food on our plates:

"*Your eyes are bigger than your belly!*" We all loved him and accepted his presence amongst us as totally normal.

Morfydd in particular became very attached to her Granshire and protector. It was to him she preferred to go for help with her "sums" homework. He had a quick mind and would recount how he had to pay a penny a time to attend school. Mammy took good care of him and provided him with wholesome meals every day. When Morfydd would scuttle behind his armchair to escape her irate mother, he would remonstrate with his angry granddaughter as she chased after her:

*"Leave the child alone, you silly woman!"* and Mammy would have to retire resignedly until her ire had cooled and Morfydd was saved yet again. In later years, dear Granshire died just around the time of Morfydd's eleven plus examination. Morfydd was devastated. She cried for days and was in no fit state to sit the all-important test. When she was not offered a place at either of the local grammar schools, Mammy managed to secure an interview with the Director of Education of the Rhondda. She explained what had happened and made a most convincing plea for her child to be given a second chance. Her determination had ensured that no child of hers was to be denied a good education. Thus Morfydd re-sat her eleven plus the following year and passed for Porth Secondary Grammar School with flying colours.

My love for reading often got me into trouble also. We sisters shared a bedroom and I would smuggle my book up with me to bed to read by the light of the candle. Tired after her exertions playing with her friends, Morfydd naturally wanted to go to sleep, but I resisted her pleas to put out the light and was determined to go on reading. Eventually, she would shout downstairs to Mammy.

"Pat's reading again!" and heavy footsteps would soon be heard coming up the stairs and my book would be taken from me, the candle blown out and after a stern scolding, Mammy would tuck us up again. Enraged for being told off 'for nothing' in my opinion, I retaliated by slapping Morfydd for getting me into trouble. The receding steps on the stairs quickly returned to the bedroom and this time I received a smack on my bottom. Finally I gave up and we settled down to sleep at last.

I must have inherited my love for reading from Mammy. However, although Daddy was proud of the medal he had been awarded at school for one hundred percent attendance, it appeared that he must have slept through the reading lessons. Mammy was horrified at the hesitancy he displayed when reading a newspaper article aloud when they were first married. She encouraged him to read more, imbuing him with a love of books, especially history books, which he continued to enjoy reading avidly over the years. His maths, on the other hand, was always of a good standard which enabled him to help his young children with their homework.

Every Saturday afternoon after finishing work on his allotment, Daddy would start on the long walk to Penygraig where he would serve behind the bar in the Adare Hotel, run by his brother, Uncle Mark. This not only brought in a little extra money to ease the family budget but also a little treat for us all. We could look forward to some crisps, lemonade, or even a small glass each of Bulmer's sweet cider with our Sunday lunch as we grew older.

Later, when Morfydd and I became teenagers, I was always expected to take Morfydd with me when I went dancing to the youth clubs. Though she was only fifteen months younger than me, she was quite a bit less mature and tended to report everything that happened to Mammy which occasionally got me into hot water. As we grew, things became easier and a very close and loving relationship developed between us, even if I was somewhat authoritative and bossy and Morfydd more amenable.

* * * * *

Our home at number 7, a sturdy little miner's cottage built of stone and red brick around the windows and door, was towards one end of a long row of terraced houses near *The Oval,"* a dusty coal-black football field where we played as children and watched soccer and cricket matches. At the other side of the field was the "park," the children's playground furnished with a slide, swings and roundabouts. Behind the row of houses opposite No 7 and along the side of the Oval and the park, flowed the River Rhondda, its swirling waters black with the coal dust from the collieries' washeries. Above the street and the river rose the green mountainside, below which our little valley nestled and over which we roamed freely as children. What a mammoth task it was for our mothers to keep us clean and healthy in such an environment.

Our house had changed little from the days of our grandparents, Dai and Lizzy. We entered the house through the front door, painstakingly kept painted by Daddy. I remember admiring his skill in achieving a wood-grained effect. The bricks surrounding the windows were also painted a bright red while the sills were in a matching colour. We were all proud of the final result. The door led into a long dark passage, at the end of which stairs led to the three first floor bedrooms. Half-way along the passage on the right was a door opening into the *"front room"* or *"parlour."* This room was the only downstairs room with wooden floorboards. Otherwise, the flooring was stone throughout.

At the stairs end of the corridor, a second door, also on the right, gave access to the middle room (living room), the largest in the house. Here there was a black-leaded open grate surrounded by a bright brass fender and, on the wall opposite the door, a window looking into the back yard between our house and Number 8. This room had a square dining table with matching chairs and a sideboard to store our crockery and cutlery. Mammy used to tell how I would empty the sideboard of her best cups, saucers, plates etc and then replace them carefully without breaking a single thing. It was my favourite game as a toddler. There was also a small comfortable three-piece suite which gradually began to look the worse for wear as we children clambered over it as we grew. Cushions were then used to camouflage small holes and tears. The stone floor was partially covered by rag mats made from multicoloured old clothes by a skilful neighbour.

There was a "*cwtch*" (store) under the stairs behind the middle room which housed cleaning materials and had numerous hooks from which coats, satchels etc. were hung. This led directly into an ample kitchen with its huge ancient black-leaded grate and integrated oven. In the left hand corner, stood a recently installed large stone sink (called the *bosh*) over which was a cold water tap. The kitchen was furnished with a scrubbed wooden table, a bench against one wall and some wooden kitchen chairs. There was also a small gas stove. Off the kitchen was a pantry used for storing all our perishable foodstuffs, as no one had refrigerators in those days. Our milk bottles stood in bowls of cold water which was changed frequently to prevent the milk from turning sour. At the end of the pantry still sat the old stone slab on which rested a massive brown earthenware pot, the usual repository for the day's bread and which became the cake and pudding mixer at Christmastide. We children loved to watch our mother fill it with mixed dried fruit and add all manner of mysterious ingredients, finally stirring it all together and wetting it with beer or brandy when available, to make our festive puddings or cake. We were all allowed to have a stir and make a wish as we hung precariously one by one over the enormous pot clutching the huge wooden spoon.

Outside in the rectangular back yard was one cold water tap, a drain, another *cwtch* for Daddy's tools, our few toys, a set of ladders, buckets etc., and an outside toilet. This "ty bach," as it was known in Wales, had a scrubbed wooden seat and was set beneath a flushable water cistern activated by a long chain. It was furnished by neatly cut-up newspapers and sometimes with de luxe squares of tissue papers that had passed a previous life as wrappers for oranges. This may not have been the most salubrious or comfortable of places, but I often took refuge there when there were jobs to be done. Deaf to Mammy's calls, I would settle down to read "on the throne" until Morfydd grumbled that I was locked in the toilet with my head in a book again while she was left to do all the chores. Rumbled, I was forced to emerge and do my share of the work.

On the yard wall hung a large oval tin bath, and behind the yard at the end of the house was a small piece of ground. This had been Dad's vegetable patch but as Daddy now had a large allotment on the mountainside in Wattstown, it was left to run to seed at first. Later on during the war, a chicken coop was constructed there to provide eggs and chickens for Sunday dinner when their laying life was over. It was not until much later when we were young schoolchildren that Morfydd and Jane, our cousin, persuaded Daddy to dig out some plots for us to make flower beds that we could proudly begin to call it our back garden. It developed gradually into a small square of green lawn surrounded by pink and white rose bushes, a deep red peony bush with sunny yellow daffodils and multi-coloured tulips in season.

At the far end was a back door leading into a back lane or gulley, next to which sat the coal shed housing the ton of coal per month allocated to all mine workers. This was delivered in a coal lorry and dumped in a huge black pile outside the back door until my father returned home after work to hump it all into the shed. Coal was never scarce, so we had three huge welcoming fires throughout the ground floor in the winter months. The kitchen fire was kept going even in the summer and a kettle was always singing on the hob to provide a warming cup of tea for any family members or friends who came to visit. On this roaring fire, too, was boiled all the hot water needed for cosy baths beside its soaring flames as well as for washing the clothes and scrubbing the stone floors.

To us children bath nights were joyous affairs. Mammy would bring in the long tin bath from the yard and place it in front of a bright crackling fire. After first half filling it with cold water from the tap, she would then stagger with a huge bucket of boiling water from the fire which she then emptied into the bath. It was a wonder that over the long years there was never an accident as she was always careful to keep us all well away until the water was at the right temperature for us to jump into the warm bath. Fortunately, pit baths had been added to the National Colliery where Daddy worked so that he did not have to walk home blackened from head to foot from dealing with coal all day. We children went in one after another and when young, we girls could go in two at a time, one at each end of the long bath. After splashing a little and playing together for a while, we loved to soak luxuriantly in the warm water, watching the multicoloured flames shooting up into the chimney.

This system continued for many years as we had no money to build a bathroom and the landlord was certainly not prepared to put one in for us. Thus it was that years later when I was a student at University, I invited my best friend to visit us in Ynyshir. She lived in a large, comfortable country house near Stroud with her parents and elder sister.

"I'm afraid that our house is very small and crowded, and I'm sorry but we don't have a bathroom," I explained to Vendla.

"That doesn't matter," she replied. "I'm really looking forward to meeting your family and going for walks over the mountains with you."

So we arrived in my simple but welcoming home to spend a weekend together amongst my large, lively family. During her stay, of course, Vendla experienced bath time in 7 William Street. There had been no need for me to have worried. Vendla really enjoyed this new experience. To this day, she still contrasts the warm cosy bath in front of the leaping flames of an open coal fire with the shivering that came over her when coming out of her "posh" ceramic bath in that huge draughty bathroom at home.

Although bath-time was very pleasant for us, it was hard, heavy work for Mammy. Life was extremely hard for both men and women in those days. Daddy worked as much overtime as he could get to provide adequately for his growing family, often doing a double shift as well as working in his allotment and carrying the precious produce on his back on his way home to Ynyshir. For years, he refused promotion to the rank of colliery "official" because the post would not have allowed him to work the extra time so essential for catering for all the needs of his large household. Instead, he did the job as a stand-in so as he could continue with the onerous overtime. Eventually, by the time Morfydd and I were working and able to contribute something to the family income and the younger ones had grants or were in training for their future careers, Daddy became a colliery official and was able to contribute towards a pension for his retirement.

Mammy worked at least as hard as Daddy. She it was who had the massive headache of trying to stretch the pay to make the money go round each week. Daddy kept nothing back for himself and was content that Mammy always managed to provide him with his "little bit of satisfaction" of a packet of Woodbines or a tin of Bondman's pipe tobacco. She herself had no such little luxuries. Mammy would fill up on potatoes, bread and vegetables when there was little meat to go round. I remember her suddenly realising she had put on weight when she caught sight of her reflection in a shop window and, for a brief moment, thought that it was her stout mother with her severe bun and drab clothes coming towards her. She immediately decided to diet as best she could and soon returned to her trim pleasantly plump figure.

* * * * *

On 15th August 1941, my sister Ann was born. Morfydd and I went to stay briefly with my father's family in Wattstown for the birth. I was quite happy and content with the spoiling and attention I was receiving there but Morfydd was not. She was a real "Mammy's girl" and suspected she was being kept out of the way for some dark purpose. On hearing that a baby had been born, five-year-old Morfydd took to her heels and ran all the way back home to Ynyshir all by herself. She had managed to give her aunties the slip and careered through Wattstown Park and all along Standard View to arrive panting from her exertions at 7 William Street, about a full mile away! She rushed in to find her mother with the new baby in the cot beside her. She clung to Mammy and then sat glowering at the tiny girl in the cot. It was some time before her jealousy subsided and she accepted and came to love her little sister Ann dearly.

Mammy was not quite so ill this time but the baby was small and puny. Mammy had difficulty in getting Ann to eat properly and we two older sisters remember staring wide-eyed at the tiny waif placed on the kitchen table and painted almost all over in a bluish hue reminiscent of the ancient Britons, as Mammy tried to treat her many boils and carbuncles. However, with tender care she made gradual, if slow, progress and when later I was taking her to school, a classmate pontificated solemnly:

*"Your mother will never rear her."*

I hotly responded *"Of course she will – she's improving all the time and my mother's a very good nurse!"*

By the time Ann was born, my parents, hoping for a boy, had given up the name of Michael and the new addition was to be named "David" or "Ann." Now a fourth child was on the way, they were still hoping for a boy and chose the name "Thomas" with "Mary" as the female option. Mary was born on 9th December 1942, a healthy happy little girl. This time both mother and child were fine, due to the fact that they both had the same rhesus negative blood. It was so nice to have another sweet baby to coo at. However, with this pleasure came responsibility. Being the eldest, I was not only expected to help my mother with the household chores, but also to help look after the babies.

When Ann and Mary were very small, they were content to sleep for hours in their cots in Granshire's room. As they grew and began to crawl about, they became a bit too lively for an eighty-year-old. Therefore, after school and at weekends, Morfydd and I were required to take the babies out for a walk in their prams until they went off to sleep. Once they were sleeping, we were allowed to bring them back to park them outside the front door before running off to play with our friends. Although Mammy always ensured that the sun canopy was set to protect the babies from the glare, it was strange how the sun always managed to shine directly into their eyes. We two big sisters would coo consolingly and rock the prams gently so that the tired, wailing babies would eventually give in and drift off to sleep. Prams safely parked, we dashed off to play.

There were a number of girls of our age living in neighbouring houses in our street with whom we would play happily. One of these went by the name of Sister Roberts. Her first name was actually Margaret but few knew that as, when she was born, her brother, David, was told that he now had a new sister. Delighted, he spread the word around that there was a new baby in his house called Sister and the name stuck. When the weather was fine, we all played together in the street or in the park on the swings, slide or roundabouts. Morfydd could not wait to be free to play with her friends "over the stones," a flat, smooth piece of concrete at the foot of the mountain, where we used to play making houses. They would also make mud pies, cakes etc. using the crystal clear water that gushed from "the spout," a long metal pipe that protruded from the mountainside producing a never-ending source of fresh, cool spring water. This spring was most valuable if ever the domestic supply was cut. Queues of people carrying a variety of containers would form in front of the spout. I also enjoyed playing "house" at times so long as I was the child of the family and did not have to dirty my hands making mud pies for the family to eat! More often, however, I was to be found climbing up the side of the mountain to balance on pipes, or playing in the park at the end of the football ground at the bottom of the street.

When it rained, we had to make do with playing in some one's passage-way (corridor leading from the front door to the stairs and the living rooms). As we had the largest number of children in any of the houses, it usually fell to our mother to allow our friends to play in our "passage." Those mothers with only one or two children were often too house-proud to welcome a gang of lively, twittering children into their homes. Mammy would serve drinks of water or squash and snacks of thick doorsteps of bread and butter and homemade jam to one and all as we played. I came into my own on these occasions as I liked to organise everyone and had a vivid imagination which allowed me to devise little plays to enact together. Mostly the other children went along with my bossy ways but sometimes squabbles would break out when someone was dissatisfied with the part allocated to her. These even escalated into little fights occasionally when some pulling of hair and slapping etc. occurred.

After one such squabble, Maureen Lloyd dashed home to no.11 in floods of tears. Shortly afterwards, Mrs. Lloyd came to complain to Mammy that I had pulled a large clump of hair from her daughter's head and she had the proof in her hand. Mammy looked at the blond hair that Mrs. Lloyd was thrusting at her and jumped to the conclusion that I was the culprit. With a sharp slap on my leg, I was instantly bundled up to bed in front of all my friends, despite my pleas that Maureen had pulled my hair also. The bunch of blond hair could just as easily have been mine and taken from Maureen's fist when she got home. Anyway, that was my story and I was sticking to it! Fortunately, this was a rare occurrence as we normally played cheerfully together with little disruption.

In those days, children were allowed a lot more freedom. There were no cars in our street. We children were able to skate up and down the middle of the road on our roller skates and sometimes we would play "kiss, bump or torture" with the boys. This game entailed the girls being given a short start to race down the street chased by the boys. When caught, a girl had to choose "kiss, bump or torture" according to how attractive the girl rated the boy. One of the leaders of the gang was a very handsome boy called Howard Waltham who often chased me down and caught me without difficulty. I secretly found him very attractive but never admitted it, as he was considered to be a bit rough. It was not until many years later when I was retired and he already dead, that his elder brother, Ivor, told me that Howard was always talking about a girl called Pat Stevens. He would have certainly been more my choice than the more molly-coddled Elwyn Thomas whose mother bought some raffle tickets that I was selling for the church.

"You are Pat Stevens, aren't you? I'll buy some tickets from you because you're our Elwyn's girlfriend," she informed me. I soon put Elwyn right on that count in school the next morning.

We played ball, skipping and hopscotch, also on the road. We were even allowed to roam in groups over the mountainside and to paddle in the reservoir where some even dared to swim. We made dens amongst the ferns and played all sorts of imaginative games together. We were sturdy, healthy self-reliant children not confined indoors by TVs, game machines or computers. Naturally, accidents sometimes occurred. Once when climbing the rocks with my friends Gaynor and Jill, Jill fell down and had to be carried home, quite the wounded soldier. Fortunately, no permanent damage was done and once her bruises and scratches had disappeared, she made a rapid recovery. Another time, whilst balancing on the wide pipe near the river, I slipped and fell. When I looked down at my right wrist, I noticed that it was a very peculiar shape. So that was why it was hurting so much! I walked home bravely holding up my fractured wrist, flanked by all my friends competing to give the most graphic account of the accident to my mother.

*"Pat fell off the big pipe by the river and I heard her bone crack!"* Sister Roberts informed my mother. A second time I managed to fall from the top of the slide injuring the same wrist. Dr Orr diagnosed a greenstick fracture each time and tugged my disfigured wrist back into shape before it was set in plaster of Paris. I was then allowed back into school, a wounded heroine, with my arm in a sling, and, as we had recently moved to a new class, the teacher referred to me at first as the "little girl with the broken arm" when requiring me to read. However, these accidents, along with all the other bumps, bruises and grazes were shrugged off by us sturdy valley children as part of the ups and downs of life. We needed to be tough if we were to compete with the shrill-sounding evacuees who came to live in our streets and swell our school classes during the war.

\* \* \* \* \*

Mammy kept our home spic and span and as Morfydd and I grew older after the younger children were born, we each were given certain chores to do before being allowed out to play with our friends on Saturdays. The hardest jobs were the scrubbing of the stone floors. One of us would do the pantry and kitchen and the other the passage and the "front." This entailed swabbing down the pavement outside the front of the house with soapy water and a hard broom, wiping down the windowsills and scouring the front step with sand and stone. I found the latter the less onerous job, as the kitchen and pantry entailed moving and dusting furniture as well as scrubbing the floors on hands and knees. Morfydd usually opted for the kitchen, as she didn't like being seen washing down the pavement in her "working clothes" so we were both relatively happy. Dusting and polishing was easy compared with that, even though we used solid wax polish which needed quite a bit of elbow grease to create the desired shine.

As the eldest child, I also had to do almost all the family food shopping at the local Co-op. Mammy would write out a long list of all the necessary provisions which I would take with our "book" to the store. When the list had been completed and all the items set out on the counter, the grocer would call out the prices to the cashier across the shop after she had called,

*"Mrs. Stevens, Please!"*

The order would be written up and totalled in the "book" until payday when I would return with the money, often not enough to pay it all off. This was a great worry to Mammy. I would frequently catch her sitting with her purse open and all the money emptied onto the kitchen table. Try as she might to arrange the pounds, shillings and pence in different piles, it was not enough to cover all the various household expenses. Many were the times I would come in to find her quietly weeping.

"What's the matter, Mammy?" I'd ask.

"Oh Pat, I just don't know what to do. The pay won't stretch to cover everything. I can only pay £3 off the Coop bill today. We'll have to leave the rest until next week."

"It's all right, Mammy. They won't mind at all," I'd say.

"But Pat, it will be even worse next week if we have to pay extra," she said.

I had no answer to that, of course. She would then try to put on a brave face, dry her tears and say:

"Never mind, something will come. We'll pay it off somehow." She always had faith that "something would come" to enable her to pay the bills in full in the end. Indeed, the "divvy" was a great help at the end of the quarter and when things were particularly bad, Daddy would often come home with a beaming smile and say,

*"I've won the tote, May. Here's the money to pay the Coop."*

A bright smile would quickly transform her worried face as she threw her arms around her beaming husband and thanked God for their good fortune.

I had every confidence in my parents to be able to overcome any problems together. We children never seemed to go without any of the necessities of life although we understood that we could not expect to have expensive toys or treats. One Christmas, Morfydd and I asked if we could have a toy sweet shop for Christmas. It was out of the question to go out and buy one of those smart toy shops displayed in shop windows, so Daddy set to and made a beautiful sweet shop out of some wood that he found lying around. He then painted the shelves in bright colours and hung a natty sign over the top. Bottles and jars were found from somewhere and by Christmas they were all filled with a variety of colourful sweets. Father Christmas also filled some of Mammy's old stockings with chocolates, oranges and one or two small knick-knacks which we found on the foot of our bed in the morning. Our joy was complete.

Christmas dinner was always delicious too. We all tucked into a plump roast chicken that had been fattened on Uncle Ted's smallholding in Wattstown. It was garnished with sage and onion stuffing and we had plenty of fresh vegetables grown in Daddy's mountainside allotment. To finish it all off, we dived into the rich Christmas pudding which Mammy never failed to produce for us every year. I remember how assiduously we searched every little portion of our pudding hoping to find the silver sixpence which was always hidden there for the lucky finder. Once everything was cleared away, we would settle down to play traditional parlour games together and entertain one another with songs accompanied by Daddy on the violin. Morfydd and I also dressed up in some of Mammy's clothes and high heels to perform little sketches that I had written for us. We children were always happy and content with our lot and blissfully unaware of the sacrifices our parents made to protect us from the harsh realities of life.

With labour-saving devices for the home virtually non-existent, and certainly no money to purchase them, the physical work was very onerous. Not only did Mammy have to prepare massive amounts of fresh vegetables to cook nourishing meals for her large family, she also had to do all the washing by hand. She prepared a huge tub in the back yard and would stagger out from the kitchen with steaming buckets of hot water. She had a small rubber sheet which she pinned to the front of her dress under her piny in the vain hope that it would protect her chest. Into the tub went all the sheets and pillowcases from our beds and she would rub them with "Fairy" soap over her washboard until they were clean. Next went in the towels and tea-towels, and, finally, Daddy's coal-black working clothes. They were all then rinsed in turn and put through the mangle which we children liked to help to turn, when Mammy had enough patience.

Finally, fresh water was boiled to wash all our good clothes which were then hung out on our clothes line which Daddy had erected on a pulley so that they soared up to blow in the wind high up along the length of the yard and the garden. As the Lady Lewis pit had closed in the 1930s, we were not plagued so much with the black smudges that had soiled our grandmother's washing in the past. However, the hard toil on washdays every Monday had a detrimental effect on Mammy's health and she regularly succumbed to nasty bouts of bronchitis every winter. This finally became chronic and was worsened by her asthma. My father's pipe did not help matters and she suffered even worse symptoms because of passive smoking. My father, however, never seemed to inhale it himself. None of us children ever smoked.

Although Mammy suffered dreadfully from chronic bronchial asthma and emphysema, yet Daddy, with a lifetime of working in clouds of coal dust and who was a lifelong smoker, never succumbed to the miner's disease of silicosis. Weak from a hacking cough, Mammy would always say "a creaking door never breaks." So it was that despite frequent severe illnesses, including bouts of pneumonia and acute arthritis, she always pulled through and eventually outlived her fitter husband by two years. Daddy retired at sixty-four when Wattstown Colliery closed in 1968. From then on, with Daddy's small miner's pension to supplement their state retirement pension, life became easier for them enabling them to live more comfortably. Furthermore, having children living in different parts of the world, they also began to grasp the opportunity to travel widely outside Britain for the first time in their lives.

# Chapter 6
# The War Years

I was five years old at the outbreak of World War II in 1939. Since we were a mining community and coal was essential to the war effort, there were only a very few people we knew from our valleys who were called up to serve in the armed forces. On the contrary, those 'Bevin Boys' who had not joined up were conscripted from around Britain to work in the pits in wartime, and school children from all over England were evacuated to live amongst us in our remote valleys. As a young man, my uncle Will John, my father's eldest brother, had volunteered to serve in the army towards the end of World War 1. In 1939 he had a responsible job as Under-Manager of the National Colliery, thus since he was employed in a reserved occupation, he was not called up to serve in the army this time. For the same reason none of my other uncles working in the mines were conscripted into the armed forces either. In our family, nevertheless, we had three members who served in the army during the Second World War.

My cousin Marco was a young man working in Ynyshir Co-op when he was called up to fight in Italy. The son of my father's brother Mark, he was a kind, friendly young man who often called to see us at lunchtime or after work. I remember being spoiled by him and standing on his feet as he held me by the hand and waltzed me round the kitchen, teaching me to dance. During the Italian campaign, Marco was employed as a motorbike courier and was wounded during a sortie. The wound became infected and when they operated it was found that he also had cancer. It was a terrible shock to us all to hear that he had died of his wounds in Italy just before the end of hostilities. He was survived by a young wife, Shirley, and a new-born baby girl called Eirlys.

Aunty Selina's husband, Bill Evans, living as they did in London, was conscripted early in the war and was sent to fight in Burma. Although he was not killed in action, he nevertheless lost his life in the jungle where he had contracted malaria. My Uncle Davie, my mother's only brother, was conscripted when he left the mines following a tragic mining accident in 1943. He was also sent to fight in the torrid jungles of Burma. Uncle Davie was the only one of my relatives to survive the war to return safely to his family. Although the war ended in 1945, Davie was required to attend the Japanese War Crimes Trials and so had to wait a further two years before being demobbed as a corporal. He visited us soon after his return in 1947 and presented Morfydd and me with a small very squashy black soft fruit. When the skin was peeled off, we were persuaded to taste it and were delighted with its sweet exotic flavour. It was the first bite of a banana that I can remember.

Apart from these events and the influx of raucous *"vacuees"* in our streets and schools, the war had little effect on us children in the Rhondda. These city kids loved the unaccustomed freedom they enjoyed roaming with us over the mountains dotted with sheep. Indeed it was the first time they had ever laid eyes on live sheep wandering around the streets as opposed to the dead carcasses they had seen hanging in the butchers' shops at home. The only experience we valley kids had of bombs was second-hand from the vivid accounts of the shriek of sirens, followed by the drone of aircraft overhead before the whistle and crash of exploding bombs igniting buildings and lighting up the London skies, as recounted by our new cockney pals.

They painted a truly horrific picture of falling debris everywhere, the putrid smell of burning and the terrifying dash to get to the comparative safety of the underground shelters where they huddled together awaiting the sound of the All Clear sirens. True, we had blackout imposed on us all and after a long day's work, Daddy had to tour the streets in the vicinity as a warden to ensure that no chink of light showed through the heavy dark curtains. Everyone was told to take cover in the safest part of the house if a raid was imminent. As we had no basement, a mattress was placed in the *cwtch* under the stairs where we could all take refuge if necessary. Since Daddy was usually in work and we children in school, Mammy ended up alone sheltering under the stairs clutching baby Mary to her breast. When she realised that none of her neighbours bothered to take shelter, she soon gave up and just carried on with what needed to be done in the house.

When the sirens wailed, we school children had the excitement of dashing out from school with our gasmasks at the ready to shelter in basements or under the stairs of nearby homes of friendly ladies who spoiled us with biscuits, cakes, squash or pop. Our gas masks were hideous and uncomfortable, making it difficult to breathe and giving us the appearance of creatures from outer space. Tiny tots were given Mickey Mouse gas masks to avoid frightening them and to encourage the little ones to wear them. It took great patience and skill to get Ann to don hers, while Mary was enveloped in hers like a cocoon. Only one stray bomb dropped in our area. It fell on the mountainside and shattered some of our school's windows. What a commotion it created! Each over-excited child either:

*"heard the plane roaring overhead,"*
*"saw the flash as the bomb hit,"*
*"was almost deafened by the explosion"* or
*"was nearly caught by flying shrapnel narrowly escaping death."*

Such a rare, one off incident was not the case for my grandparents living in Nuneaton, of course. Being so close to Birmingham and Coventry, they regularly experienced bombing first hand. In fact a small fire bomb fell through their bedroom roof and landed on the foot of their bed while they were in it. They escaped death through the quick thinking of my grandfather, Dai Davies. He jumped up, grabbed the smoking bomb and threw it into the full chamber pot which was under the bed. Perhaps due to his rapid reaction, a fault in the bomb or just pure luck the bomb did not go off and the family escaped unharmed.

Sadly, their luck did not hold. A tragic accident was soon to deprive us of our much loved grandfather. His son, Uncle Davie, had married Ethel and was living with their infant daughter, Rona, in Greenmore Road just a short distance from College Street where Dai and Lizzy lived. On 22 June 1943, Davie was ill in bed with a nasty bout of bronchitis. Dai decided to pay his sick son a visit, so he walked across from College Street to see how he was, before going to his shift in the mine. He brought Davie a yellow rose from his garden and made a great fuss of his granddaughter, little Rona, then sixteen months old. With a smile and a wave, he left them, promising to call in again on the way home from work.

Later that day, however, it was a coal board official that called at Davie's house to say that there had been an accident at work and that his father had been taken to Nuneaton hospital. Davie got up from his sick bed and went immediately to the hospital expecting injuries, but had to formally identify his father instead. The shock left Davie a shattered man for many, many months and Aunty Ethel said that it was like living with a stranger for a long time. It transpired that as the shift finished, my grandfather was walking with two younger miners towards the exit, when a loud screech and thunderous rattling sounds were heard rushing towards them. At this point it was so narrow that it was awkward for two men to walk abreast.

"Watch out, boys," shouted Dai. "Something's up. Sounds like a tram's broke loose."

All three immediately jumped back against the rough stony wall as trams came jolting and hurtling over the uneven rails towards them down the drift at breakneck speed.

"B--- hell! Those b--- trams have come loose!" screamed Jimmy.

With that, a journey of trams containing a full load of coal broke away and pinned the three men against the wall. When the rescuers arrived to get them out, they went straight to Dai who was badly injured and started to try to free him.

"We'll soon 'ave you outa 'ere, Dai, just you 'old still 'til we prise this damn wheel offa you," said Joe.

"No! Don't you bother about me. I'm alright. Just you see to them youngsters first."

Reluctantly, Joe turned towards the other two injured men and worked quickly with his mates to free them. When they turned back to Dai they found that he had lost consciousness and was bleeding profusely.

"This looks very bad," shouted Billy. "Help me get this off 'is chest quick!" The men heaved and pulled with all their might and finally managed to lift the massive broken tram off the badly injured man.

All three injured men were rushed by ambulance to hospital and on arrival Dai was pronounced dead while the other two survived. He died at the age of sixty, a strong, active, fearless and selfless man with so much life in him. As Mammy always said, he was *"a marvellous man"* so no one who knew him was surprised to hear of his heroic sacrifice. My grandmother Lizzy never got over the shock of his sudden, premature death and died, some say, of a broken heart just a few years afterwards.

Also unable to come to terms with this dreadful tragedy, Uncle Davie took the decision not to go back down the mines. He knew well that by coming out of a reserved occupation, he would be conscripted to serve his country in the armed forces. He was called up in Spring 1944 and so exchanged the dangers of the pit for the dangers of combat in Burma where he fought until the end of the war, returning home to Nuneaton as a corporal only in 1947. Mammy, of course, joined her grieving family to say her sad goodbye to her adored father. Daddy and I held the fort during her absence.

On her return, life had to go on again despite the family's personal tragedy. It was war-time. Everyone had to take setbacks on the chin and carry on regardless. Amongst the hordes of evacuees who invaded our valleys as the war progressed, were two very special ones. These were our two cousins, Jane and John Davies, the children of Aunty Rosie who lived in Kent. They were sent to safety in the Rhondda at the very beginning of the war. Jane went to live with my Aunty Florrie (Bopa) and Uncle Dan in Treorci near the top of the Rhondda Fawr while John was sent to live in the old family home with Aunty Nan and all the uncles in Bailey Street, Wattstown. However, Jane came down from Treorci with Bopa to spend the whole weekend from Friday evening to Sunday evening, as well as most of the holiday periods, in Bailey Street with the large Stevens family. I wonder now how they managed to accommodate everyone in that one small house but they did so happily and without any fuss. Jane was the same age as Morfydd and John almost two years younger. They spent six of their most formative years amongst us in the Rhondda and subsequently retain an enduring love for Wales and feel that they are as much Welsh as English. In fact when they eventually returned home to Kent, Jane was actually sent by her English teacher for elocution lessons to try to eradicate her strong Welsh accent.

It was only natural that two little children amongst so many doting adults should be spoiled by their uncles and aunts. At Christmas, they were showered with expensive presents. Morfydd and I couldn't help noticing the contrast between what they received and the one small token present we each received from the same uncles and aunts. We had already come to understand that when Daddy had left the Stevens clan to get married, he had to "*paddle his own canoe,*" so this preferential treatment didn't worry us at all. They were often taken to Cardiff for treats. They visited Cardiff Castle, Castell Coch (Red Castle), Roath Park Lake and were also treated to pantomimes and musicals – something quite beyond our family's reach. Jane and John would have preferred to share some of these treats with us and once even managed to persuade Aunty Nan to invite Morfydd and me also. I well remember the one musical that we saw in Cardiff as children. *Carrousel* was such a lively colourful show and its catchy tunes still live in my memory. We all went around singing them together for ages afterwards.

Living in such close proximity with us and being so close in age, a very close bond of affection was forged between us four children. We saw each other every weekend and during school holidays and played happily together. As usual, as the eldest, I was in charge. Jane and Morfydd did not question my authority and John was always keen to ally himself with the leader. On Sunday mornings, dressed in our Sunday best, Morfydd and I would walk up through Wattstown Park to Bailey Street to visit our father's family and to play with our cousins. Then the four of us would skip back down to William Street to have Sunday dinner (the main meal of the day, usually served at lunchtime) with our family before running off to Sunday school in Saint Anne's together.

When it was time for Jane and John to go home, we two would accompany them to Wattstown once more and stay for tea with our uncles and aunts before setting off through the park again on the familiar route home. Bopa was adept at cutting the thinnest and daintiest of slices of bread and butter and we children would keep her going for some time with our healthy appetites. There would often be juicy red tomatoes from Uncle Ted's greenhouse to tempt us too. We certainly had plenty of exercise walking up and down between Wattstown and Ynyshir when we were young, but we enjoyed it and took it all in our stride.

Many a time, Jane and John would spend the whole of Saturday with us in Ynyshir as well as Sunday. On these occasions we would play together in the street, in the park, on the mountains or in the house if it was raining. Sometimes we would go to the Saturday matinee together in the nearby Ynyshir Workman's Hall. We enjoyed being frightened by such horror films as *Frankenstein* and *The Werewolf* when they were shown and these gave

John and me the chance to play tricks on Morfydd and Jane as we walked through the park at twilight on winter evenings.

"Boo! Frankenstein's coming!" John would shout out as we dashed off together with the other two careering after us as fast as their legs could carry them, uttering shrill cries of fright.

When it rained, we were allowed to play in our bedroom. We played all sorts of quiet indoor games together and loved to make tents with the sheets of our roomy double bed. Inevitably, I was asked to tell the others a story. I did not need asking twice. If I had exhausted all the fairy stories that had been requested, I would regularly make up new stories. Using my imagination I could keep them happy for hours recounting the very varied fairy tales they wanted to hear. As recompense for my labours, I would often get one of them to tickle my back and when the first one got tired, the next one would take over. We could keep going for ages like that so my mother could get on with her work without being disturbed. When the night came, we all four slept in our double bed, top and tailed. Again this was an opportune time for more stories including frightening ones but eventually finishing off with fairy tales with happy endings so that we could all drop off to sleep after a long and energetic day.

One day during our cousins' stay in Wales, a nasty accident occurred. John loved to play on the mountainside with his friends in Wattstown. As now, little boys liked to play with matches and some very naughty ones even deliberately set fire to the grass on the mountains. On this particular day, John was wearing his new cowboy suit with long trousers made of inflammable cotton. Matches were struck, grass was burning and all of a sudden John's long trousers were aflame! He and his friends struggled to tear off his trousers and somehow they eventually succeeded but John was badly burned. Fortunately, they were not too far away from Bailey Street so the uncles were quickly alerted. Uncle Ted ran to pick up John and, carrying him in his arms, dashed up the road to the bus stop to take him to hospital. There, some kind neighbour gave them a lift in his car and John was swiftly taken off to Porth Cottage Hospital where he stayed from January until late August.

John's parents were not told of the accident until they were due to come down to Wales for their son's fifth birthday in late February. John was very badly scarred so his father offered his skin for skin grafting, but as the procedure was so new, it was not attempted. He eventually had a graft sixty years later after ulcers on his leg began to erupt. A near tragedy had been averted and although John was left with lifelong scars on his legs, he was otherwise unharmed. He and his friends had learnt a salutary lesson and never risked playing with matches near the tinder dry grass on the mountains again.

Having spent most of their infancy with us in Wales, Jane and John became like members of our close family. Jane in particular loved our mother very dearly and was always willing to help her whenever she could. She would shame us by actually volunteering to brush up the crumbs after Sunday dinner or to wash up before being asked. She says today that our mother had a very great influence on her life, including her faith, and that she considers herself more as a fifth sister to us rather than a cousin.

When they returned to Kent after the cessation of hostilities they had no cousins to play with since Uncle Glanville's children were not yet born. They missed their free and easy life and all their many relatives in Wales, as we did them. They continued to come back to the Rhondda for the long school holidays for many years so we spent much of our time as teenagers together, too. Morfydd, Jane and I went to our church youth clubs and dance halls together and had great fun dressing up, learning to put on makeup and trying out different hair styles on one another. Once in the dance hall, I would suggest that we all remove our glasses and stand there smiling to encourage the local boys to ask us for a dance – a ploy which often worked for all three. We cousins all trooped off also to the "Pictures" (the local cinema's Saturday matinee) every week and watched with bated breath the progress of the war on the Pathe News reel.

Towards the end of the war, my parents made a last effort to provide a little brother for us four sisters. Mammy was older now and much less fit, so she was taken into Llwynypia Hospital to await the birth. At ten years old, I was placed even more in charge of the household while Daddy was in work. I bossed and organised my younger sisters, allocating simple little tasks even to Ann, as well as to Morfydd. We could not wait for the baby to be born and Morfydd and I were regulars queuing outside the one and only red telephone kiosk situated next to the cenotaph in the centre of the village, with our pennies ready to ring the hospital. I would put on my most grown-up voice when I got through to inquire,

*"I am ringing to ask how Mrs. Annie May Stevens is. Could you tell me, please, whether she has had the baby yet?"* The understanding nurses were gentle in reply and told me that

*"All is well but these things cannot be hurried and we must be patient."* Nevertheless, I continued to pester them with calls until the glorious day when they replied:

*"Yes, Mrs. Stevens has had her baby. It is a beautiful baby boy and mother and baby are both doing well."* We were over the moon and ran headlong home spreading the good news to everyone we met along the way.

*"Mammy has had the baby and it's a boy. We have a new baby brother!"*
Our home was in turmoil of delight. Even two-year-old Mary clapped her hands and sang out "Baby brother!" to everyone she saw. We cleaned and

shone the house and prepared the baby's cot for the much-awaited homecoming. Mammy was ill again after the birth and had to stay in hospital for some time with the new baby, a healthy bouncing boy. Although the preferred name reverted to Michael once more, there was hot discussion amongst us all as to what the baby was to be called. Eventually, it was decided that he was to have the accolade of having two Christian names, Thomas, after his father, and then Michael, although we girls had had to be content with one.

Born on Empire Day 24th May1945 between VE Day and VJ Day, the new baby was christened Thomas Michael Stevens. I was determined to call him "Tommy" whilst the rest of the family opted for Michael. I doggedly stuck to Tommy whilst he was Michael to everyone else until, months later, I capitulated and he became Michael to everyone. My mother was weak when she returned home and it was I, at ten years' old, who carried the baby everywhere, upstairs and down and placed him in his cot. Soon, I even learned to bathe him and change his nappy under instructions from Mammy.

He was a strong lively baby with a will of his own. He was not too happy about being put down to sleep at a regular hour and would show his dissention with hearty yells as he fought off the bedclothes I tried to tuck around him. Mammy had always been strict on this count and, after a few returns to check he was not getting cold by kicking off the blankets, I would sometimes resort to flinging him back down unceremoniously and telling him sternly that he had to stay there. One day as I was bringing him down from his bed, my open sandal caught on the stairs and I went flying, baby in arms. My shrieks and the thump, thump, thud as we landed together at the bottom of the stairs caused great consternation.

*"The baby's all right!"* I insisted as I staggered to my feet clutching a squalling baby to my chest. Mammy arrived panting and coughing in a state of great agitation.

*"I kept the baby inside my arms and he's not hurt at all,"* I reiterated, and, indeed, Michael had already stopped crying and was obviously none the worse for wear, to the great relief of Mammy.

Despite her positive attitude towards the daily grind, the stress of running a household of seven, plus Granshire, on a shoe-string meant that Mammy's health remained poor for many years. Not only did she suffer from chronic bronchial asthma, but her osteoarthritis caused her great pain also. I really had to take charge of baby Michael for most of the time. When I was in school, he would at first sleep in his cot under the watchful eye of Granshire, but as soon as he started to move under his own steam, he proved too much for the old man, unable to chase him around the room or keep him from wandering off. Michael was therefore tethered loosely to the foot of Granshire's brass bedstead until I got back from school. I suppose it was good that I learned child care from an early age so that, when I had my own children later on, I coped with them confidently from the start.

Of course we, like everyone else in wartime, were subject to strict rationing with food and clothes coupons to ensure fair sharing. We children had to hand over coupons to buy a few sweets from Anne's front room shop at the top of our street. We would run up the street clutching our ration books and precious pennies. The bell tinkled as the shop door opened. Once inside, we handed our money and ration books over the wooden counter to Anne who then cut out the appropriate coupons with her scissors. Next came the difficult part – choosing from amongst the dazzling array of brightly coloured bottles and glass jars along the back wall. Gobstoppers – boiled sweets so big they could hardly fit in the mouth at first – were regular favourites. They changed colour as we sucked them and lasted for ages, as long as you didn't bite into them and crunch them away fast.

Another favourite was a paper bag of sherbet which came with either a lolly to stick in it or a liquorice "straw" with which to suck it up. With lips pursed, our eyes watered as the sharp-sweet lemony powder dissolved on our tongues. I was also allowed to have sweet-smelling, pink bubble gum occasionally but Morfydd was too small at first. My friends and I would have competitions to see who could blow the biggest bubbles. If you blew too enthusiastically the bubble would burst resulting in a sticky pink mess all over your face and hair and a good telling off from your mother and a very unpleasant face scrub to follow. Sometimes it also entailed the cutting off of a chunk of hair, so it was no wonder Mammy was not too happy with this choice.

Somewhat more nutritious were our own fresh eggs. Daddy had constructed a hen coop and run at the back of our house so that we could have real eggs as well as the dried variety that could be bought in the shops to supplement our war-time diet. When a hen became too old to lay, Daddy had the unenviable task of killing it so that Mammy could pluck it and cook us a delicious chicken stew. Always a gentle, peaceful man, he hated this job but it had to be done. The designated chicken seemed to have a premonition that something was up and would dash around frantically clucking loudly before being captured and eventually slaughtered.

We children felt sorry for the chicken at first and could even be known to shed a few tears on its behalf, but that didn't stop us from thoroughly enjoying the resulting stew put in front of us at the dinner table. An excellent cook, Mammy made us a cooked breakfast (porridge), dinner, as well as a lighter tea or supper each day, from scratch and not a crumb was wasted as we wolfed it up. The chickens were fed on boiled vegetable peelings mashed up with bran – yet another regular task for my mother. One day, little Michael toddled after his mother as she fed the chickens. In the twinkling of an eye, he had grabbed a handful of the steaming mash and thrust it into his mouth to find out for himself what generated the hens' excited clucking. We sisters were disgusted and I grabbed him and pulled him away as he screamed for more.

* * * * *

After the long stressful and meagre years of the war, great rejoicing marked the end of the conflict. Multi-coloured buntings sprouted at every window and criss-crossed the narrow terraced streets. Union Jacks appeared in window and flags were waved everywhere by all the small children. Tables were set up along the middle of the streets and people somehow managed to pile them high with good things to eat: homemade Welsh cakes, jam tarts and fresh, plump sandwiches. Sports were organised in the streets and competition was fierce for all who wished to participate. My three younger sisters wanted to race in everything. With great enthusiasm they put their names down to run in sprints, three-legged races and egg and spoon races and each managed to win something in their age category.

Now a very grown-up twelve-year old, I had given up careering down the street in races. However, there was one competition I could enter. The local doctors announced that they would judge an Ankle Competition. Old blankets were hung over the football goal posts leaving only a space to disclose the leg from the knee down. Contestants had to walk slowly between the posts, stopping in the centre to show off their ankles to their best advantage. Alma Waltham, elder sister of Howard, was a very attractive teenager of about sixteen and was said to have the best chance of winning. However, I had to enter something so I borrowed Mammy's best pair of high heels and paraded with the other contestants between the goal posts. To my great surprise and joy, totally unexpectedly, I was judged the winner. I was as pleased as punch. Maybe Dr Orr as the main judge recognised my slightly unsteady walk and thought it judicious to allocate the prize to a child so that he did not have to choose between the older more competitive contestants. Whatever the case, all the Stevens sisters came away with a victory in something or other, even if mine was only for walking slowly between two posts.

The evening closed with dancing in the street and my best friend, Gwen, and I were thrilled to be asked to dance by one or two of the slightly older boys, as those of our own age had no idea of how to dance. We were all allowed to stay up later than usual and mothers put each sleepy child to bed as soon as exhaustion set in. It was indeed a most exciting and memorable experience for us all. We felt we could now look forward to a period of peace and prosperity when anything and everything would be possible.

In addition to our street celebrations, the whole Stevens family rejoiced together to mark the end of the war at Christmas 1945. Although Uncle Mark and Aunty Rosie lived their lives a little apart from the hub of their nuclear family, close links were always maintained. For many years, any of the family members who were in Wales at the time, would converge on Uncle Mark's pub in Penygraig after closing time on Christmas Eve to join in a most enjoyable private function. The most memorable party took place after the end of World War II on Christmas Day. There was both happiness and grief at that party. Mark had lost his only son Marco in Italy early in 1945. His sister, Aunty Selina, had suffered a triple blow, having lost her mother, her husband Bill (who died at thirty-six years old in Burma) and her five-month-old baby in a cot death in quick succession. Mammy was more fortunate, having been re-united with her brother, Davie, who had returned home safe and sound from Burma.

It was perhaps the only time that all the eleven Stevens siblings had come together in their maturity. Tears mingled with joy now that the terrible war had, at last, ended. There was much jubilation and joyful singing and music into the small hours. While my three youngest siblings were put down to sleep upstairs in the private part of the pub, Morfydd, Jane, John and I were far too excited and determined not to miss any of the fun. At the age of twelve, being the eldest of the children, I was allowed to help Daddy behind the bar. I felt very proud and grown up indeed. I have a vague memory of mixing a rather lethal cocktail of fruit juices laced with small amounts of any alcoholic beverage I could lay my hands on and administering it to a twelve-year-old male relative. Luckily no harm came to him but he dropped off into a sound sleep soon afterwards!

My mother was naturally prevailed upon to sing at the party. "Come on Annie May, give us a song!" was repeated time and again. Always one to oblige, she struck up into all the favourite wartime tunes. Vera Lynne's well-loved airs such as "The white cliffs of Dover," "We'll meet again" and many others rang out to enchant us all. She sang many duets with Uncle Ivor, too, as well as everyone's favourite traditional Welsh folk songs. There was no dearth of drinks placed on the piano to reward her efforts. Thirsty after prolonged bursts of singing, Annie May knocked them back without realising what she was doing. No sooner was her glass empty than it was refilled and replaced on the piano. Unused to consuming any alcohol, her head began to swim and she finally had to retire early to an upstairs bedroom where her three youngest children, Ann, Mary and baby Michael were sleeping peacefully. I, her eldest daughter, was left feeling a mixture of pride tinged with concern as I watched my wobbly mother being escorted out of the room. After a few hours' rest, the four sleepy heads were helped into Uncle Ted's car and driven home none the worse for wear. Now that the war was at last over, just like the street celebrations, our family party ended on a note of joy and new hope for the unknown future that stretched before us.

# Chapter 7
# Safely Over the First Hurdles

There was never a question of any one of us ever being kept home from school to help in the house, however ill or busy Mammy was. We were all regular attendees at school and Sunday School. I had been in the "A" class from the beginning and scored high marks in all subjects except for penmanship. I could never seem to keep my letters between the lines and they strayed all over the place in a spidery fashion. Mammy became concerned over this and took me to see an optician. Sure enough I was myopic, to such an extent that when I first looked through my new spectacles down at the floor of my school hall, I was amazed to see that there was not a single plain surface beneath me but serried ranks of floorboards I had never been able to see before. I was also able to see the lines on the leaves of my exercise book and the words more clearly on the blackboard, though I had always sat at the front before.

This was another unexpected expense for my poor parents. Although I could have been given the little round National health spectacles, Mammy would not contemplate my wearing such unflattering glasses and somehow found the money to buy me a more attractive pair. Even though I was able to see more clearly, I was not prepared to hide behind my glasses all the time. Besides, I did not want to look different from my friends who did not need to wear glasses. I would always remove them if I had been chosen to play Cinderella or Queen Titania in school plays in the Junior School and, later, to go dancing as a teenager.

The time to sit the eleven plus scholarship examination was drawing near. My mother talked confidently of when I would be going to Grammar school. There were a number of secondary schools in our valleys. In Porth, the next village, there were three grammar schools: The Porth County Grammar School for Girls, The Porth County Grammar School for Boys and The Porth Secondary Technical Grammar School which was mixed. Children throughout the valleys sat the same examination. Those who passed at the top of the list received two papers offering them a place in both the Porth County Grammar and in the Secondary Grammar School nearest their home. We were all keen to pass, so competition was fierce. Education was the way out of the pits and out of poverty. Being almost uniquely a working class area, the children of doctors, solicitors, business people or engineers had no option but to play with us or go without friends. Subsequently, there was very little class system amongst us, quite unlike the situation in Bournemouth where my cousins on my mother's side were growing up. It became apparent how lucky we were in the Rhondda when my cousin Raymond, only six months' younger than me, was refused entry to a local grammar school after passing the scholarship examination because of his working class background.

My Junior School in Ynyshir was perched on the mountainside on the other side of our narrow valley. I had a good view of it from my back bedroom window, as well as of the isolated hill farm silhouetted against the sky line at the top of the mountain. I liked to draw these two buildings and try to imagine who lived in the farm and what their life would be like so far away from the village. It was a very rare occurrence to see any sort of truck or farm vehicle winding its lonely way up the empty road towards the farm. The school building was divided into two sections. The ground floor housed the Nursery and Infants' School which we all attended from the age of three years. The first floor was divided between the Elementary School comprising the Junior Girls' School and the Forms where those who failed the eleven plus entrance examination continued their education until the age of fourteen. My mother never contemplated any of her children ending up in the dreaded "Forms."

I had many different teachers throughout my schooling in Ynyshir. I liked and respected them all and was always happy and usually had good end of term reports from them. During the last two years we kept the same teacher for continuity while preparing for the eleven plus. Our class had a new young teacher called Miss Jones. The appointed day came, the papers were distributed and I settled down to answer the questions. I was totally engrossed in my work when I gradually became aware that someone was whispering my name. I looked up and was horrified to realise that Enid Williams, one of my classmates, was trying to attract my attention. I tried to ignore her but she persevered and I was terrified that we would both be sent out of the room for talking. She was having problems with her arithmetic and wanted me to tell her the answer to a sum. In the end, fearing to be caught if she continued, I told her the answer and kept my head well down and away from her until the end of the examination.

As soon as the exam was over, I dashed out and started telling Enid off in no uncertain manner. She slapped me and a fight ensued with much pushing and shoving and pulling of hair. I made it quite clear that if she tried the same thing again, I would immediately tell the teacher about her. I would never have been able to face my mother if I had been prevented from sitting the scholarship examination for "cheating!" The rest of the time passed without further incident, so all we had to do was to wait for the results and hope.

When the day arrived, the rattle of the letterbox at the end of the passage signalled the passing of the postman. There on the floor lay two envelopes addressed to Miss Patricia Stevens. I tore open both letters and let out a shriek of pure joy. I had received an offer of a place in both the Porth Grammar Schools! Our prayers had been answered and our dreams had come true. I was over the first hurdle. We all jumped for joy.

"I knew you'd do it, Pat. I'm so proud of you," said Mammy giving me a big hug.

"Well done, Pat," Daddy said. "My chest is out. We'll have to go up to Wattstown to tell your uncles and aunts. They'll be so pleased. You've shown the way for the others to follow."

Shortly afterwards we walked up through the park to Bailey Street imparting the good news to friends and neighbours along the way. Indeed, my aunts and uncles were delighted to hear of my success and promised to buy me a leather satchel to carry my books to school. This satchel did valiant service throughout the whole of my school career.

Out of the thirty-four girls in my class, only three of us passed for the top grammar school, Porth County Girls – my friend Gwen Stinton from number 24 William Street and Margery Humphries from Gynor Avenue. I don't know if it was because our young teacher was inexperienced or whether that was about the correct percentage. Miss Jones got married that summer and lots of her pupils went to the church further up the valley in Pontygwaith to see the wedding. The bride was beautiful and was pleased to see her young 'ladies' come to wish her well.

During the preceding year, Morfydd and I had been attending Saint John's Ambulance Classes every week. We had learnt to give first aid, to apply bandages and to use slings etc. The summer before I was due to start my new school, the Saint John's Ambulance Brigade organised a huge children's camp at the seaside to reward all those who had worked so well over the year. Children came from all parts of the Rhondda valleys. We all packed into a special train which took us down to the coast. The train had a corridor running along its length and children ran up and down it to see who was in each carriage. A group of noisy boys arrived in our carriage and said that they were deciding who they were going to choose to be their girlfriend for the duration of the week. We girls felt a bit like slaves must have felt when put up for auction as the boys haggled over which of us they liked best. Of course, we sisters had made choices of our own. I was pleased to end up with John Moxham, one of the more confident and very good-looking boys. Almost twelve, I felt very grown-up as we walked together in the moonlight over the cliffs, arms around one another. All too soon our innocent and very fleeting romance was over and we were back home preparing for the new school term.

Before I could start attending my new school, there was the question of uniform to be addressed. We received a long list of clothes to be bought and of shops where they could be purchased: navy-blue gym slips, long sleeved white blouses, a green blazer with the appropriate badge, a navy mackintosh and a navy beret with badge. We would also need white gym shoes and socks and navy knickers. For the summer term, we would also need green and white gingham dresses. This was surely going to prove to be a problem for our impecunious family. However Mammy's "something will come" philosophy turned up trumps once more.

Bopa's niece, Valerie Radcliffe, came from an affluent family of gentleman farmers living in the Vale of Glamorgan. She was a few years older than me and had grown out of her current school uniform which, apart from the badges, was identical with mine. It was in excellent condition and of top quality so I considered myself lucky to be the recipient of such a fine ready-made uniform. Hand-me-downs were a normal state of affairs in families of our sort, but as not only the eldest in our nuclear family, but being the oldest of our near cousins, I myself had not experienced it much. However, I was not proud and was absolutely delighted to accept a second-hand uniform from Valerie which would spare my hard-pressed parents so much worry and expense. We bought brand new badges and I settled down to remove Valerie's badges and sew mine neatly on the garments instead. The gymslip was far too long for me too, so I set to and made a large hem which was let down bit by bit as I progressed through school. Although the gymslip became thin and shiny with wear, it actually lasted me for the whole of my school life.

At the start of term, greatly excited, Gwen and I set off for our first day in our new school. As pupils came from all over the valleys to attend this school, most of them were allocated free bus passes. Porth County was situated just over a mile from our home so we lived just outside the area qualifying pupils for bus passes. This meant that we had a long walk of over half an hour every day, except when the weather was really too bad. Our route took us around the Oval, up Jacob's ladder (a long flight of stone steps leading from the main road up to a higher one) and along the streets past "Porth Sec." and "Boys' County" and up a long final hill to reach "Girls' County." This we did to and from school every day and, though it was quite pleasant in good weather, it was quite a hard trek when it started to rain en route. However, as time passed, we met up with friends, both boys and girls, on the way and even got to have our heavy satchels carried for us at times.

Most of my friends had bikes. Somehow my parents managed to buy me a brand new drop-handled BSA bike for my birthday on the strict understanding that it was to be shared between all us children as time went on. It was not possible to use it to go to school for me, as the last part of the route consisted of a very steep hill and my bike did not possess any gears. Later on, other siblings attending Porth Secondary Grammar would sometimes ride to school, as their school stood at the bottom of the hill and was that much nearer home. In fact all my siblings got more use out of my bike than I did in the end. Ann used it to get around Cardiff when she was at university there and even Michael deigned to use a girl's bike before he managed to acquire a proper boy's bike.

One time, he let it free wheel down the steep hill leading down from Heath Terrace and ended up cracking his head against a stone wall which emerged unexpectedly round a sharp bend at the bottom. Fortunately, he had a hard head. We girls were just as concerned about the state of our precious bike as about the big blue lump on our brother's forehead! It was difficult to find the money for bus fares and for school dinners, especially when several of us were of school age, so we all walked and took packed sandwiches for lunch. This gave us good exercise and good appetites for the delicious cooked dinners, usually made with cheap cuts of meat stewed slowly over the fire until tender with plenty of fresh vegetables, that Mammy always had waiting for us when we got home from school in the afternoons.

There were two classes of over thirty pupils in each year of my new school. At first, Gwen and I were placed in Form 1B. There were examinations at the end of each term and at the end of the first year, pupils were re-assessed and there was great movement between the A and B streams. Gwen and I were promoted and, having come eighth, seventh and fourth in 1B, once in the A class, I progressed to being always in the top three and had book prizes every year for "merit." I settled well and made many friends. I liked almost all my subjects and found that I was very well suited to academic work. I did well in most of my subjects at one time or another, my work being criticised for untidiness rather than for academic standard. Though I was often scolded for chatting, I concentrated well on my work and never found it a real grind. Mammy often used to recount how I would do my homework quickly while standing at the wide windowsill of the middle room with the 'wireless' (radio) going full blast and all my noisy siblings playing around me. I loved school.

In 2A, we had to choose between Welsh and French. I would have very much liked to be able to continue with both, but I eventually decided on French. Those in the A classes had to take Latin and those in the Bs, German. Although Latin became one of my favourite subjects, I very much regret not being offered the opportunity to study more modern languages since I ended up following a career in languages.

We had an excellent English teacher who taught us the ins and outs of English grammar before the days when teaching pupils about nouns, adjectives, prepositions and tenses of verbs was frowned upon. I loved it all, especially the academic exercise of parsing the whole sentence. My spoken English improved quickly and so did Mammy's as she was eager to learn from me and wanted desperately to know the *correct* way of speaking. She had already picked up quite a bit of good English from paying close attention to the families she had worked for in London. In fact she had never spoken with the thick Welsh accent full of colloquialisms of her neighbours, though she retained the melodious Welsh lilt, of course. Years later when I was teaching, my English teacher colleague asked,

"Why does your mother speak differently from all the other mothers around here?" and was particularly impressed to hear her using such vocabulary as 'transmogrify' when threatening to punish her children! Daddy, however, was a different kettle of fish. He preferred to speak in the same vernacular as his butties in the pit and resisted our efforts to improve his speech. This in-depth knowledge of the English language stood me in good stead when learning foreign languages, especially when studying in France in later years.

Needless to say, I chose all the academic subjects. I often chose them according to whether I liked the teacher or not and ended up finding that I was studying almost all Arts subjects. In fact, my only science subjects were Maths and Geography. I dropped needlework in which I had come top, to the great disappointment of my teacher, Miss Griffiths. This did not seem to matter in the end, as, being keen to be well-dressed, I built upon what I had learnt. I never had a single lesson of domestic science, either. This was not a problem because, as far as cooking was concerned, Mammy was an excellent role model and I was always one who "lived to eat" rather than one who "ate to live." Mammy's Welsh cakes were absolutely delicious and we all used to stand close to the fire (later the Rayburn stove) as she dropped the soft mixture onto the hot bake stone to cook the little round cakes. Hot as they were, they disappeared as fast as she could cook them so that only a relatively small plateful finally remained for tea. She was always very successful in the cookery competitions for Saint Anne's Mothers' Union. One year, her friend and neighbour, Marion Pike, asked her if she would make her some Welsh cakes to enter the competition, as she was not quite such a good cook. That year, Mrs. Annie May Stevens took second place to Mrs. Pike!

If not the happiest days of my life, school days were certainly some of the best. I blossomed in every way, making lots of new friends and tried to follow my mother's adage of making the most out of whatever life had to offer, gaining new social and cultural experiences along the way. I joined in all aspects of school life. I liked sports even though I was only average in most of them. I did, however, manage to gain a regular place in the second eleven hockey team, but as most schools in the area only had one team, I rarely had the chance to play for my school at sport. I did represent Penrhys, my House, in Netball and Country Dancing and often emerged on the winning side.

Early on in my first year, I had been performing some country dances with my class. My Headmistress Miss Hudd was watching. Suddenly, a loud voice rang out,

"That girl with the long curls! - get them tied back immediately!"

Suddenly everyone was looking at me. Three rows of blonde ringlets had caught the sun as I bobbed around the court and caught Miss Hudd's attention at the same time. Our Headmistress was very strict about hair being plaited or neatly tied back. I suppose it was partly for tidiness and partly to avoid the spread of nits through loose long hair flying about. That morning as usual, I had stood patiently next to the kitchen sink while Mammy had curled strands of my hair around her finger, dampening it with cold water until my head was covered with a mass of springy ringlets, held off my face by a slide at each side. Then she had plaited Morfydd's luxuriant chestnut hair into two thick plaits tied with white ribbon at the ends. She was proud of our healthy hair and used vinegar in the last rinse to make it shine. However, after this incident, she did not want to risk my getting into trouble at school, so she tied my hair into two neat bunches from then onwards.

Homework was done quickly as soon as I got home. I was totally absorbed in it, anxious to finish fast in order to return to the book I had been reading or, after I had joined the tennis club, to meet Gwen to play tennis in Wattstown Park. We had formed a nice mixed group of friends there and enjoyed socialising with them as much as actually playing tennis. One of the boys, Maurice Williams, the son of the owner of the local Dairy business, became my first real boyfriend. We played tennis, went for walks and to the cinema together. He carried my satchel to school for me and waited for me to walk home with him. He was very sporty and played fullback for the County Boys' first rugby team. He also played cricket in the summer and I would often watch him on the Oval at the bottom of our street. He even invited me to go to watch him playing rugby away from home when I found myself to be the only girl on the bus, as I was when he took me to see our national team playing in the famous Arms Park, Cardiff. The other players had to curtail the bad language and the crude rugby songs they normally sang rowdily together in deference to the "lady" present. Maurice was not the most popular boy on the bus on those occasions!

Maurice lived in a comfortable detached house in Gynor Avenue on the opposite side of Ynyshir, overlooking the valley. It was certainly grander than our family home, something I soon realised when I was invited to tea there one day. I was not at all ashamed to invite him back to tea with us, despite the holes in the rag mats and the worn furniture. He had to take us as he found us and indeed he was happy to do so. I never rushed around tidying everything up before his visits as my more house-proud sister, Morfydd, did before her friends arrived. We went out with one another for almost two years. During that time, I would often finish with him after a little tiff, confident that he would soon come crawling back. I made the mistake of doing it once too often, for I had told him that another girl was sweet on him and when I broke off with him the next time, he asked Nettie John out. The worm had turned and we never made it up after that, though there was always an underlying attraction between us quite noticeable to our friends. I then started going out with different escorts, changing them frequently at first. Maurice and I often walked and talked together affectionately within our friendship group but I am now thankful that we never got back together.

Sometime later when I was nineteen, I learnt of a terrible tragedy that had occurred after a rugby match in Pontygwaith. Maurice had taken a bad knock during the game but continued playing until the end of the match. It appears that he went into the toilets and passed out there. His friends left the club without realising that Maurice was missing, so that when he came round he was all alone. He managed to make himself heard to the caretaker who immediately dialled 999 when he saw the state Maurice was in. When help came, he was rushed home where he died shortly afterwards in his mother's arms. He died of a ruptured spleen. His death affected us all deeply and his friends blamed themselves for not realising that he was missing after the game. I went to express my condolences to his parents who asked me to continue to call on them when I was home, as they had learnt from Maurice's diary how fond he had always been of me. I went on visiting them for some years afterwards.

* * * * *

Life settled into a fairly regular routine during my first five years in Porth County. It was certainly very full, divided as it was between school work, family duties and social commitments. However, a possible tragedy was avoided through Mammy's constant vigilance. One day she was watching Ann and Mary playing in the back garden. As they ran towards her she noticed something odd about the way Mary was walking.

"Go back down the path, Mary, and then walk back slowly towards me," she instructed her youngest daughter, watching her carefully as she approached. She was very concerned to see that Mary appeared to be limping and further scrutiny revealed that one of her legs was slightly shorter and thinner than the other. Without delay, she took her to the doctor who sent Mary to the hospital for further tests where polio was diagnosed. She was immediately put on a course of treatment. This included sunray therapy and Ann was allowed to receive this with her.

As it took place at Trealaw Clinic which was close to my school, I sometimes took the two girls there for their treatment at weekends. Mary made a full recovery and became the sportiest of all us sisters. Mammy had averted a catastrophe which would have changed Mary's life. At the very least, she would certainly have become disabled at an early age with the likelihood of having to wear heavy callipers on her leg for the rest of her life. Many years later, I got to know that we four siblings were often referred to by outsiders by the attribute that most suitably described us. Of the Stevens Girls, I was known as *the academic one,* Morfydd as *the singer,* Ann as *the musician* and Mary as *the sporty one.*

Until now, I had concentrated my spare energy on the Church where I became a Sunday School Teacher in my late teens. My little sisters, Ann and Mary, were keen church goers and very lively too, so I took on a new role. I became a sort of producer/director of a band of energetic urchins desperate to perform. Rev. Pugh, our well-loved Vicar, had every confidence in me and allowed us the use of the Church Hall as often as we wanted it for rehearsals and performances. This activity usually went on during school holidays and kept us off the streets by providing something interesting to do. There was a stage in the hall and parents were soon roped in to put up make-shift curtains and props. I produced Music Hall type programmes where the children sang and danced together dressed up in colourful costumes fabricated from any bits and pieces their parents could lay their hands on.

Once, Ann put rather too much enthusiasm into dancing the French can-can and ended up in an untidy heap on the stage, causing some hilarity. Flushed with embarrassment to have fallen when her "boyfriend" John Cull was in the audience, she soon got up again and continued her performance none the worse for her fall. Mary once starred singing the solo "I'm Forever Blowing Bubbles" dressed in a long flowing dress, swaying gently on a swing hung up securely over the stage while soap bubbles of every hue were blown from the wings. I also had to create sketches for them to act at times. In the most memorable one, Ann and her best friend, Christine, took the main parts as scarecrows in a Worzel Gummidge play which went down very well indeed to roars of appreciative laughter. We always had a full audience of parents, uncles, aunts, friends and church goers who generously paid their pennies to see the show. The collection was used to provide little treats for the young performers and any money remaining was given to church funds.

Miss Osman, my geography teacher, ran The First Porth Rangers Company and along with many of my school friends, I joined the Guide Movement enthusiastically. Although there had been scout packs, there had been no Brownies or Guides in Ynyshir. Encouraged by Miss Osman and by Daddy, I threw myself into the guide movement. I walked to Porth one evening a week to attend First Porth Ranger meetings. We did all manner of exciting and interesting things together and went on outings all over our area, marching briskly together, merrily singing our jolly guide songs at full throttle.

Our company went camping under canvas and to specially built camps such as Gorseinon in the Vale of Glamorgan and further afield. Our Captain sent us out on interesting projects for which we had to plan routes and draw maps to illustrate our journeys. We were encouraged to go on expeditions singly or in pairs. It was necessary for us to prepare meticulously in advance, drawing maps to scale, estimating accurately the time necessary to complete the expedition and writing it all up neatly on our return. My expedition entailed drawing an accurate map of the Rhondda valleys, travelling to Maerdy by bus where I met my friends, Lonwy and Meryl, who lived in the village. They then accompanied me over the mountains and down into the neighbouring valley of Aberdare and back over to Maerdy again. In Aberdare we searched out the most interesting features such as the old church and park and noted them down. It was a valuable experience in acquiring life skills and becoming independent and self-reliant.

Towards the end of Form 4, there was talk of our Ranger Company having the opportunity of going to the South of France in the summer holidays. I knew that I could not ask my parents if I could go. One day however, Miss Osman called me to her room to ask why I had not put my name down to go on the trip. I explained our financial situation at home and, to my surprise and delight, she said that certain grants were available for families in our position. She helped me to apply and I obtained a full grant which enabled me to take part in the two-week holiday free of charge. All we had to do was to save up enough for me to have some pocket money to spend and to have a few new clothes to take with me. As we would be wearing uniform most of the time, this did not prove too much of a problem. My parents were as delighted as I was that I was to be given such a wonderful opportunity and the first real holiday of my life. Previously, holidays for us had consisted solely of a week or so with relatives in Nuneaton or Bournemouth or a day-trip to Barry with the church in the summer.

On one memorable occasion when we were all sunbathing on the beach in Barry (a rare occurrence when we didn't need to shelter from the wind and rain), Mammy suddenly looked up from making the sandwiches.

"Where's Michael?" she inquired.

"He's just over there playing with his bucket and spade," replied Mary.

But when we looked he was nowhere to be seen. There was just a small pile of sand and a hole where he had been digging. The beach was absolutely packed with very little space between family groups. It was like looking for a needle in a haystack. Consternation reigned.

"He can't have gone far. We'll soon find him."

93

"Perhaps he went down towards the sea to fill his bucket."

"Spread out and ask everyone if they've seen a little boy wandering about with his bucket and spade. I'll go to the sea," I said.

In very little time we had all returned empty-handed.

"Now don't panic," said Daddy. "Idris just told me there's a *Lost Children's Place* up on the prom. Let's go and 'ave a look, see if anybody's taken 'im there. You stay here with Ann and Mary, May, in case he finds his way back or someone brings him. Pat and Morfydd come with me and help look out for him as we go."

We set off immediately shouting his name and scouring the beach around us as we went. As we approached the Lost Children's Centre, we had no doubt that we had found Michael, as we heard loud cries and sobs emanating from the room where carers were trying to pacify frightened children until they could be reunited with their parents.

"Mammy! I want my Mammy!" three-year-old Michael was repeating between gulps and sobs until he caught sight of us and rushed headlong into Daddy's arms. We were so pleased to find him safe and sound that he escaped any recriminations and was soon tucking into a big strawberry ice-cream in consolation.

None of us ever had regular pocket money but we contrived to earn a little money in any way we could. I often tried out new hair styles on my mother and sisters and even gave them a trim occasionally to save money. When neighbours complimented them on their hair do, I was asked to do their hair and they were willing to pay me for my efforts! Thus I became the local hair dresser, going into several houses in the street to wash and set some of our neighbours' hair in their kitchens. In this way, I managed to earn a little much needed pocket money and this I saved up ready to spend in France.

My most regular customer was a lady called Cassie who lived just a few doors up from us. She was disabled and suffered from a degenerative disease called muscular dystrophy so she was totally incapable of washing her own hair. She was lonely too as she lived alone and greatly appreciated the little chats we had together when I visited her at least once a week. Even after I left home, I would call on her as regularly as I could to give her an extra special hair do. The disease eventually progressed to such an extent that she had to go into a care home. I always kept in touch with Cassie, but my visits became rarer as she lived quite a long way away in Radyr in the Vale of Glamorgan and this entailed a long bus ride and a walk. I would take her a small gift at Christmas time though and once she gave me an Ali Baba wicker basket that she had woven for me in activity therapy at the home. I still use it in my bath room to keep my dirty washing in all these years later. When she died, her nephew Gordon presented me with a beautiful little claret-coloured antique vase which she had left me as a keepsake in her will.

Then came the longed-for day when we Rangers left for France. Rucksacks stuffed full, we set out by train and ferry for the South of France. First stop was Paris where we stayed in a youth hostel in the centre of the city. I was totally overawed by the beautiful, elegant city with its wide tree-lined avenues, its fashionable shops, its impressive arches under which flowed the majestic River Seine with its *bateaux mouches* (Parisian sight-seeing boats) taking tourists all around its winding water-ways. We were taken to see the Louvre museum and visited the great cathedral of Notre Dame. I remember being given large chunks of tasty French baguettes with lumps of delicious chocolate to eat as a snack as we strolled through the Tuileries gardens. That was much more appreciated than dreary sausage rolls or doughnuts. Before leaving this fascinating city, we were let loose in cheap souvenir shops where we bought tiny metal replicas of *Notre Dame, the Eiffel tower, etc.* as presents to take back home.

Our brief stay over, we packed into our reserved carriages on the fast train to take us down to the famous French Riviera. We continued by coach to the little town of Grasse in Provence Verte, perched on the lower slopes of the Alpes Maritimes. There we got out of the coach and were told that we would have to walk the rest of the way to our destination. Our heavy luggage was loaded onto a four-wheel-drive vehicle to be taken up the steep mountain road. We, however, were expected to walk up a winding track that pointed straight upwards under a blazing hot sun in the middle of August! "Les Courmettes," *Une Colonie de Vacances* (a sort of holiday camp for French children,) was situated high up in the middle of nowhere on the steep mountainside. We were soon huffing and puffing and complaining bitterly:

"I can't go much further. My feet are killing me."

"I can't carry this bag any longer. It's as heavy as lead."

"You should have left it in the luggage van with the rest of the heavy stuff."

"I can hardly breathe. The air is so thin up here. It's so hot."

We were urged on and at last the first glimpse of the camp came into view. What a welcome sight that was! We all heaved a general sigh of relief and gulped down thankfully the cool refreshing water that awaited us. We could finally relax after our long, tiring journey. Our holiday had begun.

We just had time to find our beds in the large, airy dormitory, freshen up and pack away some of our things in the small spaces allocated to us when a shrill whistle announced that supper was ready. We trouped outside to find a long table laden with all sorts of fresh salads dressed with tasty *vinaigrette*, different varieties of pâté and crisp French baguettes laid out under the shade of the trees. The long walk and the mountain air had sharpened our appetites and we fell to with gusto as soon as we had sung our grace together. To our surprise and delight, this was followed by a second course of pasta with a very tasty sauce sprinkled with grated cheese and finally with a little pot of chocolate mousse topped with Chantilly cream. Despite the excitement of our new surroundings and the babble of chatter in the dormitory, no one had a problem in dropping off to sleep, as we knew we would be woken up early the next morning for breakfast. We didn't want to miss a moment of our unique holiday in France.

Straight after breakfast we met our new French friends. These were young teenagers of our own age who attended these summer camps at a reduced rate to help supervise and organise games for the younger children. They were called *monitrices*. This mixture of French and British girls aimed to give us all the chance to try out our new language skills. I made friends with a pleasant girl called Huguette who was very sociable and lively. We chatted together about our homes and families when the little children were in bed and we could enjoy free time together in the cool of the evening. The French girls taught us some French songs and we taught them many of our guide songs which we all sang lustily together. I was not slow to try out my schoolgirl French on her either and we communicated very well from the start. Both my French and her English benefitted from our two-week association. It certainly increased my enthusiasm for the subject, too.

We Rangers also had certain chores to do each day but they were quickly done and didn't detract in any way from the enjoyment of the holiday. We were taken on short trips, went swimming and visited the Fragonard perfume factory in Grasse where we were shown the process of extracting the scents from the natural herbs which grew prolifically over the mountains. Although it was too late to see the lavender fields in bloom, their scent and that of the pungent wild herbs was everywhere so that the perfume factory had a continuous supply all around it. It was there that we bought little bottles of *eau de toilette* or small tablets of perfumed soap for our mothers and sisters. This wonderful, never to be forgotten holiday first gave me the travel bug which drove me to explore ever widening horizons in my future life.

On my return home, it was time to think seriously about O Levels. This new examination had just been introduced for the first time and our Form teacher told us that it was now possible to drop any subject with which we were experiencing difficulty. Immediately, there was an avalanche of undesired subjects on her list.

"What are you going to drop?" my friends wanted to know.

This posed quite a problem for me as I liked all the subjects I had chosen so I really didn't want to drop anything. Nevertheless, I didn't want to be looked on as a "*swot*" so I said quickly,

"I think I'll drop music."

We had acquired a piano just under a year ago from my great Aunt Annie, my grandfather Dai Davies' sister, and Mammy had enrolled the three oldest girls for piano lessons with Mrs. Griffiths, Graig Road. My six-year-old sister Ann took to the piano like a duck to water and was always tinkling away whenever she got the chance. The tradition of a love for music was strong in the family in my generation. We all sang regularly in Mr. Ardwyn James' Co-op children's choir when young and competed most successfully in *Esteddfodai* all over Wales. Mammy also served on the choir committee for several years. From tiny children, Ann and Mary ended each concert by singing the closing prayer as a duet, Ann singing alto and Mary soprano. My grandfather had been right when he had forecast that Morfydd would have a beautiful voice when she was only a toddler. Mammy was able to relive her early success as a singer, sitting in the front row of the audience mouthing the words, as Morfydd won prize after prize in competitions.

My brother, Michael, still continues to sing tenor in a Welsh choir in Canada where he brought up his family. Although Daddy did not have a violinist to follow in his footsteps, he was equally proud to accompany Ann when she competed in piano solos. He was eventually able to bequeath his beloved violin to Nicola, Morfydd's youngest daughter, who became as competent on the violin as on the piano and went on to teach music. Our cousin Pam, Aunty Iris' daughter, was also a gifted pianist. She played piano solos with youth orchestras and had an ambition to become a concert pianist before following the family tradition into teaching music. All this musicality was finally to culminate in the fourth generation when my son Mark would attain his ambition of becoming a professional operatic tenor.

When we first acquired the piano at home, I was studying music in school. All the other pupils in the class had been playing the piano for years. I had been down to sing a traditional Welsh folk song, *Y Fywalchen* (The Blackbird) for my practical examination. However, now that we had a piano, I was making great strides and was soon put in for Grade 3, as I already had a good knowledge of theory. This obviously entailed a lot of practice which interfered with my tennis club and other social activities. I did not really want to drop music but could think of no other subject that didn't seem essential to my future career so, when asked in my turn by my teacher,

"What subject do you wish to drop, Pat? You must say now or it will be too late." I replied,

"I *might* drop music."

I had decided to ask my music teacher whether she thought I would do well in the subject and if she encouraged me, I would tell my Form Teacher that I would be continuing with music after all.

What a shock I got when I walked into my music lesson as usual later that day! My teacher, Miss Harris, had already been told that I had decided to drop music and she was absolutely fuming.

"Why are you dropping music?" she inquired sharply as soon as I entered the room.

97

"I thought that I wasn't good enough in music," I stammered. "All the other girls have been playing the piano for years and I won't be able to catch up in time."

"That's nonsense," she retorted. "You can sing for your practical. You already know your song. I expected at least a credit from you if not a distinction. You are nothing but a lazy good-for nothing! Bring back all your books and leave the room immediately," she stormed, as she grabbed my books from me.

I was utterly dumbfounded and slunk from the room in shame. I was so upset that I stopped my piano lessons and never played again.

We sat the O Level examinations in June and went for our results in August. I had passed everything comfortably and Miss Hudd congratulated me.

"What are you taking for your A Levels?" she enquired.

"I'm not quite sure yet," I replied. "I would like to talk to my subject teachers before making up my mind."

"You must take Maths," she said. "You have gained a high distinction in all three papers."

"I like Maths very much," I said, "but I don't have enough science subjects to go with it." At that time, you either studied Arts or Sciences and you could not mix the two so my choice was partly made for me already.

\* \* \* \* \*

I became a prefect on entering the Lower Sixth and now had to decide which subjects I would study for A-level. We were allowed to take three subjects for A Level but after consulting my teachers, I was still in a quandary. Five of them were quite happy to have me in their A level class, so I began by sampling lessons in French, Latin, History, Geography and English for almost the whole of the first term in Lower Sixth before settling on French, Latin and History. I never regretted my choice although I loved English Literature.

I had always devoured books from an early age. When we were young, there being no electricity in the house, gas mantles were fitted to give us light downstairs. I was always in trouble for reading in bed by candlelight or for reading in the toilet to avoid washing up. While still at primary school, I had got to know that Aunty Nan had a complete set of the works of Charles Dickens on her shelves, so I borrowed them one by one until I had read them all.

I had also had ambitions to take a main role in one of the school plays. Alas, this was not to be. We had just started to have violin lessons in school, and as my father was keen to help me, I was the only one advanced enough to be able to play the violin in the school play. A good part was out of the question for me – I had to play the court musician. When "the Duke" turned to me as I was playing and said,

"Enough! – 'tis not so sweet now as 'twas before!" my proud parents were none too pleased to hear someone in the audience behind them say:

"It never sounded sweet to me!"

In the fifth form, I had auditioned for the part of the chirpy maid in a translation of Moliere's *Le Bourgeois Gentilhomme*. I found that, for the life of me, I could not master a cockney accent, so I was relegated to dancing as a Turk, like a whirling dervish! Finally my chance seemed to have arrived at last in the sixth form, when two pupils who resembled each other were needed to play the twins, Viola and Sebastian, in Twelfth Night. Hannah Jones and I were being seriously considered, but at the last minute, Linda Milliner returned to school and, as she was not only an excellent elocutionist but also had almost a double in her class, they won the parts.

Our Geography mistress, Miss Osman, had now become the chief Guider for South Wales and had inspired me with a love of far-away places, peoples and map-making. Geography was yet another subject I really enjoyed, as was French too since that fantastic holiday in France with First Porth Rangers. I loved to practise my French on the *"Shunny Onion Men"* who called at our doors. They came from Brittany on their bicycles selling long strings of firm, round onions which would keep all winter. Though Breton as a language was akin to Welsh, they also spoke fluent French and were always happy to chat with me on the doorstep as they toted their wares.

Miss Davies, the Latin mistress, was a real academic. In the lower school, she would swing on her chair at her desk, after having set us an exercise, while we competed to be the first to finish and rush out to get it marked. We ended up in a long line at the front of the class but there was never any noise or indiscipline at all. Later in the sixth form, some pupils would buy a crib copy of our Latin set books, Caesar, Livy or Catullus, and learn it by heart. However, I always so enjoyed the challenge of translating the Latin text, I never resorted to that myself.

We had had a motley assortment of French teachers during my school career. Madame Roberts, who lived in the big house near the church in Ynyshir, left at the end of my first year to become the first Headmistress of Ynyshir Girls Secondary Modern School. After that, we had one French teacher after the other, one often away during long periods of illness and one pitiful supply teacher from Australia who was unable to keep order in her classes. This was most unusual in our school, especially in the 'A' classes which were normally taught by the best and strictest teachers. There was pandemonium in Miss Lauder's French class. No-one listened; everyone talked and laughed, ignoring the poor teacher. Although I was really interested in the subject, to my great shame now, I also found myself crawling up and down in the aisles between the desks. I was especially contrite when, at the end-of-term exam, I received top marks and the comment "Works well!" The situation was eventually saved by the arrival of Miss Llewellyn from Swansea in time for our O-level year. Teacher and class had to work very hard to make up for lost time, but fortunately, I had not lost my enthusiasm for the subject.

Miss Lloyd, our History teacher, inspired me with a great love of History. We were never given long lists of dates and reams of notes to learn by heart. From the beginning, we were encouraged to discover the causes and consequences of great historical movements. We were encouraged to use our brains to compose our own essays using specific examples to illustrate each point made in our arguments. I am eternally grateful to her for the insight she gave me into History. To this day I still very much enjoy reading historical novels when they portray the period in an authentic way.

Towards the end of my first year sixth, a troop of singers and dancers from Yugoslavia came to tour the Rhondda. It was the era of Marshal Tito, head of this communist state. The Rhondda was Labour to a man and was suspected of having strong communist leanings. Maerdy at the top of our valley was often referred to as *Little Russia* at that time. It was not surprising then that they were welcomed with open arms. They were to be put up in our homes and although our little three-bed-roomed house was almost bursting at the seams, Mammy had volunteered to take two young Yugoslav girls. Morfydd and I were to sleep on the studio couch in the front room so that they could have our bedroom. We were all awaiting their arrival with eager anticipation.

On the appointed day, Gwen and I rushed home from school to hear Daddy shouting in a loud voice as we entered the house,

"You are very welcome in my house. I am Tom and this is May, my wife. What's your name?"

In front of him were two athletic young men, smiling broadly with puzzled looks on their faces. Taken aback initially, we too were soon smiling broadly when we realised that we had hit the jackpot. It seems that everyone had opted to accommodate girls, so Mammy had been persuaded to take two handsome young male dancers instead.

"Don't shout, Tom. You'll give them a headache and they still won't understand you any better," Mammy was saying. We quickly resorted to sign language and were soon sitting around the table enjoying a hot meal together. Daddy went on trying to hold a conversation with them at the top of his voice. He wanted to make them very welcome and to be sure there was nothing more he could do to make them comfortable.

"Have you had enough to eat? There's plenty more vegetables if you are still hungry. I grow them all in my garden," he informed them.

By smiling and tapping their extended stomachs they indicated that they had enjoyed a more than adequate meal. Assuming that they would be tired after their long journey, we showed them their room and they were greatly relieved to leave the problem of communication until they had had a good night's sleep in a comfortable bed.

Being keen to communicate with our guests, I searched out the set of ten *Books of Knowledge* that we had in our cupboards. I flicked through them to see if there was anything to do with Yugoslavia in them. All I found was a smattering of Russian there so I tried it out on them in the morning. Luckily they understood it, so we were able to converse by pointing to the words in the book while they told us how to pronounce them. We got on very well like this and were invited to join them in their bus when they went further afield to give a concert. They had wonderful voices and sang enthusiastically on the bus, obviously very proud of their leader Tito and their native country. Their concerts were colourful and fascinating. They harmonised in many parts and the acrobatic dancing of the men was absolutely incredible. Their tour was a great success and we were all sorry to say goodbye to our first ever foreign guests when the time came for them to depart.

Now that I was only studying my three best subjects which I really enjoyed, it was easy for me to excel in my examinations. I came top every time throughout the First Year Sixth. Academic excellence was all that counted in our school, so I was appointed Head Girl with certain specific duties. This was not a sinecure and I was entrusted with much organising and disciplining of the younger pupils. Amongst my duties, I had to make short speeches to thank visiting dignitaries at Prize-Giving Day and always led the "Three cheers for the holidays, girls!" at the end of each term. I also became the right-hand girl of our Headmistress, Miss Hudd. I had to stand next to her with the bell in my hand, ready to ring it when she gave the signal for all the girls, lined up with their teachers in the corridors, to enter their class rooms. While standing there, I was sometimes embarrassed when the Headmistress gave a severe dressing down to an unfortunate young teacher in my presence.

"Now you can see what I have to put up with, Pat," she would say, as the poor red-faced teacher trembled in front of her. Miss Hudd could be very strict and hard with her pupils and equally hard and even cruel with any inexperienced teacher who put a foot wrong.

My two years in the Sixth Form passed very quickly indeed. I worked hard and concentrated well in school so that I still had plenty of time to enjoy myself in the evenings and weekends. In addition to my commitment to Rangers and Tennis club, Gwen and I, together with our other close friend Clarissa, frequented the local dance halls: the Rink in Porth and the Library in Tonypandy. Since my romance with Maurice had ended, I was now free to go out with other boys. One of my friends, Enid Franklin, was raving over a popular and good-looking boy called David Boor. One evening, I was dancing with a new partner, having stowed my glasses away in my hand bag, when I noticed Enid making signs to me over his shoulder. When I returned to my place next to her, she asked breathlessly,

"Do you know who that boy is you were dancing with?"

"No, who is he?" I replied.

"That's David Boor! All the girls around here are nuts on him. He's a real smasher, isn't he?" she said after he had left us.

Being so myopic, I did not go looking for possible dance partners to stand near them and ogle them as did many of my friends. Smiling broadly and hoping that I looked more attractive without my glasses, I waited for boys to search me out instead and this time at least it had worked. I danced several more times with David and he asked to walk me home. After that we went out regularly together.

Later David was called up for his National Service and he looked very handsome indeed in his smart RAF uniform. We were only able to go out together when he was on leave. However, I had other male friends to keep me company while he was away, two of whom also happened to be called David! David Davies would sometimes escort me home from a dance but soon skedaddled when his friend David Boor turned up unexpectedly. The third David, David Enock, was studying French in the adjoining Boys' School and we liked discussing poetry together. He had a friend, Trevor Fudge, who was also keen to take part in our poetry readings and discussions. We needed to find a suitable venue for our Poetry Club, so I asked Vicar Pugh if we could use the church hall. He agreed readily and so our exclusive little club was swiftly established. We three met regularly to declaim emotive poems written about the war, of which one of our favourites was Rupert Brooke's *The Soldier*. We would often discuss too the French poems on our A Level syllabus. Our preferred poets were Baudelaire and Verlaine.

One clear evening after reciting Verlaine's *Clair de Lune* (moonlight) together, we went for a walk and ended up near the disused Lady Lewis colliery. It was abandoned and derelict but the old pit wheels still rose temptingly above the mine shaft into the night sky. I had always wanted to climb up there so now, encouraged by my two friends, I dared to mount to the very top. It was such an exhilarating feeling to stand right up high surveying all around us beneath a starlit sky. Thank goodness that Mammy never heard of this exploit! I was surprised to learn many years later from my daughter that a certain Trevor Fudge, a colleague she had met when she first took up a post as a lecturer in Cardiff, had mentioned to her that her mother had been his first girlfriend.

One Sunday afternoon not long after that moonlit walk to the old pithead, as the family was finishing tea, a knock came on the front door.

"Go and answer it, Michael," said Mammy.

Two minutes later a treble voice piped up from the passage way: "It's David Enock for Pat" sang out my little brother. It was not David Enock at all who was standing there at the door looking rather put out when I got up to meet him, but David Boor. He had unexpected leave and had dropped in to surprise me but it was he who had got the surprise and not a very nice one. I had quite a job to convince him that David Enock was just a pal with whom I discussed poetry. Little brothers are such a bind! Why couldn't Michael have just said that David had called and left it at that.

* * * * *

The time was fast approaching when I was to sit my A levels which I hoped would open the door to a University education and a whole new life of opportunity denied to my parents. I had worked assiduously in all my three subjects throughout the last two years but had left most of my revision until lessons were finished. My father used to get up very early to light the kitchen fire before setting off for his morning shift which started at 6 a.m. I would get up in time to begin revising by 6 a.m. also. The whole house was quiet. There was no chatter of children running about or the sounds of Mammy clattering in the kitchen preparing meals. I made fast progress before breakfast and then it was time to get ready for school.

All was going swimmingly until, one morning, I started to feel unwell. My head ached and I had a slight fever. Mammy dosed me up and sent me to bed at the weekend but was forced to call the doctor when I had obviously got worse by Monday morning. My throat was very swollen and sore and my head was throbbing so much that it was impossible to even look at a book. Dr Orr diagnosed tonsillitis with a high fever and prescribed antibiotics and a fortnight in bed. It was a catastrophe - my first exam was in ten days' time! Despite Mammy's expert nursing, I was still feeling very ill and running a high temperature the day before my exam. My Headmistress said I could be brought to school by car, wrapped in a blanket, to sit the exam, but Dr Orr said that I was in no way fit enough to leave my bed. I had to resign myself to missing my Latin exam and concentrating on getting better in time to take my French and History exams later, but I needed all three A-levels to get into university.

On the day of the exam, I was lying despondently in bed when my friend and neighbour, Elfed Lewis, came over to console me. Suddenly there was a second knock on the door and my needlework mistress, Miss Griffiths, appeared unexpectedly. My Uncle Ivor had told the story to the Matron of Porth Cottage Hospital where he worked as an engineer.

"Pat is a very good, hardworking pupil and she is ill in bed and will not be able to sit her A Level exams. All the family are very upset about it and worried that it will spoil her chances to go to university."

"That's ridiculous," said the Matron. "When pupils are ill in hospital, an invigilator is sent to enable them to sit the exam in bed. They can do the same thing for your niece at home. I'll ring the Director of Education immediately and see what can be done."

She was as good as her word and soon the Director had telephoned Miss Hudd, my Headmistress, who, unknown to us, had dispatched Miss Griffiths with a copy of the Latin paper without delay. Elfed soon made himself scarce and no time was lost in starting the exam. Miss Griffiths settled herself comfortably on a chair by the window with a hot cup of tea and a Welsh cake provided by my delighted and very relieved mother. Without more ado, I sat up in bed and began my Latin translation paper. Luckily very little revision was necessary for this paper and I loved getting to grips with translation. As I had had no time to prepare myself before starting to write, I soon began to feel rather uncomfortable. Eventually, I was forced to say,

"Excuse me, Miss Griffiths. I'm afraid I need to go to the toilet."

This posed a problem, as I was not allowed to leave the room. This was overcome when my ever practical mother fetched a chamber pot for me to use while Miss Griffiths waited outside the door, having first checked that there were no Latin books in the bedroom.

Fortunately, the rest of the exams passed off normally in school and when the results came out we were all delighted that, thanks to the Matron, I had achieved the three A Levels required to go to university. The only blot on the landscape was the fact that my best friend Gwen did not pass enough of her exams to enable her to go off to university that year, but had to return to school to re-sit the following year. Thankfully, she was successful then and went off to study Geography at Aberystwyth University as planned, just one year later.

Mammy's dreams of education opening up the world to her children were to be fulfilled at last. I was set to take my place at university, having won a full scholarship from Mid-Glamorgan County Council as well as the Evan Williams Memorial Prize from school. Not only was I the first person in both my parents' families to go to university, but I was also the first girl from William Street to win a scholarship. I was quite undecided which of my three subjects to study at university. Each of my three subject teachers had encouraged me to choose their own specialism. During the year, I had applied to three London colleges, University College, King's College and Bedford

Ladies' College in Regent's Park to study History. I had even sat a scholarship entrance exam for Bedford College, the standard akin to that of the Oxbridge entrance, and had been successful. Miss Lloyd (History) and Miss Davies (Latin) had both studied at Bedford College, London.

I was called for interview at all three but I was not offered a place at any of them for the following October. Fortunately, one of our neighbours had relatives living in a flat in central London and I was offered a couple of nights' accommodation with them to enable me to attend my interviews. Gwilfa John, an ex-student of Porth Secondary Grammar, who was studying medicine there, met me and showed me around. I went first to the Bedford College interview. I had to take my birth certificate with me. This showed my father as a "labourer on the surface of the pit." I felt that my working class background went against me at that interview. Having rarely travelled by train, I had no idea that the Cardiff-London train was known as "The Red Dragon" and felt humiliated and was left tongue-tied when asked if I had come up on the Red Dragon. I was told that I had passed the written examination with a high grade. Nevertheless, they asked me to stay in school another year to "become more mature" before they would offer me a place at college. Financial circumstances made this impossible, of course.

As for University College and King's, although I felt I had done quite well at these interviews (indeed King's told me I had written the best application letter), I was also asked again to stay on another year in school. The reason for this was possibly that I had applied to all three colleges as first choice, having received little university application advice from school. When asked why I had particularly wanted to come to King's, I emphasised that, having been in an all girls' school, I would prefer to study at a mixed college. Imagine my consternation when I was asked why I had applied to Bedford Ladies' college as first choice also!

Nevertheless, all was not lost. I had decided to apply to Bristol University (also as first choice) to study French, realising that, if successful, I would be sent to the Sorbonne in Paris for most of my first year. This time, the interview went well and I was offered the option of reading for a joint French and Latin degree. However, the family asked a university graduate living in Gynor Avenue for her advice on the subject and so it was decided that I would follow the Special French course with Latin as a subsidiary.

Now preparations had to be made to fit me out to go to Bristol which would be costly. Through Uncle Ivor's influence, I obtained a holiday job as a nursing auxiliary in Porth Cottage Hospital for three months from July to September. I was put to work in a men's general ward. I nursed all sorts of illnesses from cancers to young miners who had been brought in after being trapped by a fall of coal in the pit. I really enjoyed working there and was nicknamed *"Smiler"* by my patients who teased me a lot and begged me to take out their stitches etc. It was easy to become too attached to the patients as I got to know them. One dear old gentleman suffering from throat cancer had to be fed regularly through a tube and when I had finished ministering to him one day, he said,

"Diolch yn fawr (thank you very much), young Smiler. You are so gentle and good to me. God bless you, cariad."

I was so touched by his expression of gratitude for something which was really no more than what I was being paid to do, that I could barely stop myself from breaking down in tears.

Young nurses were sometimes required to help in the operating theatre. Most of the trainees were dreading this and were hanging back. I saw my chance and volunteered and was allowed to assist for a whole morning. I was not allowed to do much but I was thrilled to be asked to hang on to a muscular rugby player's foot while the surgeon tugged a damaged cartilage from his knee. This experience fired my imagination and had I had three sciences amongst my A Levels, I would not have hesitated to change my plans and opt for a medical degree with a view to becoming a surgeon. I was still excited about the prospect of studying languages at Bristol though and saved up the money that I earned to provide pocket money to see me through until my grant arrived.

I set to making myself a wardrobe of new clothes from material bought from a local factory or from unpicking hand-me-downs from relatives to make more fashionable models. My parents bought me a beautiful new red and grey woollen coat from Aunty Rosie's shop while a new trunk was purchased from money given as congratulatory presents. Daddy's pianist friend, Griff, gave me a smart leather brief case in which to carry my books. This was so strong and sturdy that it lasted me all through my professional life later on, though it did look a little the worse for wear by the time I retired! I was now ready to take my first steps into the wide world far from my dear familiar valleys.

# PART 3

## Expanded Horizons

# Chapter 8
# Reaching the goal: Bristol University

I set off by train with two local lads, one a second year and the other a third year student at Bristol. We three were the only students from the Rhondda going to Bristol that year. It seemed that it was not easy for Welsh students to gain a place at Bristol in those days. I had obtained digs in advance by writing to the University accommodation officer. When I arrived at the address at Cotham Vale, I was met at the door by the landlady, Mrs. Wise. It appeared that Marion, an English student from the North who had arrived earlier, had opted to take the second best room rather than share with a French girl. I, of course, jumped at the chance to share with a French girl. You can imagine my delight when allocated the nicer room and a French room-mate, Hélène Klauber from Paris, to share it with! We got on like a house on fire and Hélène was to prove a real friend when it was time for me to leave for Paris. Gillian was the last student to arrive, so she shared with Marion.

Everything was so new and exciting for us four young first year students, Hélène, Marion, Gillian and myself. Throughout Freshers' Fortnight in early October, we visited all the stalls and signed up to join most of the societies. How on earth were we going to find time for study? And then there were dances and parties almost every night. When we arrived, there was only one key available for the digs, so we had to share it until others had been cut. After considering for a little while, Mrs. Wise gave the key into my custody and told the other three girls to come home with me. The dance was a great success and we four girls returned together to our digs accompanied by my new cavalier, whom I had met at the dance. From then on, we were known as the "Wise girls" (the capital letter significantly showing it related to the name rather than the attribute!)

The week progressed in a swirl of gaiety. I met many interesting students of both sexes and made friends quickly. Ration books were still being used at that time, so the "Wise girls" went to get them stamped like everyone else (although we were told when we got there they were no longer necessary). On the way, we bumped into a young man known to Marion. With him was a tall, dark and handsome young chap carrying a sports bag. He was introduced as Archie Luther and was on his way to play hockey for the University. To my friends and me, he was exotic and exciting, and, as we continued chatting on our way, we decided he was a real heartthrob. At tea-time that same day, we were talking together in the university refectory when Archie came in after his match. He joined us girls and started making conversation, paying particular attention to me, which thrilled me to bits.

We learned that Archie was a medical student on the second MB course, so I immediately started to recount my recent nursing experiences.

I explained that I had enjoyed my work experience so much so that I would have loved to switch from French to studying to become a surgeon. I went on to say that, despite being allowed to help during operations in a small way, it was only when blood was being taken that I had felt at all queasy. Very seriously, Archie enquired exactly how the blood had been taken. His big brown eyes twinkled merrily as he interjected such comments as "Really?" and "Is that so?" as I recounted how it was done. I eventually realised that he had been teasing me ever so gently as he mimicked my lilting Welsh accent at the same time. We soon ended up laughing together and a new and exciting relationship had begun for the girl who, until a few short days before, had never met anyone from outside the Rhondda, apart from the very brief encounter with the Yugoslav singers of course. Except for my short stay in Paris at the age of fifteen, I had virtually no experience of cosmopolitan cities even though Cardiff, capital city of Wales, was situated so close to my home.

Although Archie seemed to come from an entirely different, far off world, his accent was surprisingly English with very little trace of a typical Pakistani lilt. He was five years older and appeared to be a man of the world to my inexperienced eyes. He came from the north of Baluchistan, next to the North West Frontier Province of India, later to become Pakistan after independence, near the Afghan border. His family were Anglican Church Mission doctors, practising General and Eye Surgery in the Christian Mission Hospital in Quetta. He had already studied in Lahore University and had gained a science degree there. When he had enrolled in Bristol University, his father had arranged digs for him with a Miss Mattick, a Christian spinster in her forties attached to the Church Missionary Society. Archie was made most comfortable by Miss Mattick who soon fell under the spell of this well-connected and charming young man. There was one drawback in living with Miss Mattick. Although she spoiled Archie dreadfully, lavishing care and affection on him, she also tried to supervise his studies and encouraged him to bring his friends back so that she could vet them. She took him to church and to religious meetings to show off her young lodger to her friends and reported regularly to his father, Dr. Samuel Luther, in Quetta.

Archie felt smothered and soon found his position in her home quite untenable. He was a lively, fun-loving young man who wished to participate fully in the social and sporting opportunities available to him in Bristol University. As tactfully as possible, he informed his landlady that he wished to leave her home to share a flat with a friend. Try as she could, Miss Mattick could not dissuade him, so she eventually capitulated, though she continued to encourage him to treat her home as his and to bring his friends there for Sunday tea.

111

When Archie and I met, this same situation prevailed, and I was soon taken for tea with Miss Mattick. Although the male friends had always been well received and encouraged, I had a distinctly cool reception. Much later, we learned that Miss Mattick had written to Dr.Luther to say that his son was associating with a "nurse" who was taking up all his time and preventing him from getting on with his studies. Gradually, Archie escaped from the clutches of this rather possessive woman and went on to lead his own life.

Thus it was that, towards the end of the Freshers' Fortnight, we were meeting up frequently. Archie offered to show me round Bristol and to take me to the zoo. Since in Pakistan, he was used to well-brought-up young ladies being chaperoned when associating with a young man, Archie always included my friend Dorothy in his invitations. I wondered at first in which one of us he was interested. It soon became clear, however.

I had accepted an offer from a fellow first year student, whom I had met at an earlier social event, to escort me to the *End of Freshers' Fortnight Dance.* Archie had promised to take his landlady's two daughters to the dance also. However, on the night, my escort-to-be had had to cancel and his friend rang to offer to escort me in his place. The unfortunate boy had been injured that day in a rugby match. Thus it was that I had no compunction on leaving the substitute escort when Archie *pardoned* my partner[#] at the beginning of the evening. After that we didn't see much of his landlady's daughters either. The romance was off to a very promising start.

By the time my nineteenth birthday arrived on 22nd October, I had a large number of new acquaintances to invite to a celebration. Archie volunteered his flat for the venue, so invitations went out and food and drink was organised, my digs-mates and Archie all offering to help. That day, I received a large bunch of red roses from Gareth, the boy-friend I had been seeing for a while in Wales before coming up to University. I had already tried to break it off before leaving, as I wanted to be free to enter into my new life without any ties. The taxi was at the door as I explained this once more to Gareth over the telephone, and so, finally, he accepted it and I ran off into the arms of the man with whom I would later decide to make my life. That party saw our first kiss and the true beginning of our romance. I had found my "Prince Charming."

---

# In those days, when a man "pardoned" another man dancing with a lady, he was asking to replace him as the lady's dance partner for that dance.

# Chapter 9
# Archie's Story

Archie was the fourth child of Dr. Samuel Martin Luther and Edith Zenith Dean. He was born on 8th December 1929 in the Mission Hospital, Quetta, where his father was an eye specialist who also undertook general surgery. His father Samuel was born in Fort Sandeman, near Quetta, a fourth generation Christian living in the predominantly Muslim province of Baluchistan in West Pakistan. His ancestors, however, came from Amritsar, India, best known for its famous Sikh Golden Temple. Thus the family were originally staunch Hindus.

Samuel's great-grandfather was converted to Christianity by Lutheran missionaries as the province was under the influence of the Lutheran mission at that time. After his conversion, he could no longer, in Hindu tradition, be accepted by his family. He took the family name of Luther out of respect for the great Protestant leader Martin Luther. Samuel was a doctor who, working with other missionary doctors, cared for the poor and the sick of his native land as his father and grandfather before him had done, so it was not surprising that he, too, had entered the medical profession. Samuel's father, Dr Martin Luther, had eventually come to Baluchistan to work in Quetta Mission Hospital run by the Anglican Church Missionary Society. From 1918 it was there that Samuel, following his father, spent his whole working life.

The Luther family had become devout Christians and Samuel became a renowned eye surgeon, having helped to set up eye camps (mobile clinics) over a wide area to treat the poor who so often suffered from dreadful eye diseases.

He would operate for hours on end to remove cataracts, restoring sight to those who had been virtually blind for years. Samuel worked with his colleague Sir Henry Holland, and, later, his son, Ronnie Holland, for many years in Quetta Mission Hospital, or the Christian Hospital, as it is known today. Sir Henry Holland wrote about the loyalty and co-operation of his "Indian colleague, Dr Samuel Luther, both at the hospital and as a respected leader of the local church. He followed the footsteps of his father. He was a born operator and was never happier than in the operating room. Like his father he had a wonderful way with him and very soon became the most popular general practitioner in the city. We look forward in the future to more men of Samuel Luther's stamp."

British missionaries naturally helped Christian families to find suitable spouses for their children, not an easy task in a predominantly Muslim country. A marriage was arranged between Samuel and Edith Zenith Dean, also a fourth generation Christian. Her family were originally from Kashmir and, as with the Luthers, her great-grandfather became estranged from his Hindu family on his conversion to Christianity. She also came from a medical background. Her father was a well-to-do doctor in a hospital near Lahore and owned large tracts of land in the area. Zenith had a rather unhappy childhood. At the age of thirteen, she had lost her mother, Edith. As was the custom, her father then married his late wife's sister to help him bring up his four children. In the manner of the archetypal wicked stepmother, his new wife more or less drove Zenith and her younger sister Dorothy out of the family home. They were sent to boarding school and spent most of their holidays with the missionaries. When they occasionally visited their father and brothers, they received no welcome from their stepmother and were treated very badly. They were never taken around in the family car and were always made to walk to church on Sunday, where they stayed on for Sunday-School. Afterwards, when they went to visit their very good friends in the neighbourhood, they always had to go on foot, however far away they lived or hot the weather was.

By the time Zenith married Samuel, she had become a pharmacist and her younger sister a nurse. So Archie came from a family steeped in medicine on both sides. Like Samuel, Zenith was a devout Christian. The couple attended church regularly and participated fully in religious meetings and church affairs. She was a good mother and was of a cheerful and kind disposition. Both she and Samuel were possessed of good voices, and sang enthusiastically at church services. She also sang as she went about her domestic duties and always had fascinating stories to tell the children. She spread the Good News of Christianity wherever she went by her example. She would also teach the little children of the guards and house servants the Lord's Prayer and was generous in her gifts to them.

At Christmas, she regularly bought full bails of cloth to distribute to family, friends and servants alike to make up new clothes. The family employed quite a number of servants to see to their needs. The Hindu cook would arrive very early in the morning to take tea in bed to the adults. He would then stay to prepare breakfast and lunch before going home for a few hours, returning at 4pm to make tea and cook dinner for the family. Being a vegetarian, he refused to cook meat, so it was Zenith who prepared the delicious meat curries for the family.

Zenith and Samuel had four children, the eldest of whom, Evelyn Zenith (known as Eva) was born in 1924. The following year Ruth Lily was born, then Henry Martin the year after and, finally, in 1929, the baby of the family, Archibald Jonathan (always known as Archie.) Mother Zenith saw to it that her four children were always well fed and cared for. Eva remembered with distaste that they all had to eat nourishing porridge every morning without fail. The couple employed an *ayah* (nanny), a converted Christian called Nikki, to help care for the children. On 31 May 1935, a huge earthquake of magnitude 7.7 on the Richter scale, struck the area where they lived. The Quetta earthquake ranks as one of the deadliest to hit S. E. Asia. The city of Quetta suffered the greatest number of casualties and the infrastructure was severely damaged with the greater part of the city razed to the ground. Between 30,000 and 60,000 people in the region died from the impact. In Quetta itself, it was initially estimated that 20,000 people were buried under the rubble, of which approximately 10,000 survived and 4,000 were injured.

The Luther family were also badly affected by the disaster. Little Ruth Lily was killed and Eva badly hurt, while the rest of the family escaped serious injury. Young Archie was only five years old at the time but carried a vivid memory of that traumatic episode well into later life. Miraculously, very few of the Mission Hospital staff were seriously wounded so the remaining doctors, sisters and voluntary workers strove valiantly to relieve the terrible suffering of the numberless casualties. During the four days before the injured were evacuated, Samuel and the other surgeons were working night and day and gave heroic service. However, it was a long time before the city was rebuilt, the hospital fully restored and life began to return to normal.

A second tragedy struck the family only five years later. Zenith died at the early age of forty whilst undergoing an appendectomy operation. Since the children were left motherless, it was expected that Samuel would marry his wife's younger sister Dorothy. However, remembering the harrowing tales his wife had told him of her unhappy childhood under the control of an unfeeling stepmother, he refused to remarry. He employed Nikki full-time to care for his young family. She lived just outside the high perimeter wall of their house, but quite within earshot, so that she was able to attend immediately she was called. She had to bring up her own large family in just two rooms in very cramped and impoverished conditions. Even though the Luther family was always kind to her, she led a hard but uncomplaining life. Dr. Luther paid for her children to be educated as they grew.

Being a small boy of ten years old when his mother died, Archie was taken under Nikki's wing and a real bond of affection developed between them. Archie became the family prankster, but was always protected by Nikki whenever he was found out in any of his escapades. He would tease his siblings and, later, his little nieces, unmercifully, and get up to lots of naughty pranks, bringing the wrath of his strict father on his head. He had even dared to tickle the soles of his parents' feet as they prayed barefoot! He started smoking quite young and accidently burnt a hole in his quilt while secretly smoking in his bedroom. He went straight to Nicky, who always made excuses for him and covered up his misdemeanours. On this occasion, she managed to obtain another quilt so that his father would not find out what his son had done.

Dr. Luther had arranged a marriage for Archie's eldest sister Eva to Cyril Nathaniel, the son of the Rev Makham Nathaniel, a vicar in Quetta. He was very pleased to have found his daughter a good match with a Christian boy from a very respectable family. However, Cyril turned out to be the "black sheep" of the family, leaving Eva alone for months on end to bring up her four children on her own. Finally, he left her and she was forced to seek work to provide for her children. She went to train as a Sister Tutor in Karachi Hospital. Eva lived for many years as a single mother. She found it very difficult to cope with four small children whilst training in order to provide them all with a good education. The eldest was called Cynthia Zenith (known as Honey), next came the twin girls Romila Ruth (known as Baby) and Promila Amelia (known as Bunny) and finally the only son, Reginald (known as Reggie.) It appears that Archie Uncle (as they called him) had actually given the girls their nicknames and they had stuck.

Eva wished for a divorce so that once finally free of her unhappy marriage, she would be able to marry businessman Moses Daniel Kodot whom she had met in Karachi. But divorce was out of the question for Eva. Her religious father would not hear of it, as divorce was said to besmirch the family name in the Christian community. However, after many years, Dr. Luther finally relented, realising how very unhappy and lonely his daughter was, as she struggled to bring up her children on her own. Eva then re-married and found happiness and stability with Moses Kodot in later life.

Archie loved his little nieces and their baby brother, Reggie, but could not stop himself from teasing them. On one occasion he encouraged his tiny nieces in a little harmless mischief.

*"Why don't we see which one of you can collect the most shoes belonging to the family from wherever you can find them in the house?"* he suggested one day.

*"Yes, yes, yes"* they chorused together.

*"I know where Grandpa's shoes are kept,"* said Honey.

*"Me, too,"* joined in Baby, following her big sister.

*"Where can I go?"* wailed Bunny.

*"Come with me – I'll help you find Uncle Heno's shoes!"* said Archie.

All three girls scurried away to hunt everywhere and each soon returned with her booty.

*"Look what I've got"* sang Bunny with pride as she struggled with a large pair of boots, one man's left slipper and a pair of ladies' slippers belonging to Indu, Henry's wife. With a sigh of relief, she dropped them in a pile at Archie's feet before leaving to hunt for more. She was followed by Honey

116

carrying a large selection of her grandfather's footwear, both in-door and out-door. Baby trailed after her with more of the same.

*"It's not fair – Honey took most of the shoes before I got there,"* she complained.

*"Never mind,"* replied Archie, *"no-one has been to my room yet!"* In a trice, they had all disappeared in that direction, soon returning with a miscellaneous collection of sports shoes, smart modern pairs, slippers, and old walking boots.

*"Have I won?"* demanded Honey.

*"Yes,"* replied Archie, swiftly adding *"so have you, Baby, and you, too, Bunny, so there are prizes for all of you."* He then distributed the little toys he had brought home for them from Lahore.

*"Thank you, thank you, Uncle,"* chorused the delighted girls.

*"What are you going to do with all these shoes now?"* asked Baby.

*"Let's arrange them all in tidy rows all along the wall of the living room,"* suggested Archie.

*"Yes, let's,"* they agreed, and started arranging the shoes in serried ranks, military fashion, although with a more than relaxed attitude to matching pairs and to keeping all shoes of an individual together. They all seemed content with the result and continued to play happily with their new toys. The girls always had fun with their uncle and looked up to him with adoring eyes and wide smiles of pride as he congratulated them on their efforts.

Others, however, were none too pleased to see their footwear missing from its correct place. In particular, their grandfather was most displeased and both Archie and the tiny tots received a good dressing down from Dr. Samuel Luther on his return from the hospital. The escapade ended in tears for the little girls, but Archie soon consoled them with hugs and little treats.

Archie grew to become a charming young man despite, as the baby of the family, being spoilt by all and sundry. He never lacked for anything and got through his schooling with ease. He went on to study at the University of Lahore where he obtained a science degree without too much difficulty. Here he led a carefree, happy life with his friends. Although he was provided with sufficient pocket money, he spent it lavishly and often found himself short of funds. However, this never worried him as he had doting aunts and an elder sister to bail him out. His brother, Henry, was much more sober and was very conscious of his elevated position in society. When Archie needed more money from his brother, he would smoke the foul-smelling "biri" cigarettes (only used by the less privileged members of society) in front of him. Henry could not bear to see his brother letting the family down, so he would come up with the desired sub. Archie was very popular amongst his peer group and had many friends of both sexes. He was a handsome young man and very attractive to the girls. He captivated the heart of a beautiful young girl called Usha who gave him a photo of herself with the inscription "from Usha with endless love." Archie took it with him when he left for Bristol, but they were fated never to meet again. Years later, Henry told me that he had attended Usha's wedding in Pakistan and even then she had asked after Archie once again.

Archie's elder brother, Henry, had been sent to study at the Christian Medical College, Vellore, where he met his future wife, Indira. They both qualified as doctors and married in 1957 after which they went to practise medicine in Quetta where they took over the running of the Mission Hospital. Dr. Samuel Luther retired from the hospital soon afterwards and set up a small private practice. However, Archie had always wanted to travel and see the world and was deemed clever enough to be sent abroad to study at Bristol University.

He set sail for England in 1951. He had a wonderful time on the long voyage and made many friends including an attractive American girl who also gave him her photo. She was very glamorous and, in the signed photograph she had given him, could have been taken for a film star with her sultry good looks. His father had paid his course fees and gave him a generous allocation of pocket money. To ensure that his youngest son would be well looked after in a foreign country, Dr Luther had arranged digs for him with Miss Mattick, a Christian lady with whom he was acquainted through church missionary circles. He hoped that she would keep his lively and adventurous son in check while he was so far from home. This arrangement worked very well at first while Archie settled into life in Bristol.

Archie, however, having decided that he wanted to avail himself of the freedom enjoyed by other students of his age, had left to share a flat with a friend. He flung himself into the life of Bristol University with great enthusiasm. He loved sport and joined the Rowing, Hockey and Badminton Clubs. Together with his full social life, this did not leave much time for study. He sailed through life, happy and carefree. Following the family tradition, Archie had been encouraged to take up the study of medicine. The first two years passed off well but it was during his third year that he began to consider reverting to his first love, science, for a future career.

# Chapter 10
# A New Life, New Friends, Unaccustomed Ease

Meanwhile, I entered enthusiastically into all aspects of university life in Bristol. During my first week though, I had a rather unpleasant surprise. Not satisfied with having A-Level results and school reports, the "Special French" Department of the university set its own tests as soon as the students arrived without any prior warning. This resulted in several students being relegated to following a General Honours Degree course. My work was of the required standard except for the dictation. When my mediocre mark in dictation was pointed out, I politely explained that I had found it difficult to understand the lecturer's French accent. Mr. Warne, however, assured me that his strong Bristolian accent did not detract from the pronunciation of the language. He was confident that his accent (with all its diphthongised vowels) was nevertheless a very acceptable French accent. I soon became accustomed to it, different as it was from Miss Llewellyn's clear, lilting Welsh accent. To my relief, my name was safely on the list of those accepted to join the "Special French Honours" class when the results came out. The standard of my school Latin appeared to be particularly high, so I spent approximately half my Latin lecture hours drinking coffee with Archie and other friends in the refectory. It was not surprising, therefore, that my Latin lecturer was amazed when I claimed the paper with the top marks at the end of the first term.

Archie played badminton for the University, so I joined the Badminton Club too. I also joined other clubs and societies such as the History and Literary Societies together with my new friends. I began to sit with Dorothy Knowles at French lectures and made special friends of Eileen Spencer and Vendla Sorrell, particularly on the social side. I sat with Eileen when I attended Latin lectures and enjoyed a full social life with both her and Vendla in the evenings and at weekends. We three never missed a dance at the Students' Union however much work we had on at the time. Vendla was in the same Special French Department as me and conversations at the dances often went like this:

"Have you given in your essay yet, Pat? It has to be in by tomorrow morning, doesn't it?"

"No! Not yet. Have you? I've written part of it but I'll finish it off when I get home tonight."

Vendla was usually in the same boat as me, but neither of our essays was ever missing by the time they were to be handed in to the lecturer the next day. I might have had to stay up working until three o'clock in the morning, but the work was always finished and acceptable in standard.

Gradually, I gathered a reputation for organising parties for the Special French Department group of around fifty students in Archie's flat. He was always happy to give us the use of it and soon became an honorary member of the French Department. We girls would provide the food and the boys the drink. We vied with one another to make the tastiest savouries and the most scrumptious desserts. My corn beef pasties (using Mammy's recipe, of course) and sherry trifles always seemed to go down well with everyone. The French students were sometimes called upon to help serve at wine tastings, which gave them the opportunity to get to know French wines – and for some to get – regularly - a bit too merry!

Soon after the start of the Spring Semester, arrangements were being made for students studying French to leave for France in February. All students were told to apply to their respective Local Education Authorities (LEAs) for a supplementary grant to cover the extra expenses involved in travel and living costs in a foreign country. Mine, Mid Glamorgan, was not renowned for its generosity to students, but once again, I was lucky. I was the first student to be awarded a grant for foreign study by Mid Glamorgan LEA. However with my full grant and two extra bursaries I had never been so well off. I found that I could now afford to buy good presents for the family. I was also able to send money home to my sister Morfydd in Barry to provide her with ten shillings per week pocket money and her fare to and from Barry Teachers' Training College. Morfydd had left home to do her teachers' training the year after I had left for Bristol. She received a small book grant, her fees and full board and lodging in the college residence but no pocket money at all.

Since I had come top in needlework early on in the grammar school, I had soon been expected to make clothes for the whole family when I had time. This had first come about during the holidays after finishing my O Level exams. Our needlework mistress, Miss Griffiths, was a real Miss Jean Brodie type. She was most fastidious and we "gels" spent half our time unpicking work that was not up to standard and sewing it all over again. We learned how to use a sewing machine, to embroider using cross stitch and satin stitch and how to prepare a pattern using squared paper and body measurements. We made an embroidered needle case, (still in use today) a work pinafore and, the pinnacle of our achievements, a pair of voluminous gingham bloomers to wear under our summer uniform – a green and white gingham dress.

Mammy was an expert knitter so we never lacked for warm colourful woollens but she had no idea what to do with a piece of material. She decided however that after my success in the needlework class, I was now not only

120

an experienced but also an expert seamstress. She confidently invested in two remnants of different patterned red tartan taffeta which a neighbour, Mr. Jarman, had procured for her from a local factory at bargain prices. This she presented to me proudly saying,

"Here you are, Pat. You can make yourself and Morfydd a dance dress each for Christmas." As far as Mammy was concerned, if you had a good education as well as "a good head on your shoulders," you could do anything. That is how she brought us up.

At first I was aghast. What did making dance dresses alone at home have in common with making bloomers in school under instructions at every turn from my sewing mistress? Well, there was nothing to be done but to give it a try, after all the material was very pretty and we were allowed to go to dances at Saint John's church hall, Porth – and Christmas was on the horizon too! I started by perusing the Simplicity pattern catalogue from start to finish of the section for dance dresses. Morfydd was delighted with the one we chose for her, so I started work on it straight away, having checked her body measurements over and over again with those on the pattern. As we were both quite petite, it was necessary to pin up the pattern above the waist and in the skirt section before cutting out. Then, of course, there was the problem of matching up the plaid pattern on the seams. It took me a long time before I had enough courage to put my scissors into the material, but all the preparation paid dividends and the dress was a great success.

Heartened, I tackled mine and before long we had two pretty red dance dresses of different plaid patterns and different styles ready for the start of the festive season. Mammy had also bought some white linen for me to make tennis shorts for myself. The material frayed as I sewed it and was not the easiest material for a beginner to start on. Nevertheless it turned out all right in the end. From then onwards, I never looked back. Having been *"encouraged"* by Mammy into taking up dress-making, I now became the family *couturier*!

I remember going on a school trip to Swansea whilst in the sixth form. I was making spotted cotton party dresses for Ann and Mary who looked like twins. I took along the frilled tops to hand-sew on the bus. Miss Griffiths, who was supervising us that day, was delighted to see that I was using the skills she had taught me in this practical way. When curtains needed to be sewn at home too, it was Pat who sat at the old treddle machine to make them.

With five children in full-time education, it was particularly hard for our parents to manage on the small wages of my father. Daddy would very often do a double shift by working from 6am until 2pm, then returning until 10pm after walking home for a brief respite to have his main hot meal of the day at home. Although Daddy was only about five feet four inches tall, he was very fit and strong and often managed to work *"nine turns a week"* instead of the five or six normally worked by miners. That was, of course, on top of working on his allotment and serving at his brother's pub in any spare time left. Despite all his efforts however, Mammy was often reduced to tears on pay day as she still struggled to make ends meet to feed and clothe her family.

Fortunately for me, from the day I received my first grant in university, my money troubles were over. Indeed, I was then able to help out financially at home during the holidays. I also sometimes bought the materials from which I made the clothes for us all. That first year, Mammy had ordered two new costumes for Easter for Ann and Mary from Aunty Rosie's shop but when they arrived, they looked shop-soiled. Mammy was in tears when she opened the parcel as I watched on during the Christmas holidays. Luckily I had just received the extra grant to go to France in February, so straight away I took her down to the Porth Co-op. There we chose two pretty new outfits, one of which I was able to buy outright from what I could spare from my grant, while the other was put on the book to be paid for weekly by Mammy. The situation was resolved and the two little girls looked beautiful in their smart new blue costumes at church that Easter.

Every holiday after leaving school, of course, we girls had holiday jobs. I worked in a sewing factory at the top of the street, filling in by hand the *petit point* stitches missed by the machine. Morfydd and I both worked at Sherman's Football Pools in Cardiff from time to time. There we worked in a cacophony of noise as the sound of the stamps being slammed hard down vied with the shrill voices of some of the more vulgar girls who yelled and swore to each other over the din to make themselves heard. We were amazed at the large sums of money that flowed regularly from the punters in bets each week. The fact that their winnings often amounted to less than a quarter of their outlay certainly encouraged us to give betting a wide birth in later life.

Morfydd had also often worked in cafés and restaurants in various Butlin's Holiday Camps. She suggested that I join her in Filey in Yorkshire whilst awaiting my degree results. However, I was not keen to clear tables and wash up, so Morfydd, who was already working there, asked if there was anything suitable for an 'almost graduate.' She must have given a glowing reference for her sister, for I was offered a job running a sweet shop at the camp, so I was happy to join Morfydd after all. I must have shown some efficiency, as I was able to obtain overtime selling cigarettes, crisps, sweets etc from a small kiosk inside the dance hall whilst other student workers had to scurry about serving drinks and clearing tables on their feet all evening. Almost every time I passed the big, blue round tin of Cadbury's Roses chocolates, I couldn't resist dipping my hand in to find my favourite soft caramels with a nut in the centre – delicious! My luck was in yet again!

While I was at Butlin's, a beauty competition was organised between all the different departments at the camp. There seemed to be no-one suitable to represent the "Shops and Bars Department." I was young, reasonably slim and adorned with a magnificent head of fair, curly hair – a woman's crowning glory, as it was termed in those days. Unfortunately, I was not tall and willowy or platinum blonde with an ample bust. In fact, I only ever managed to achieve a height measurement of five feet two inches once and that was by stretching upwards as much as possible and the fact that the measurer landed gently on my springy hair which gave me a generous result.

However, no other candidate presented herself. Finally, I was persuaded to enter the competition but had no hope of winning, as I certainly didn't have the curvy hour glass figure that was so admired by the judges. At least I had had a go to represent Shops and Bars. The same thing occurred when I attended a school reunion dance later that summer on returning home to Ynyshir. The dance was held in Porth Rink and the main judge was a VIP star of the cinema, Julie Andrews, who was at the height of her fame after her success in "The Sound of Music." Area competitions had already taken place throughout the Rhondda during the preceding weeks. The finals were to take place that evening. None of us had entered the competition and were looking forward to discussing which of the finalists we thought should win. When I was dancing with my partner someone tapped me on the shoulder:

"You have been selected to take part in the Finals this evening," said one of the officials as he handed me a card with a number on it.

I was astounded, as were my friends. So yet again I paraded around the floor only to see a tall, glamorous, busty blonde walk off with the prize once more. My days as a failed beauty contestant were well and truly over!

February 1954 saw the start of a great adventure. It was time to prepare to leave Bristol and set sail for France where we were to stay until the beginning of October without returning to Britain. The university employed a Madame Salmon to arrange accommodation for all the Bristol students due to study at the Sorbonne. They were paired up and allocated to homes quite a distance away from the centre of Paris, necessitating a long commute by train and metro. The digs were not cheap, either, and together with the fares, gobbled up a large slice of the living expenses. I, however, had my French room-mate Hélène Klauber to help me. During the Christmas holidays, she had contacted the *Surveillante Générale* of the *Foyer des Lycéennes* at *10, rue du Docteur Blanche*, Paris 16e. This was a residence for seventeen to twenty year-old young women pupils at some of the most prestigious *lycées* in Paris. It was absolutely new and heavily subsidised by the French Education Ministry. Clever Hélène had secured me a place there in one of the best areas of central Paris, near the Bois de Boulogne. However, when I spoke to my tutor about this, he was very dubious and suggested I share with Dorothy, as already

123

arranged by Madame Salmon. I was not willing to let this golden opportunity slip away, so I used all my powers of persuasion and my tutor finally accepted the alternative arrangement. He told me later that he thought I would be living in a "hole in the ground," given the location and the money I would be paying.

Arrangements for my accommodation made, it was time to set sail for La Belle France. However, the sea voyage was anything but beautiful! In early February, the weather was at its very worst and we had to endure a dreadful storm throughout the crossing. The thunder crashed and the lightning flashed and the ship rolled precariously as the huge white-crested waves tossed it around like a little cork. We all wondered whether we would ever reach land to begin the eagerly-anticipated new life for which we all had such high hopes. Almost every one of the British students suffered terribly from sea sickness and the sick bags were in high demand. People were vomiting all over the place and the stench inside was awful. Vendla and I were the only two who escaped the dreadful sea sickness and stayed just outside on the deck to watch the rolling waves and the play of the rain and the vivid lightning flashes over the sea. We were forbidden to walk on the deck, of course, but really enjoyed watching the changing faces of the storm playing out all around us. The ship finally made it safely into harbour and all the students disembarked hastily in the port of *Le Havre* feeling a great sense of relief.

We boarded the train for Paris and arrived at the *Gare Saint Lazare*. It had been arranged that Hélène's mother would meet me outside the station to take me by taxi to the hostel where I would be staying. When the Bristol students got down from the train, there was a large reception party waiting to greet us. Madame Salmon was in charge, holding a long list of our names, matched with those of the landladies who were to receive us. She called out the names in twos and ushered each pair into the custody of the families who had come to meet us. She then came to my name. In an angry torrent of French, she made it quite clear that I was a distinct pariah. She scolded me for not going with Dorothy to a lady who had always received two students and was not happy with the reduced money she would receive from one. She then told me that she took no responsibility whatsoever for me and that I must make my own way to where I was to live.

With my heart beating fast and tail firmly between my legs, I gathered my luggage and made my way towards the exit. What if Hélène's mother had not arrived or was waiting at a different exit? What if we failed to recognise one another? All these dismal thoughts passed through my mind as I made my way out alone. Imagine my joy when I recognised Madame Klauber from the photo that Helene had given me as soon as I emerged from the station! We greeted one another warmly with the customary kiss on each cheek and lost no time in finding a taxi which took us swiftly through Paris

124

and deposited us safely at the *Foyer des Lycéennes* in the leafy arrondissement of Auteuil. Instead of my tutor's "hole in the ground," my accommodation turned out to be a sparkling new study bedroom with a private *cabinette de toilette* and a stupendous view from the seventh storey overlooking central Paris and with a distant view of the Eiffel Tower itself. There were large sunny terraces, lifts, common rooms and excellent food as well as hundreds of young French girls to get to know – and the price was really right! My luck had held.

The hostel was in an absolutely perfect location situated as it was in a most desirable area of Paris. It was close to the Bois de Boulogne where I often strolled with my friends. There, well-to-do Parisians could be seen trotting along the bridleways on their beautifully groomed horses. Many of the famous boulevards were in easy walking distance and I would often watch from our high terraces the elegant Parisian models being photographed against the unique Paris skyline and other famous backgrounds below us. It was within easy reach of the centre of the city too. It would take me no time at all to dash to the nearby metro station of Jasmin and jump on an underground train which would take me swiftly to my destination at the Sorbonne. I thoroughly enjoyed my stay in this chic area of Paris and soon many of my friends became rather envious of my superb and most convenient accommodation. However, before too long, I had managed to obtain places for the six most discontented students. Thereafter, Bristol University always reserved as many places as possible in *Le Foyer des Lycéennes* for its luckiest women students every year.

My life in the capital of France had got off to a very good start indeed. The male students that year were also lucky. As Le *Foyer des Lycéennes* was brand new, the French Minister of Education. André Marie himself, came to officiate at the opening ceremony. A great free celebration was thrown to commemorate the opening. It took the form of a dinner followed by a ball. Suddenly I became very popular, both at the hostel and with my male fellow students. The all-girl residents needed male escorts for the dance and the English students would do very nicely! I therefore tended an invitation to all the Bristol boys who eagerly accepted it. We all had a wonderful time, dancing until the early hours of the morning. There was also plenty of free wine provided which was much appreciated by the boys.

For the very first time in my life, however, I experienced the pangs of homesickness during my early weeks in Paris. Although my fellow French boarders were always pleasant and friendly during the occasions we were all thrown together, as at meal-times, after dinner they all disappeared into their rooms to chat, play games or study with their friends. At such times, I felt something of an outsider and would repair to my room alone to gaze longingly at photos of my family and, of course, of Archie. I would sit down to write

125

long letters, describing everything about my new life except my loneliness. Fortunately, this did not last long, as I soon made close friends with a young Italian and a young Breton girl, both of whom were suffering similar pangs of loneliness. Carla Modica, my Italian friend, wanted to go to England to visit her boyfriend who was studying there, but money was a problem. Having already received my grant, I was able to lend her the necessary money and was touched by Carla's insistence on leaving me a letter addressed to her parents asking them to reimburse me should anything untoward befall her on her journey so that she could not repay the loan herself.

My new friends were most helpful in guiding me through the morass of paperwork, still absolutely essential for anyone deciding to live in France! I had to pay a visit to the *Préfecture de Police* in Paris, taking recent passport photos to obtain my *carte de séjour* to enable me to live in France as a temporary resident and allowing me to follow my course at the Sorbonne. Furnished with my new official card, I was at last ready to sign on for the *"Cours de Civilisation Française"* at this prestigious university of Paris.

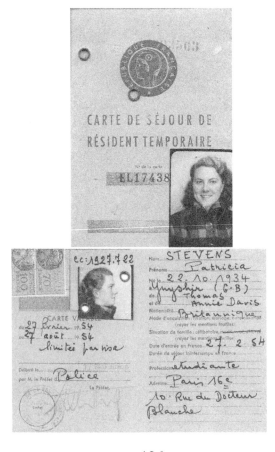

# Chapter 11
# Life at the Sorbonne

It was only a short journey by Metro to get to the Sorbonne each day, in contrast to the long journeys by train and metro undertaken by the majority of my fellow students. How well I remember that first day at the University! When we had all managed to find our way to the Lecture Theatre, we were amazed to find that it was a huge theatre with tiered seating rising in a large semi-circle towards the ceiling. We were part of a cosmopolitan group of students from all over the world who had joined the course entitled *Civilisation Française*. Instead of a nucleus group of approximately fifty in "Special 1" which at times rose to a maximum of one hundred and fifty when joined by second and third year groups studying similar texts at Bristol, we now found ourselves in a lecture theatre which held over four hundred students. Life would surely be more independent for us all. Hardly out of our tiny sixth form language classes, we had been catapulted via our British Universities, into an international arena where it felt like sink or swim for us all. The big fish lauding it in the goldfish bowl was now counted among the myriads of tiddlers trying to survive in the ocean! What an exciting - and rather scary- prospect.

As well as arranging the accommodation, Madame Salmon was tutor in charge of the Bristol students at the university. She organized us into tutorial groups for language study. The first thing we were required to do was to read a passage in our best French accents. This was taped and then played back to us individually. I was proud of my accent, as, being Welsh, my vowels were pure unlike those of my English compatriots, where one could often hear up to three distinct sounds in the pronunciation of one vowel – e.g. instead of a simple closed "o" sound, one might distinguish an amalgamation of "o," "ee" and "ou." My problem turned out to be different. My Welsh lilt accented words and phrases in a most un-French manner. In fact, my intonation was much more of a sing-song, up-and-down melody than the un-accented straight intonation of the native French speaker. We each started immediately to work on our own specific deficiencies and, by the end of the course, I was not only dreaming in French, but had mastered the intonation to such an extent that I was taken for French when visiting my Belgian pen-friend. Later, I was even given the accolade of possessing *le petit accent de Tours*, the French equivalent of the English Oxford accent, something to which I could never aspire when speaking English!

The grammar course was thorough and demanding. However, I really enjoyed this aspect of the work as I had always loved translation and French composition, and had been well trained in English grammar during my schooldays. My subsidiary subject was Latin and we were supposed to attend Latin lectures on set books and send back translations regularly for marking in Bristol. The translations were sent back, though not always on time. However, after attending one lecture on Livy, pronounced *Teet Leev* in French, I found the pronunciation of the Latin texts hilarious and the lectures boring. I decided, therefore, to forgo them, and only ever attended one more when some of the male students captured me and placed me under the nose of the lecturer so that I could not escape. I took great care thereafter to give them a wide berth whenever Latin lectures were imminent.

A large choice of subjects was available for those enrolling on the *Cours de Civilisation Française.* I chose to follow courses on Literature, History of Art, Geography and French Philosophy as well as the compulsory language courses. All these courses were given entirely in French in the huge lecture theatres and turned out to be very interesting indeed. Armed with my student's card, I was able to visit the famous Louvre Museum at least twice a week, thereby increasing the depth and breadth of my knowledge of some of the world's greatest art. The *Orangerie,* with its wide collection of impressionist paintings was another interesting visit. There were regular exhibitions of some of our favourite painters studied on our Art course. It was wonderful to be able to appreciate first-hand the original canvases, such as Monet's *Water Lilies,* as we studied them in our lectures instead of having to content ourselves with prints in books.

Paris is, of course, rightly famous for its majestic tree-lined boulevards, bridges over the Seine, elegant historic buildings, parks and squares. The contrast with Bristol was stark and even more so with my tiny mining village in the Rhondda. We all made the most of our stay, with typical visits to the Eiffel Tower, the *Palais de Chaillot,* the *Panthéon,* resting place of France's most famous citizens, and the glittering Paris Opera House. I was as much impressed with the spectacular building as with the dazzling performance of Gounod's Faust which had entranced me on my sole visit there. Of course, the wonderful cathedrals and churches, such as *Notre Dame* on the *Ile de la Cité,* the classic *La Madeleine* with its Roman columns and *Le Sacré Coeur* overlooking *Montmartre,* were high on the list. Apart from the famous church of *Le Sacré Coeur* with its stupendous views over the city, *Montmartre* is the place to go for a special night out in such celebrated (and very expensive) night clubs as *Les Follies Bergères* and *Le Moulin Rouge.*

We students spent hours also browsing among the *bouquinistes* along the *rive gauche* (left bank) of the Seine where we purchased most of our set texts second-hand. The nearby *Jardin du Luxembourg* was a favourite place for picnic lunches, especially in good weather. Gradually we became well acquainted with all the famous boulevards and landmarks of Paris – *la Place de la Concorde* with its swirling, noisy traffic, *la Rue de Rivoli* with its ridiculously expensive shops, the extensive natural parks and the renowned monuments, such as the *Arc de Triomphe* and *Le Petit Trianon*. We could find our way confidently all over the city and felt like real Parisians in no time. Like them though, we were happy to leave our beautiful city to the tourists who flooded in during the holiday seasons.

Many of the boys decided to go hitchhiking to areas around Paris at the weekends. We girls thought we were missing out, so, taking our courage in both hands and our duffel bags over our shoulders, we set out on another new adventure. We always went in twos and I well remember my first attempt at hitchhiking. Armed with maps, picnic, change of clothes, sleeping bag and a list of Youth hostel addresses, my friend Shirley and I started walking along the road in the direction of our desired destination. Cars swished past, but neither of us dared even to look towards them, let alone make any thumbing signs. We were getting nowhere, so I said,

"We'll have to indicate somehow that we'd like a lift."

It was decided that we would continue walking along the road, now thumbing for a lift, yet still with our backs to the cars. To our amazement, a car drew up alongside almost immediately and the driver offered us a lift. He was polite and pleasant and from that time onwards, getting about was easy. My friend, Vendla, often accompanied me and we visited Versailles, Malmaison, Chantilly, and Chartres, various *châteaux* of the Loire and many other sites of interest close to Paris. Drivers were often reluctant to pick up two burley boys at the roadside, so we girls generally had more hitchhiking luck than the boys, and did very well on the whole.

At Easter, I took the train to Brussels to visit my Belgian pen-friend, whom I had met at a dance in Wales during my sixth form days. He was doing his national service in the army at the time, but he had about a week's leave. He took me round all the sights and introduced me to many of his friends. His parents made me really welcome and I thoroughly enjoyed the break from my studies. They lived in the French speaking part of Brussels but there were certain differences from France apart from the accent. The food was good – especially the chocolates - but a bit stodgier with potatoes in different guises taking pride of place in the tasty dishes served up at meal times. A big, fluffy duvet was a pleasant surprise on my bed at night, as I was only used to blankets up until then. The most amusing and memorable statue of the little boy called *Manneken Piss* was pointed out to me as it is to all visitors to Brussels. The week's holiday was great fun and passed in a flash so I returned to my studies in Paris pleasantly refreshed, ready to get down to work.

We also had a few days off at Whitsun, so Shirley and I decided to try to visit other *châteaux* of the Loire we had not yet seen, then going on to Caen and even St.Malo if time permitted. This was rather ambitious as we only had a long weekend and St.Malo is right up north on the Brittany coast. Nevertheless, we set off, each carrying a youth hostel-type sheet sleeping bag, a mackintosh in case of rain and a woolly in our duffel bags. All went swimmingly at first. We toured a few of the historic *châteaux* nestling along the banks of the magnificent Loire and got to Caen, in Normandy, earlier than anticipated. We had intended to stay at the youth hostel there but, instead, had a quick look round the main points of interest and set off again towards St.Malo, quite a bit further West on the North coast of Brittany.

After one or two long lifts, we were standing at the roadside at dusk discussing whether we would make it to St.Malo that evening. At that very moment, a lorry went past carrying a large number of young men, obviously on their way home from work. There were lots of wolf whistles and shouted comments, and, although they seemed innocuous enough, we hurriedly declined their offer of a lift. What to do? We were approaching a village just as house lights were being switched on. We were getting desperate.

"There are no youth hostels within reach now," said Shirley, gloomily.

"Perhaps there'll be a B & B somewhere," I ventured.

"No hope of that," said Shirley.

Finally, in desperation, we agreed to knock at the door of the first lit-up house we came to and ask if they had a barn in which we could sleep. This we did. When the door opened, I was standing there alone, Shirley nowhere to be seen! I stammered out something about our being two British students trying to reach St.Malo, overtaken by the night and did they have a barn in which we could sleep? The man on the threshold immediately called his wife and repeated this to her. Though totally amazed, they soon recovered themselves and invited us into their home, Shirley having magically reappeared. We were ushered into their cosy home, given warm water to wash, a good, hearty meal, a comfortable bed and an invitation to return the next night on our way back if we could make it! I shall never forget the warm hospitality shown to us strangers by this kind Norman couple.

The next morning, we continued on our way and reached St.Malo before lunch. We had a dip in the sea which was quite cool at that time of the year and we could see passers-by shaking their heads in disbelief and almost hear them saying "These mad English!" The port of St.Malo was very pretty, surrounded as it is by its ancient fortified walls, so we enjoyed visiting the picturesque old town. Thus it was that we set off on our return journey rather later than intended. Unfortunately, there was no way we could make it to Caen and the comfortable bed awaiting us before nightfall so we ended up in the same predicament as the previous night. This time I refused to knock on a door to ask for shelter to be left alone on the threshold and Shirley refused to do so, too. As it was a balmy evening, we decided to kip down behind a hedge bordering a convenient field. We donned our pyjamas over our clothes and topped them off with our woollens. One mackintosh served as a groundsheet as we lay close together inside our sheet sleeping bags with the other mackintosh covering us. We both slept well under the circumstances, but awoke at first light, wet with heavy dew and gazing into the big brown eyes of one of the curious cows which had come to check out the trespassers. We lost no time in tidying ourselves up and making our getaway whilst the herd was still in a friendly mood.

Studies recommenced on our return and soon the final exams were upon us. There were written tests in all our subjects as well as oral exams which required us to recite a chosen poem and give an *explication de texte* which was totally unprepared. The Bristol contingent did very well on the whole. One of our Bristol students, Irene Burton, who had one French parent, came top of the 400 candidates. I had a *mention très bien* and was twenty-ninth overall. We all graduated happily and met together in the *Cour de la Sorbonne*, each clutching his or her attractive *Diplôme de Civilisation Française,* duly stamped by the Sorbonne, University of Paris.

# Chapter 12
# Footloose in France

Although our study period at the Sorbonne was at an end, we still had to remain in France until the end of September before returning to Bristol to resume our degree course in October 1954. Whilst I was living at the Foyer, I was given a reference by the *Surveillante Générale* which enabled me to earn extra pocket money by taking a local doctor's children, a girl and a boy, for a walk in the *Bois de Boulogne* every Saturday whilst teaching them a smattering of English. This arrangement worked well for everyone so that when the doctor arranged to do a little locum work in Beauvais, a lovely town north of Paris, I was invited to accompany them for the month of July. As an *au pair*, I had charge of the two children and two of their cousins of similar ages. This was no problem for me, having often had to take charge of my four younger siblings when Mammy was ill. There was no housework to do as the family also employed a *femme de ménage*. As in Paris, my duties involved taking the children for walks and collecting fresh produce such as milk and *groseilles* from a nearby farm. I also helped to prepare these gorgeous redcurrants which we ate as a dessert, piled high in bowls and liberally sprinkled with sugar. These remain some of my favourite fruit to this day.

While I was striving to teach them a little English during their holidays (not their favourite occupation) I, myself, acquired a large new vocabulary of "*argot,*" modern French slang. The children tried to speak as much as possible in *argot* so that I would not understand them too well. However, this was done in a pleasant, teasing sort of way and we all got on famously. I remember taking them on a favourite walk to an old quarry where we used to meet an old peasant who regaled me regularly with tales of the war and the occupation. He was glad to meet a British ally who would sympathise with his tales of suffering induced by our mutual enemy, the *Bosch.*

I got on well with the lady of the house, who taught me the trick of making real French mayonnaise by using fresh eggs and oil poured in drop by drop to avoid curdling. She also taught me a number of old wives' sayings to enlarge my vocabulary. One sticks in my memory and I still trot it out today when appropriate: *Tout bon animal s'échauffe en mangeant* which can be interpreted roughly as "food warms up healthy animals" or "healthy people are stimulated by eating." The family was on holiday and so was I. They included me in all the outings to see the sights in Beauvais, such as the beautiful cathedral and the touristic areas around the town. I was also taken to smart restaurants where I first sampled some of the very best French *haute cuisine.*

At the end of July I returned with them to Paris where I went to stay at a youth hostel in Montmartre, a very colourful, arty area of Paris. I had earned quite a nice little sum as an au pair, so I arranged to invite my sister, Morfydd, to come to France to tour around as much of the country as possible before returning to the UK towards the end of September. As I was now an experienced hitch-hiker, I prevailed upon my parents to allow my sister to come to Paris under my care for the holiday of our young lives. I gave strict instructions as to what she must bring – a change of clothes, a sheet sleeping bag, a mackintosh and something warm for the cool nights. All this was to fit into a duffel bag. It was on my second visit to *Gare St. Lazare* (I had been earlier as I wasn't sure which train she had taken) that I eventually caught a glimpse of my sister, flanked by a couple who had befriended her on the train. They were carrying between them a huge heavy haversack filled to the brim with provisions sent by our doting mother. Poor Morfydd received an instant scolding, but she was so relieved to see me waiting to meet her that it was like water off a duck's back. We both enjoyed the chocolates she had brought all the same, although they had melted and fused on her long journey. I bought her a duffel bag, and her haversack and all the unnecessary contents thereof were stored with my trunk and suitcases in the basement of the *Foyer des Lycéenes*. We were now ready to set out on our travels.

Having never ventured outside Wales, Morfydd's eyes were out on stalks as I showed her the sights of Paris. To cap it all, on my earlier trip to *Gare St. Lazare,* I had bumped into four boys from the Rhondda, all ready to take Paris by storm. Like Morfydd, none of them spoke French and all of them, therefore, were very happy to have met me. I hailed a taxi and accompanied them to their hotel. The first thing they wanted to do was to visit the famous *Moulin Rouge.* We arranged that Morfydd and I would call to collect them after dinner the next evening and that they would treat us to a night out at the *Moulin Rouge.* It was very gay and lively there with champagne to drink and the famous *Bluebelle* girls giving a fast high-kicking dance show in their glitzy, skimpy costumes. It turned out to be a really fantastic evening for us all. What an amazing start to our holidays – and so unexpected too!

A few days later, we left Paris and got our first lift. Naturally, I sat in the front to converse with the driver, while Morfydd sat in the rear, looking out at the scenery and interspersing the conversation with *"Joli, joli!"* at frequent intervals. The driver soon realised that she spoke no French and, on finding that we intended to journey to the South of France eventually, proposed that I should abandon my sister and go straight to Avignon with him! I told him in no uncertain terms that I would never accept such a proposition and that we wished to be dropped at Fontainebleau, as we had asked. He acquiesced immediately without any rancour and even stood us an excellent meal in a restaurant before going on his way. He actually admitted to having daughters

133

of our age as we conversed at table. Although lurid details of dreadful things happening to young hitch hikers sometimes filled the newspapers, it was the one and only such "awkward" incident throughout the whole of my hitch-hiking days. In her innocence, Morfydd was blissfully unaware of what had occurred and thoroughly enjoyed her first day "on the road." Fortunately, we were both safe and sound and none the worse for the experience and able to continue on our way to our intended destination.

We made our way leisurely through the changing scenery of this beautiful country, stopping at various points of interest en route and staying in youth hostels where we made friends with travellers from all over France and indeed the continent and even some from Wales. We took along our own personal cooking utensils, Morfydd feeling embarrassed to carry our saucepan hanging from the top of her duffel bag as we walked through towns.

The youth hostel in Avignon was closed when we arrived, so we slept on a bench in the train station until it was time for the hostel to open in the morning. Of course, we had to dance on the old bridge at Avignon, singing together the well-known *"Sur le pont d'Avignon ...."* We bought food in supermarkets and either cooked at least one hot meal per day in the hostels or ate in reasonable, i.e. cheap, restaurants (unless generous drivers treated us to meals in more up-market establishments.) We bought fruit, bread and chocolate to eat on route. I vividly remember visiting a melon farm in the south of France where we bought as many melons as we could carry and ate them in large quantities to assuage our thirst. The unaccustomed heat was almost unbearable at times the further south we ventured, so we also consumed large quantities of cool water in order to keep going.

Entering Provence, I was keen to see as many of the famous Roman remains as we could. En route, our driver stopped at a pretty little lake that he knew in the area. There we all had a quick swim before settling down to a very welcome picnic together. Refreshed, we were taken to visit *St.Rémy de Provence* and *Les Baux de Provence,* as well as the impressive Roman amphitheatres at *Arles* and at *Nîmes*, the largest and most well-preserved outside Italy.

Our thirst for culture momentarily assuaged, we carried on down to the French Riviera, the *Côte d'Azure,* the playground of Europe. Here, progress was slow due to the extremely heavy traffic. We stopped at many resorts, big and small, along the Mediterranean coast. We both loved *Cassis* with its well-known *calanques* and *La Ciotat*, where the hostel was particularly nice, so we lingered there, making friends and sharing our enjoyment of the white sandy beaches. Being fair-haired, I had to be careful of the hot sun, but still managed to get sunburnt at times, though thankfully not too severely. Brunette Morfydd, however, had no problem in developing a really lovely tan. Making our way all along the coast, sampling the delights of *Toulon,*

134

*Hyères, Le Lavandou,* and marvelling at the huge ocean-going yachts moored in swish St.Tropez harbour, we eventually arrived at *Fréjus* and *St.Raphael.* From there, we were driven along the fabulous *Esterel,* the twisting road following the rugged coastline towards Cannes where the famous film festival takes place. The scenery along that section of coast is absolutely stupendous where the *Alpes Maritimes* sweep down almost to the sea and provide awe-inspiring views around every corner, the red and brown of the sheer cliffs covered with lush green vegetation making a vivid contrast with the deep blue of the glistening sea.

From *Cannes,* we passed through *Antibes* en route for *Nice* and strolled down the famous *Promenade des Anglais* before leaving for *Monte Carlo. Nice* itself is a very lively and varied town with lots to do for the tourists but we both agreed that the sandy beach at *Cannes* was far preferable to the pebble beach of *Nice.* The little princedom of *Monaco* was next on our list as we passed through *Monte Carlo* with its famous casino (not for the likes of us penniless students, however) and ended up at *Menton.* We were now almost in Italy, so, sadly, we realised we would have to start on our long return trip to Paris.

We back-tracked to *Nice* and *Cannes* and looked for cars going over the Alps towards *Grenoble.* Passing through the quaint town of *Grasse* nestling in the Alps north of Cannes, we visited the Fragonard perfumery there and took small perfume samples back with us. This brought back memories of my first visit there with First Porth Rangers. Crossing the Alps was memorable, as was the youth hostel in *Grenoble,* where all the girls bedded down in a sort of long *mezzanine* lined with sweet-smelling straw mattresses. The extra warm blankets they provided were certainly needed, as we gazed in wonder at the snow-capped mountains surrounding us.

From *Grenoble,* our journey took us north to *Lac Léman* and across the border into Switzerland. The festival of *Geneva* was in full swing with a fantastic parade of floats all through the town. Petals from multicoloured flowers were raining down on us from all sides creating a perfumed, fairy-like atmosphere. Being small, we had to try and hold our cameras over the heads of the crowd to get our shots. Nearing the end of our holidays, it looked as though we might even have enough money left to buy a few gifts to take back for the family. The opportunity to buy some real Swiss watches had to be seized. I purchased two wrist-watches, one for my mother and one for my thirteen-year-old sister, Ann, her first timepiece. Although not top of the range, they were real Swiss jewelled watches which I was very proud to offer as gifts to my dear ones. The next problem was to get them back to Wales without having to pay customs duty on them. They were rolled up tightly in socks and underwear and our hearts beat furiously, as, trying to look pictures of innocence, we crossed each frontier.

From Geneva, we made straight for Paris where we arrived safely after a truly unforgettable holiday. Relaxing for a few days in the same comfortable youth hostel in the *Place Pigalle* in Monmartre where we had stayed before, we started to make arrangements for our return to Wales. From the *Foyer des Lycéennes,* I retrieved my luggage and Morfydd's overspill. I sent my trunk on ahead and we gathered up the rest of our luggage and started out on the last long stamina-sapping leg of our journey home by train and boat. After four fabulous weeks our great French adventure was finally over. I had been away for a total of eight whole months and only now realised just how much I had missed my parents and little sisters and brother. I was really looking forward to returning home to see my family in Ynyshir and soon afterwards Archie and my friends in Bristol.

# Chapter 13
# Graduation, Teacher Training and My First Job

A warm welcome awaited us when we arrived back in Wales after our fantastic holiday in France. Mammy and Daddy had a lot of trust in us two teenagers to let us loose hitch-hiking around France, but it must have been hard for them not to worry in the periods between the infrequent post cards which reassured them of our safety. The whole family was agog to hear of our adventures abroad. Questions rained down fast and furious and Morfydd and I had our work cut out to answer them in the detail required – how did we manage to get such long lifts? What strange food did we sample in the restaurants? Did the Bluebelle girls actually dance with nothing on but colourful boas to cover their modesty?.......and so on.

It was like Christmas all over again when the presents we had brought back for everybody were handed around. A gasp of amazement greeted the Swiss watches that we had managed to smuggle successfully through the customs. Mammy put hers on immediately and was thrilled to be able to tell her neighbours later that they had actually been bought in Switzerland. Ann ran straight out to show hers to her best friend, Christine. Daddy was delighted as usual with the large pack of Bondman's tobacco he received, this time with an unusual Swiss pipe in which to smoke it. Mary and Michael, however, must have had mixed feelings about their gifts, which were more educational than frivolous as big sister, Pat, wanted to encourage an interest in things French. Mary was given a French version of the Monopoly board game and Michael a wooden puzzle of the map of Europe, also in French. At first, I had to translate each card as we played, but later they got to know more or less what each one meant so were eventually able to play without me. I also gave Ann and Mary a little French doll each dressed in Provencal national costume and Michael a small puppet, so everyone was happy.

Morfydd and I had hardly unpacked when it was time to gather our things together to return to Bristol and Barry to start the new semester of our second year. Archie met me at Temple Meads station in Bristol and accompanied me to my new accommodation. This year I was to share a flat with my friend and fellow French student, Vendla. We settled quickly and found it easier with respect to our social life and, of course, we could also discuss our work together at times. Life soon settled into a routine and time just flew. We attended all our lectures, gave in all our essays in between spending much of our time socialising in the Victoria Rooms (our Students' Union) and philosophising and putting the world to rights around a coffee table in the Berkley café.

Meanwhile, Archie was finding that his studies at Bristol University were not quite going as planned. Although he was enjoying certain aspects of his course and was doing well, he began to feel that it was his family's expectations that had led him into choosing medical studies while his real interest still lay in science in which he had already obtained a degree before coming to Britain. He had become very accustomed to his life here and was very happy. He felt that he wanted to settle down permanently and eventually establish a home for us together in Bristol. He then took a final decision to look for a job using his scientific qualifications.

In the meantime, he continued living in Clifton and playing sport until one day during a fiercely contested Badminton match, he collapsed suddenly on the court. He finished the game in a bath of cold sweat. I had been watching and was most concerned, so together with one of his male friends, we ordered a taxi and took him to his flat. We called the doctor who diagnosed inflammation of the diaphragm – a not too infrequent an occurrence in athletes. Archie did not wish to go to hospital, so his flat mate watched over him at night and I called in every day to make his meals and care for him in general. Gradually, he recovered and I invited him to visit my family with me during his recuperation. We went to Wales in the Easter holidays and Mammy was quite concerned with the state he was in. He had a pasty colour and got breathless when going for walks up the mountain with me. He went to see our local doctor, Dr. Orr, who told him to take things a bit more easily for a while. He agreed to consult his doctor again on his return to Bristol. This he did and soon began to feel better and gradually returned to lead a normal life as before.

During the holidays Archie continued to visit us in Wales. He became very popular with my three youngest siblings. He also made quite an impression on my teenage cousin, Rosemary, who had a little crush on him – "Oh, he's so handsome," she was wont to say. Travelling circuses and fun fairs would be set up on the oval at the end of our street and merry tunes such as "Bye bye, Blackbird" rang out constantly encouraging us to spend time and money on the many rides and side shows. Archie was a good marksman and his prowess at the shooting booths earned us many coconuts and prizes and hero worshiping from Ann, Mary and Michael. In turn he invited all four of us for weekends to Bristol where he always managed to give us a very good time. The children were very happy and excited to spend a whole day at the zoo where they saw so many new and exotic animals. Gradually Archie was making a place for himself in the midst of our family.

I took the first part of my degree exams at the end of my second year and all went well. I passed my Latin and was able to concentrate solely on French in my third year. Vendla had promised to share a flat with Irene Burton in the third year, so I shared with Hazel who was studying English. We got on well but were more independent of one another. In particular, I remember what a good mimic she was. At the time, Princess Margaret was in a relationship with a Peter Townsend. Hazel used to amuse us all by jumping up onto a chair and declaiming in a loud voice,

"I do not intend to marry Group Captain Peter Townsend" giving a marvellous imitation of Princess Margaret and other members of the Royal family.

During these last two years Archie had gone through an extremely difficult time in his life. He was struggling with a period of poor health and had begun to look for a suitable job, so that he could become independent of his father's financial support. However, it did not prove to be easy. As a foreign national and a mature man without any previous employment in Britain, it was difficult to persuade firms to even consider his application. Some of his friends were thinking of trying to set up restaurants to introduce curries to the British public. Archie seriously considered going into business with them. After our family's struggle to send me to university in the hope of securing an academic career, I was not keen on the idea. Looking back now on the way Indian restaurants took off, it might have been a big mistake.

His father urged him to return to Pakistan and since he was not a student any more, was no longer willing to go on sending Archie an allowance. Twice there was talk of his packing his bags to go back home but Archie managed to stall things. Then strong pressure was put on him to return and a passage was actually booked. As a result we talked of my following him to Pakistan when I would have finished at Bristol University but the future seemed so insecure for us. On this occasion Archie actually started to pack his things ready to leave Bristol, but at the last minute he cancelled the ticket for the voyage home. He could not risk leaving me for good, as circumstances might prevent me from joining him in Pakistan in the future. His father, of course, lost quite a lot of money from this last-minute cancellation, so Archie was now on his own with no financial support and no job.

Fortunately, he was not thrown out of his flat but started to accumulate debts and had scarcely enough money to buy food. He tried to hide his desperate position from me but I soon realised that he needed help to survive. Once, I found out that he had been reduced to eating a raw onion and bread for lunch. Things had got very bad indeed. I insisted on lending him money which he wrote down scrupulously in a little book so that he could repay it when things were better. Archie continued applying for jobs in earnest. Although this very difficult period seemed to drag on forever, it came to an end when he finally got a suitable job at the National Smelting Works, Avonmouth. His scientific qualifications were accepted and he was taken on to work in a laboratory specialising in the new field of spectrometry. He was paid a good salary and was soon able to pay off all his debts and start to save money. Archie's father gradually accepted the new situation and was glad to know that his youngest son was happy and was now able to stand on his own feet. Archie put down firm roots in Bristol where he envisaged spending the rest of his life.

Now that I was approaching the time to sit my final degree exams, Archie began to encourage me to aim for a First Class Honours. He was keen that neither my parents nor his father should be able to say that he had disturbed my studies. It did not seem to be a total impossibility, as I had sometimes achieved high marks in important essays or end of term translations. Perhaps his insistence and Mammy's always high expectations started to cause me stress because just before the start of the exams, I began to get severe headaches. I had never suffered from headaches before but was forced to go to the doctor for tablets. This did not let up and I went to my first paper with a throbbing head. It was a three hour essay paper and I could not think clearly. Half way through I tore up my work and started on a new subject in a panic. I had messed up my chances right at the beginning! A First Class was out of the question now. I just had to make sure that I did not fail. I pulled myself together and my headaches receded and all went well afterwards.

Fortunately, I managed to achieve a BA with Second Class Honours which is still considered a good degree. When my professor spoke to me about my results, he said,

"Whatever happened to you in that first paper? It was nowhere near your usual standard." On my reference he was kind enough to write:

"Miss Stevens' work is always at least of this standard, often better."

Before going down finally from the university it was a tradition that the students of Special Three would entertain the first and second year students at an end of term party. We discussed it at great length and it was decided that we would all take part in a sort of cabaret on a simple literary theme. The portrayal of *Love throughout the Ages* was chosen as our theme. Each scene was to be linked to the following one by a couple of lovers. There was no question about who was to play the male lover. Gerard Farrell was an attractive and popular boy. Now we needed to choose a girl with long flowing locks to epitomise the traditional ideal of medieval beauty. Margaret Brown had long platinum blonde hair and was keen to take the part. However, some said that my long thick golden curls were more appropriate for the era and it was left to Gerard to decide. Thus it was that I was accorded the honour of strolling through the ages on Gerard's arm as we linked the various scenes together.

That summer I worked in Butlin's in Filey, North Yorkshire, but returned in time for my degree ceremony in July. The whole family was very happy.

140

My parents and Morfydd were to come to Bristol for the ceremony. Since Mammy wanted a new outfit to attend my graduation, we both poured over the catalogue until we chose a smart dress and jacket which I made up in firm pink striped cotton on a white background. At my graduation ceremony in Bristol in 1956, Daddy was very proud of his elegant wife and equally of the daughter who had "*forged the way*" for her siblings to follow. Mammy felt very smart in the "*costume*" I had made for her and Daddy wore his dark wedding suit. They were both as proud as punch. The ceremony was to be held in the Great Hall of the university. The occasion could have been marred for my parents by the rudeness of a Bristol bus driver. Since they were strangers to the city, they had asked him for directions. Their obvious Welsh accents drew an impolite response from the driver which dampened their spirits momentarily. However, despite his unhelpful attitude, all was well, as we met up in good time for them to take their seats in the Great Hall to enjoy the ceremony. Photographs were taken to mark the occasion and we splashed out on a special meal in one of Bristol's fine restaurants to celebrate.

I had decided that I wanted to become a teacher and had already secured a place on a one-year post-graduate teacher training course at Bristol University. Vendla was to spend a year as a Reader at Bordeaux University in France, so I joined up with three other friends who were also signed up for the same teaching course. Eileen, Joan, Tessa and I were lucky to find a particularly spacious and attractive flat at the top of Whiteladies Road. We organised ourselves well and spent a very pleasant year together.

All four of us had regular boy friends who visited us at the flat and we each got engaged to our respective escorts the following year. We all opted for training as secondary school teachers and enjoyed the course and training sessions in various schools. Eileen met her future husband, Andrew Trott, at Kingswood Grammar School during her teacher training there. He was a young Maths teacher. They both had a penchant for jazz and would return home quite late at night and put on their favourite record, forgetting that we three flat mates were tucked up in bed. Then the floor would start to rock as they could not resist jiving to the strains of Chris Barber or Acker Bilk. As these sessions normally occurred on a Saturday night nobody really minded. We just settled down to listen to whatever new records they played.

We had to have teaching practice in different kinds of schools. Before returning after the summer holidays we were expected to do three weeks' practice in a school near our home. I did mine in Ynyshir Secondary Modern School which had replaced the old "*Forms*" and had been extended to take up the space of the former Girls' Junior School which had been amalgamated with the old Boys' Junior School in the centre of the village. The Head Mistress was Madame Roberts (pronounced à la française, as she had married a Frenchman) who had been my first French teacher in Porth County. She

141

had left Porth County after my first year to take up her new post leaving us to the tender care of a succession of incompetent teachers until Miss Llewellyn finally took us in hand in Form Four. As the school was so close, I went home daily for dinner cooked by Mammy. My young brother who was in Porth Sec, would dash back at top speed in order to secure his favourite place at table or the biggest junket dessert! He was happy to get some pocket money and a treat to the cinema from his big sister when she was around.

My main teaching practice took place for almost the whole of the middle term in the convent school of *La Sainte Union* in Bath. This meant that I had to be up early in the morning to take the bus to Temple Meads station to go to school every day. It was a wonder that I ever got there in time as it was always a mad dash to catch that train. I think the guard got used to looking out for a frantic student rushing in to jump onto the train as it was about to move off. At the other end I had quite a long walk past the stunning Georgian crescents to get to my school. I got used to the journey and did not really mind it at all in the end.

Students were put under the charge of a specific teacher who had to monitor them throughout their time in school. We had to follow them around and observe their methods and ask their advice. I saw my teacher a few times during the first week before she went off on sick leave for the rest of the term. I was then asked to take over her teaching commitment and had full responsibility for all her French classes and very little free time to prepare my lessons. It was a nice, friendly and well-disciplined school so, in fact, I learned to stand on my own feet and obtained some very good experience there. I particularly enjoyed training some of these talented pupils to enact a French version of Cinderella which I had written for them. It was quite a success when performed for the whole school.

Towards the end of the course we all started to apply for our first teaching posts. As both Archie and Andrew were in Bristol, Eileen and I applied for schools in the vicinity. Eileen secured a job in Mangotsfield and I at Kingswood Grammar where Andrew taught. All was now set for the start of our careers as qualified teachers. However, I decided to have one last fling before settling down to a routine job as an adult. Although our ways had parted when Vendla had taken up her post in Bordeaux, we had always kept in touch. We decided to spend the month of August hitch-hiking around Europe. Money was obviously needed to fund this plan. An advert was put in *Le Figaro* (one of the big Paris newspapers) offering my services as an *au pair* for the month of July. I had a flood of replies, so I chose a business lady living alone with two teenage children who needed supervision during their holidays while she was at work. They lived in a swish apartment in Neuilly, an upmarket area of Paris. However, it seemed such a pity not to make use of some of the other very interesting offers.

My sister, Ann, was about to begin her O Level year, so I thought that she would jump at the chance to live with a well-to-do French family to spend July in their holiday home in Dieppe. They owned a book shop in Place de Wagram in Paris, so when I arrived to take up my position as au pair in Neuilly, I arranged to call on them. At first they were disappointed to know that they were not to get a reasonably mature and experienced student to help improve their two daughters' English during the holidays and were very dubious about accepting young Ann in my place. However, I managed to convince them that although Ann was about the same age as their girls, she would arrive with plenty of lessons prepared by me and, being the talented musician she was, would be able to teach them lots of songs and play the piano to entertain everybody. Ann also needed quite a bit of persuading too, but it all turned out well in the end and everyone was happy. In fact, Ann now recognises that the experience of living in a foreign country at such young age gave her confidence and maturity.

Already settled in my job as an au pair, I had the weekend off to go to Dieppe to meet Ann and take her to her hosts' house at the seaside. I couldn't help thinking how much she must have resembled Mammy at that age with her petite frame, expressive brown eyes and long dark hair tied up in a pony's tail. She however, unlike Mammy, was not going away to work permanently in someone else's home far from her family. She was embarking on an exciting holiday in a new country with a different culture where she would improve her French and be able to speak as much English as she liked with her new charges and their friends. Of course she was very nervous to start with, so it was good that I was there to help settle her down.

She got over her initial homesickness as she got to know lots of their friends and was thrilled to be allowed to play on a grand piano in one of their homes. She had a great time with this pleasant family and returned home looking like a gipsy with her flashing white teeth contrasting with a dark brown tan. The only slight fly in the ointment was that her two pupils felt that their noses were put out of joint at times when their male friends paid a bit too much attention to the lively little Welsh girl. Towards the end of her stay, we arranged for her to come to Paris later to spend a weekend with me. She thoroughly enjoyed her short trip to Paris and took in as many sights as possible.

When she had returned safely to Wales, I met up with Vendla and started off on our tour of Europe. Our main objective was to make straight for Yugoslavia where we intended to stay for at least a week. We set off east from Paris towards Strasbourg where we stayed overnight to enable us to see the wonderful cathedral with its famous clock where little scenes were enacted every half hour to enthral sightseers. Next we headed towards Germany and passed through the beautiful Black Forrest, dense with trees of different hues overhanging the narrow winding roads. Here Vendla's fluent German proved indispensable. We had a lift with a young German who succeeded in frightening the life out of us as he careered round sharp bends on the steep and narrow roads through the forest. We clung to our seats and managed not to scream aloud as he jovially regaled us with anecdotes about the area. We were very relieved indeed to emerge safe and sound, although rather shaky, in the charming town of Freiburg.

Our journey continued eastwards through ever changing scenery in Germany to Austria. From Salzburg just over the border, we headed south towards Yugoslavia. Until then, we had breezed through all the countries experiencing absolutely no difficulty securing lifts. In the little border town of Villach, however, we came to an abrupt stop. We ended up at a crossroads with signs pointing one way towards Italy and the other towards Yugoslavia. Traffic flowed constantly towards Italy and we could have easily jumped into smart fast cars going in that direction. Unfortunately, the only vehicles turning into the road to Yugoslavia were rickety old farm trucks laden with animals or hay or small overloaded family cars whose occupants smiled and waved cheerfully at us on the roadside. The hours dragged out as we waited hopefully at the junction. As dusk began to descend in the early evening, Vendla asked,

"What shall we do? We don't look like getting a lift tonight. We're stuck here in the middle of nowhere."

"There's nothing for it but to throw ourselves on the mercy of the Austrian farmers we've just passed down the road. We can ask them if we can sleep in their barn. When Shirley and I did that in Normandy, the kind people gave us hospitality in their home with a good meal and a comfortable bed for the night," I suggested.

We had no alternative but to knock on the door of the farm and ask for help. We had to skirt round fierce dogs chained up to warn of approaching strangers, so we were soon confronted by a suspicious looking farmer's wife. As Vendla spoke fluent German, it was she who hesitantly explained our situation. The woman called her husband, who, having looked us over carefully, decided to offer us his barn for the night. We were to bed down in the hayloft over the part where the animals were housed, so we laid out our sleeping bags and made ourselves as comfortable as possible for the night. A warm, pungent scent arose from the cows below. We had certainly slept in fresher, sweeter-smelling places. There was no light in the barn but we were given a lamp to help us settle in before it was swiftly removed leaving us in pitch blackness. Dismayed, we cuddled together and tried to sleep.

"What's that noise, Vendla?" I whispered fearfully.

"It's only the cows shuffling about down below," she reassured me.

"You don't think there may be rats in here, do you?" I asked in terror.

144

"Of course not," Vendla replied bravely. I wasn't convinced, however, and passed a restless and almost sleepless night until we were rudely awoken in the early morning. Suddenly something soft and vaguely fresh-smelling was raining down on us from above. We were both up with a start pushing the stuff off our faces before it could smother us and yelling our heads off. Hay was being shot into the loft through a trap door above our heads. Suddenly, the heads of two rustic farm hands appeared in the aperture laughing in amazement to find two young students staring up at them. They thought it was all a great joke and paused long enough for us to brush ourselves down, gather our things together and scramble down from the hay loft. The surly farmer showed where we could wash under a cold tap over the trough from which the animals drank and then we were off to try our luck on the road once more. There had been no luxury, as in Normandy, but at least we had been safe in the shelter of the barn for the night and, thankfully, we had lived to tell the tale.

Back at the crossroads, our frantic thumb signals were eventually rewarded when a loaded car stopped and the driver asked us where we were going. We explained our problem and the good natured family squashed up to allow us to get in with them. They were only going to a little village just below the border with Yugoslavia but we accepted the lift. On leaving them, we put our best feet forward and started to climb up a steep path leading up to the top of the mountain which marked the boundary between Austria and Yugoslavia. We arrived red and hot at the customs frontier to the great surprise of the two officers who were manning the post. They assumed that we had walked all the way up and were much impressed with our determination to get to Yugoslavia. They sat us down with cooling drinks and assured us that they would find us a suitable lift to take us to our destination. True to their word, they returned with the good news that they had found a lift. They grabbed our duffle bags and slung one into each of two cars which were ready to leave.

"Oh, don't do that," we chorused in unison. "We always travel together in one car. We won't go separately."

"Don't you worry, young ladies," they said. "We have the drivers' names and addresses and their car registration numbers. You will be quite safe with them." Relieved, we got into the cars and set off one behind the other.

On conversing with them, we learned that our drivers were students travelling home to Athens from Heidelberg. It appeared that they were taking a lot more money than was permissible with them hidden in the cavities in the sides of the car. Because they had readily agreed to give us a lift, the custom officers had not bothered to search their cars properly. They were really happy to have got away so easily and to have acquired two young girls for company. We stopped for a swim and a picnic together on the banks of

145

a river in the city of Ljubljana in the north of Yugoslavia. The men offered to take us all the way to Athens with them. It was tempting, but Yugoslavia was our goal, so we politely declined and parted with them in the centre of Ljubljana.

No sooner had they shot off than Vendla realised that she had left her passport in the car. We looked at one another in consternation. We were in a communist country without a passport! The police must have been keeping a wary eye on any strange, foreign-looking individuals for almost immediately we were accosted and asked for our passports. There was no alternative but to explain as best we could what had happened. With descriptions of the two cars and the two men along with their route, the officers took charge of the situation. They placed us in a forbidding-looking Youth Hostel for the night.

"Oh, I feel terrible," said Vendla. "That poor guy will think I set the police on him when he hears the sirens and is stopped by the police, and after they were so kind too!"

"Not at all," I replied. "Just think how relieved he'll be when they just ask him for your passport."

All must have gone off without problems, for a smiling police officer returned Venda's passport in the morning. Thankfully he did not arrest her for complicity in smuggling money, but did advise her to be more careful next time.

We continued south until we came to Rijeka, a small town on the Adriatic coast. Here we decided to rest and spend a holiday. We found places in a youth hostel run by two male students. After our long journey, our clothes needed a good wash so we asked for some hot water. The boys seemed to think that cold water was adequate but agreed to heat water for us in return for a promise to accompany them to a dance taking place on the terrace of a seaside hotel that evening. Only too happy to agree, we spent the evening discussing the differences between life in a communist country and Britain. We soon realised that we had much more freedom than they had. We learned that they were only allowed passports to travel abroad when representing the state.

The next day I ventured down to the beach for a swim while Vendla was to join me later. The sea was blue, warm and inviting, and the sand was soft and clean on a beach which was not too crowded. Suddenly my peace was shattered by the arrival of a group of boys who had just come ashore from a small boat. They tried all sorts of languages until we found that one of them spoke reasonable French. They invited me to go for a sail in their boat but I declined saying that I was waiting for my friend. They refused to take no for an answer promising to bring me back in time to meet her. They had a small child with them and seemed to be genuine, so I allowed them to pack my things into the boat and set off for a quick sail just offshore. Meanwhile, Vendla was searching the beach for me and was surprised to hear herself being hailed at full throttle by a band of boys in a boat. She was soon introduced to them and we spent the rest of our time in Rijeka together.

One of the boys spoke German and hit it off with Vendla but one vociferous young man was determined to attract my attention, although we had no common language. Alexander spoke fluent Italian and I had recently attended an Italian course from scratch in Bristol University. My Italian certainly improved immensely during our stay. We swam and played together on the beach, went dancing and were taken for a sail on a friend's yacht. The boy who owned the little rowing boat invited us all to his home where we feasted on grapes and took many more with us when we went for a midnight sail.

The moon was shining over a silver sea and it was very romantic indeed. In such a glorious, carefree holiday setting, we were enjoying the company of our new friends so much that Vendla and I began to feel a little guilty remembering our boyfriends back home. Alex told me that he was studying to become a doctor and that everything he would do in the future would be for me. On hearing such an unexpected declaration, we thought that we had better move on, regretfully. Although nothing untoward had happened between Alex and me, I felt that I had to admit to a little romantic adventure when Archie questioned me on my return. Naturally, this led to a rift between us which was only reconciled when Archie knocked on my door with the eggs he usually brought me from a colleague.

"Do you want eggs, today?" he enquired.

"Oh yes, of course." I jumped at the pretext and ushered him in. We soon made it up on the understanding that I would have no further contact with Alex. I was sad to destroy Alex's photos and optimistic letters without being able to offer him an explanation.

Our tour continued into Italy via Trieste to Venice with its unique beautiful waterways and Saint Mark's Cathedral. We were shocked to find that the two friendly policemen with whom we were chatting were carrying loaded pistols in their belts. Then we went on to Milan where we stayed in a convent enjoying the hospitality of the nuns. After visiting the famous "*il Duomo*" (cathedral) we spent a day or two at Lake Como. On leaving, we secured a fantastic lift with a French/American couple who were going all the way to Paris via Switzerland. We settled happily into their luxurious car when

"Oh my goodness," said Vendla. "I can't find my passport."

"Don't say you've left it in the hotel this time," I exclaimed

"I could have sworn it was in my bag but it's not."

"We'll have to go back for it. Could you please drop us off?" I asked despondently.

"What a shame," said the lady.

"OK," said the driver. "We'll be staying in Geneva for the night. If you can get to the hotel by 10am tomorrow we'll take you back to Paris with us." We parted, thanking them effusively and clutching the details of their hotel, to hitch back to our hotel. Later, with the passport safely tucked away, we set off once again with little hope of catching up with our lift in Geneva. Amazingly, a luxury coach picked us up to the annoyance of some of the passengers who had paid for their trip. However, one couple was most friendly and on hearing of our predicament, offered us hospitality in their home in Evian and told us how we could get to Geneva in time. Our luck held and the French/American couple drove us back to Paris in comfort with a stop and meals on the way, all paid for by our generous driver. With yet another fantastic adventure behind us, we were now ready to start our working life.

Back in Bristol, Eileen and I found a convenient flat in Aberdeen Road and worked hard to bring it up to a standard as befitted our new status as teachers. Both our schools were on the same side of Bristol and entailed quite a long bus journey. My school was huge with an intake of five streams in each year. The Headmaster was a most unpleasant man who terrorised the staff rather than the pupils. I became friendly with another first year teacher called Josefa Burger who taught Latin. She was a Polish refugee whose whole family had been deported to Russia to work under dreadful conditions. However, one sister had escaped this fate and had joined the Polish Free Army and had managed to secure the release of her surviving relatives at the end of the war. Her mother was still living in a refugee camp in the South of England at the time. The following year they were able to emigrate from the UK to Canada where, reunited with other family members, they settled permanently.

Our Headmaster had no regard for the well-being of his staff and most of the young teachers were very unhappy there. He was a poor disciplinarian and so did not support his staff when they experienced problems with unruly pupils. It was well known that he would never expel a pupil under any circumstances, since it would reflect on the reputation of the school and of him as Head. Unhappy teachers who wished to leave found that they were unable to do so without a suitable reference from him, so they felt as if they were caught in a trap. Most of my classes were pleasant to teach and willing to work at first until I came up against a pupil called Stephen Bird in the bottom stream of the third year.

I had been forewarned about this boy who played up every teacher who taught him. He was a particularly unprepossessing youth – tall, skinny and spotty - with dark, greasy hair. Apparently he had been reported regularly but no action was ever taken, even after he had sexually assaulted a girl. I was advised to allow him to leave the classroom on any excuse (as he often wanted to smoke) to avoid confrontation. However, he never asked to leave my class but instead would wait for me at the door and, towering over me, make suggestive comments such as,

"Me and you should get on well together, Miss. You being Miss Stevens and me, Stephen," after which he would pretend to swoon before me as he almost fell into the room with a disgusting leer on his face. This had an adverse effect on the behaviour of the class of course. It all came to a head one morning when Bird put up his hand to ask a question. I tried to ignore him but it became impossible.

"Miss, Miss, Stephen's got his hand up," chorused the class.

"What do you want, Bird?" I was forced to respond.

"Can I sharpen my pencil, Miss?" he asked innocently.

This request was totally unexpected, as he rarely deigned to do any work but I had to give him permission to do so. He then sauntered to the back of the room, opened a locker and took out an axe encased in a leather shield. A loud gasp escaped from the class as, mesmerised, we watched him taking out the axe from its protective case and walking insolently towards me swinging it before him. My anger overcame my fear as, instead of backing off, I went towards him and grabbed the axe behind the head and tore it from his grasp. He was dumbfounded, as was the rest of the class. I marched him immediately to the Headmaster who appeared to be more concerned as to why the little harmless boy scout had the axe in his locker rather than the use Bird had made of it in an effort to intimidate me!

When word got around, it had a detrimental knock-on effect on other classes. A low fourth year class became more troublesome. I responded by keeping these two classes in detention after school as a punishment for misbehaviour and a very hostile atmosphere arose between me and them. It ended up with two fourth form boys walking past me in the corridor one day muttering threateningly while handling a cut throat razor in full view. On hearing this, Archie was utterly incensed and it was only with great difficulty that I prevented him from storming up to the school to teach them all a lesson. Obviously, things could not go on in this way. For my own safety and peace of mind, something had to be done. I decided that somehow I would have to find another post without delay.

Archie and I had recently become engaged, so we thought it would be a good idea for me to look for a job near home in Wales for the time being. This would enable me to save towards our wedding and contribute towards the family income instead of paying rent. A French post was on offer in Whitchurch Grammar School in the Vale of Glamorgan. It had an extremely good reputation and was only a short train journey from Ynyshir. The real problem was how to extricate myself from my Headmaster's clutches. Being in my probationary year, I was inspected several times. On the last occasion, the inspector informed me that he was pleased with my progress and indicated that I was likely to pass my probation year. However, when I informed the Head that I wished to leave for another post, he tried to thwart me, saying that I had received a bad report from the inspector and would therefore fail my probationary year. Nevertheless, when I insisted and told him that I had already secured an interview, he was forced to agree to provide me with a reference. At the interview I was disconcerted to be asked why my Headmaster had not sent a reference. I decided to come clean and described the situation at the school in full and was subsequently offered the job to my great joy and relief.

Shortly before leaving Bristol during my final term at Kingswood, I was summoned from my class to the Head's office. I was shocked to be told that my mother was critically ill and that I was to pack my things and leave for home immediately. I went straight from school without going to collect anything from my flat. On arrival I found Mammy in a dreadful state. She was sitting in a chair before the fire unable to move at all. She was in terrible pain from a severe attack of osteoarthritis and was also suffering with her chronic bronchial asthma as well. The doctor was worried that she would not survive. He dosed her up with antibiotics, cortisone and all sorts of medication and together with our constant nursing and Mammy's fighting spirit, yet again the "creaking door" did not break. Gradually Mammy recovered and we all heaved a collective sigh of relief.

However, during her illness I had had to take over the running of the whole household once again. My sisters of course helped as much as they could but it was the washing that I found most onerous. Mammy had by now acquired a twin-tub washing machine but this entailed humping out lots of wet heavy washing to change it from one tub to another. During this procedure there was a great deal of steam generated. This was obviously detrimental to Mammy's health. I discussed the situation with Morfydd and persuaded her that we needed to buy Mammy an automatic washing machine if we wanted to prevent her from dying early. It was decided that I should go ahead and buy the machine and that Morfydd would give me her share of the price later. When the machine was delivered I found a competition enclosed with it. You were asked to make up a pithy publicity statement extolling the properties of the product in a few words. I filled it in and sent it off thinking no more about it until I received a letter informing me that through "my skill and judgment" I had won the competition! The full price of the machine was refunded so Mammy benefitted from a splendid new washing machine and Morfydd and I had nothing to pay in the end. Lady Luck smiled on us once more.

The one really bright spot for Archie and me in this otherwise turbulent period was our decision to become officially engaged to be married. Although we had been an "item" for over four years, we had never talked of

150

an actual engagement. I was only just starting out on my longed-for career and the idea of an early marriage had not really entered my head. I knew also that my parents expected me to carve out a good career in teaching after the years dedicated to getting my qualifications. However, one day as we were admiring some beautiful jewellery in the window of an antique shop, an unusual gold ring which was intricately carved and set with blue sapphires and tiny diamonds caught our eye.

"Do you like it?" asked Archie.

"It's really beautiful," I replied.

"Then let's go and get it before someone else buys it," said Archie.

I was stunned, as I was not expecting such a suggestion at that time but I agreed without a second thought so we entered the shop and bought the ring.

It was a Victorian ring which had worn thin in parts so we had my finger measured and Archie gave the jeweller a gold ring he had brought with him from Pakistan to remedy this. We were now engaged and all that was left to do was to go to Wales and get my parents' approval before wearing the ring.

Of course they were surprised, but as I would be continuing my teaching career after marriage, they soon gave us their blessing. For us two young people the sun had broken through into a cloudless blue sky and the future looked very rosy indeed.

01 Florence Wood and Henry Gerrish,
maternal great-grandparents

02 David John & Selina Dix, paternal
great-grandparents

03  James Stevens, grandfather

04 Selina Jane Stevens, grandmother

152

05 Dai Davies Singer, grandfather    06 Lizzie Davies, grandmother

07 Daddy with violin

08 Billiards Club Daddy Row 1 far Rightt

09 Nurse Annie May

10 Tom & Annie May's wedding
26.12.33

154

11 Dave & Ethel's Wedding; Morfydd & Pat as flower girls

12 Outside St. Anne's Church 1948

13 Pat & Morfydd on Barry Beach

14 Mary, Michael & Ann (sun-dresses made by Pat), back garden

156

15. Daddy in his mountain allottment

16 Gwen & Pat at Wattstown Tennis
Club

17 First Porth Rangers in Les Courmettes - Pat & Huguette top Right

157

18 Pat as au pair in Paris

19 Ann & Pat on steps of Sacré Coeur

20 Diploma Day at the Sorbonne - Pat front right

21 Louis, Vendla, Pat and Archie at Rag Ball, Bristol UV

22 Pat & Morfydd, S. France

23 Pat & Vendla hitchhiking around Châteaux de La Loire

24 Pat waiting for lift to Yugoslavia

25 Eileen in our student flat

26 Pat & Archie Wedding Group 29.03.59

160

27 Pat & Archie cutting wedding cake

28 Honeymoon Porthcawl (outfit made
by Pat)

# PART 4

## A Twist in the Road

# Chapter 14
# The sun is shining, the sky is blue, and all is right with the world

In September 1958, I returned to take over my familiar childhood bedroom in 7 William Street, back with my family once more. I started teaching in my new post at Whitchurch Grammar School, Cardiff. This proved to be a complete contrast with my experience at Kingswood Grammar. I was happy in my new school from day one. The Headmaster was a strict disciplinarian who supported his staff at every turn. He warned new teachers that he was likely to come into the class and observe them teaching at any time or that he would listen unobserved outside the classroom door. This he did to ensure a high standard of teaching throughout his school and was always prepared to offer help and advice to any teacher who was experiencing problems. Any pupil sent to him for misbehaviour was quick to reform. My teaching improved by leaps and bounds and my pupils made good progress too.

I made friends with another young teacher who was also a Bristol graduate. Shirley Hughes was an ex-pupil of the school too, so was well known to most of the staff. Here it was the teachers who acted in the plays that were produced for public showing. I had a second chance to try to fulfil my ambition to act. I auditioned and secured the role of Aunt Lucy in J.B.Priestley's *Laburnum Grove*. Shirley landed one of the main roles in the play. This entailed lots of rehearsals after school but it was great fun for all involved so well worthwhile. Like all previous performances our play was well attended and deemed a success. My family and Archie were at last able to see me strut my stuff on stage without being embarrassed by comments from other members of the audience.

Like me, Shirley made most of her own clothes and was an extremely proficient dressmaker. She readily agreed to make my wedding dress for me. My dress was to be in heavy white brocade with long sleeves and a deep V-neckline which was in-filled with delicate white lace. I did all the hand sewing on it myself and covered the row of buttons made to fasten the lace insert at the back of my gown. It was a real labour of love to sew up the yards and yards of the hemline by hand. There was interest at the back too with several deep pleats fanning out from waist to hem. To finish off the outfit, I was to wear a small silver tiara to hold in place a short flared veil. I had chosen a simple bouquet of sweet smelling white and pastel coloured freesias to carry.

My three sisters were to be my bridesmaids. I undertook to make their dresses myself, ably helped by my youngest sister, Mary, also trained in Porth County Girls School by Miss Griffiths. We chose white flocked tulle over turquoise taffeta for their long dresses. The simple sweet style suited my pretty young sisters very well indeed. Our house became a hive of activity as Mary and I cut, measured and sewed the dresses, hunched over the old treadle machine Mammy had inherited from someone or other but which had remained unused in the *cwtch* under the stairs until I had sought it out. My thirteen-year-old brother, Michael, was keen to help. He was allowed to turn the handle instead of my using the treadle as I sewed, until he went far too fast and was banned from touching the machine again.

At the same time I got down to building my "bottom drawer." I ordered matching sheets and pillow cases from Auntie Rosie's shop in candy pink and peach. I then set about embroidering them on the half an hour journey by train to and from school every day. I also bought satin-trimmed blankets to match them. I kept myself busy embroidering table-cloths and a set of settee and chair backs for my intended new home. Mammy and I planned the wedding and reception together. It was to take place in Saint Anne's Anglican Church which we had all attended regularly as a family. The reception was to be held in the church hall. There was no shortage of volunteers to help to prepare the wedding breakfast and serve at table. Mammy could count on her many friends and neighbours as well as on her fellow members of the Mothers' Union. All the arrangements were now in place ready for the big day. The whole house was filled with anticipation and happiness.

Vicar Holtham had replaced our beloved Vicar Pugh when he had been elevated to the position of Canon of the Diocese of Llandaff, Cardiff. Reluctant to take over the more important parish of Aberdare, Canon Pugh had died suddenly before having to leave his Ynyshir parish. I had always assumed that I would be able to hear the banns of my marriage called in my local church when the time came for me to wed. However, since Archie came from abroad, it appeared that this was impossible. We were interviewed by Vicar Holtham and gave him all the details of Archie's family and of their strong links with the Church Missionary Society and with Britain. It then became easy for our vicar to check up on what we had told him. Shortly afterwards he was able to reassure my parents that Archie did indeed come from a truly Christian family.

"You needn't worry, Mr. And Mrs. Stevens," he said. "Your daughter's fiancé comes from a very good and highly respected Christian family. Pat is marrying a real gentleman in Archie. They will be married in church, of course, but we are unable to call the banns for someone who comes from abroad."

The problem solved, we then discussed the sanctity of marriage and the vows we would make at several talks we held with Vicar Holtham who was happy to marry us in Saint Anne's.

Though everything seemed set fair for the wedding to take place shortly in Saint Anne's, a slight hiccough occurred unexpectedly. For some time my wisdom teeth had been troubling me. After repeated consultations with the dentist, several doses of antibiotics seemed to have solved the problem. At just the wrong moment, however, the pain and inflammation suddenly reoccurred. As a child, the orthodontist had removed two impacted teeth growing behind my upper row. This had totally corrected the problem without the need for braces, leaving my top teeth perfectly aligned with no gaping spaces between them. There was equally no room for my wisdom teeth either which were pronounced impacted. It was decided that they needed to be removed without delay. The dentist was unable to remove them in his surgery, so I was admitted to Cardiff Royal Infirmary for the extractions. I was glad to think that the problems with my teeth would now be solved before my wedding in four weeks' time.

The surgeon who spoke to me before the operation pointed out that I also had impacted fives which had grown behind my bottom teeth without causing me any trouble. He suggested extracting them at the same time to avoid possible problems in the future. Bowing to his superior knowledge, I agreed. How I wished later that I had not done so! When I returned to the ward after a three hour operation, eight teeth had been removed – four wisdom teeth, two impacted fives and the two teeth with which they had fused over the years. Counting the two removed from behind my front teeth, I had lost ten teeth in all, leaving me with only two small spaces in my bottom row which, fortunately, didn't show. My mouth was obviously too small for the generous size of my teeth. What a shock I got when I looked in the mirror after coming round. My face was badly swollen and discoloured. I was aghast to see the red, yellow and purple disfigured mess that met my eyes – and it was just four weeks to my wedding!

It didn't help when my sister, Ann, who was studying music in Cardiff University, visited me and blurted out:

"Oh Pat - you look terrible!"

You can imagine my reaction to that. She got the sharp end of my tongue and spent the rest of the visit trying to console me by saying that it wasn't really so bad and it would be better in good time for the big day. Nevertheless, I was inconsolable. I burst into floods of tears when Archie phoned me after her departure.

"I'll look an absolute mess on our wedding day," I sobbed.

"Don't worry, darling," he said. "The mouth heals fast and you'll be as right as rain in a few weeks. I'll come down tomorrow evening to visit you."

166

I was horrified at the thought of his seeing me in such a state, so I cut him off swiftly.

"Oh, no! Don't come down for just an evening. Visiting hours are not very long so it's a waste of time and money. Wait until I'm out of hospital then we will be able to spend the whole weekend together."

Reluctantly he agreed. In the end it all worked out for the best, as I could only drink soups and other liquids through a straw at first, then gradually return to solids. This meant that I lost weight without having to stick to a harsh diet so was neat and slim for my wedding day – and my face had healed completely too.

The day we had chosen was 29 March 1959. The wedding was to take place on Easter Saturday at 2 pm. This meant that all the church ladies came after midday to decorate the church for Easter Day. Fresh flowers and green foliage adorned every corner of Saint Anne's and perfumed the church. Not only did numerous representatives of our large Stevens' and Davies' families, members of Saint Anne's and invited guests come to wish us well, but the back pews were filled up with neighbours and villagers come to attend the wedding and to catch a glimpse of their first ever "foreigner." Others stood outside the old church wall to watch the arrival of the wedding party and, later, the photo sessions after the ceremony.

Daddy was so proud to walk down the aisle with his eldest daughter on his arm, radiant with happiness and veiled in pure white. Mammy had tears in her eyes as she watched us process down the aisle with her three pretty younger daughters in attendance. Archie looked up and met my eyes as the strains of the traditional Mendelssohn's wedding march heralded the arrival of his bride. Our church organist from Bristol had made the journey to Wales at Archie's request to play at our wedding. Archie had always loved organ music, especially Bach, and would slip into cathedrals and churches to listen to organ recitals at every opportunity. Vicar Holtham joined us in Holy Matrimony before all the witnesses then we made our Easter communion together as the first act of our married life. Love shone all around and about us.

The day was fine and, after the photographs were taken, we gathered in the church hall just next door for the reception. The tables had been set out and a real feast of salads, cold meats and cheeses etc. had been prepared by Mammy's church friends. Wine was also available and a splendid three-tiered wedding cake took pride of place in the centre of the top table. Speeches were made, toasts were drunk to the happy couple and gifts were given to the bridesmaids and other family members by the groom. Archie gave me a gold locket to wear at the wedding and my sisters received silver lockets. Time flashed by as we chatted to the well-wishers surrounding us. Then we changed into our going-away outfits in 7 William Street, ready to

167

set off on a week's honeymoon. I had made a very smart two piece suit for myself out of some expensive *Rodier* material in a fine Bordeaux wool with a bag and gloves to match. I had also bought a fake fur coat in a silver grey colour in case it was cold at that time of the year. I was certainly glad of it when we walked along the promenade in windy Porthcawl where we spent our honeymoon.

By this time we were the proud possessors of a small car. We had bought a "sit up and beg" Ford Popular about a year ago. While it went very well, it needed a lot of loving care to renovate it to a reasonable standard. We had set to work at once. Archie cleaned his car from top to bottom and rubbed it down to remove all the rust from the body. He was helped enthusiastically in this by my young brother, Michael, who was so happy that someone in the family now owned a car. Then it was given a protective coat of rust proof paint before Archie gave it a final coat of shiny black paint. The inside also needed renovating and that was left to me. I obtained some strong firm material and made a sort of lining for the panels of the whole car which Archie cleverly fitted to the insides of the four doors. We were now roadworthy and could shoot off on trips to all the beautiful tourist attractions in the West Country and South Wales. As Ann and Mary had flown the nest by this time to study in Cardiff and London, Michael was able to reap the rewards of his labours as he often accompanied us on these outings with Mammy and Daddy. Thus our guests saw us off in style in our little beribboned black car to drive to the Esplanade Hotel on the front in Porthcawl for our honeymoon.

We returned to Bristol for the second week of our holiday. We had found a lovely garden flat in Clifton Park Road for our first home. It was a two storey maisonette consisting of a living area with two spacious rooms, a small kitchen and a narrow store room at garden level and two double bedrooms and a bathroom on the ground floor above. Archie had moved in previously and had been busy renovating and decorating it ready for my arrival. I was delighted with it and set about making curtains and cushions to brighten it up.

Archie's father had given us a generous wedding gift of £1,000 so this had enabled us to buy all our furniture brand new. We had chosen it together on my weekend trips to Bristol and it was delivered bit by bit until we had created a delightful home together. Archie had never learned to do anything practical in his youth. However, he soon asked his "do-it-yourself" friends for advice and was quick to learn. He surprised me by even fitting skirting boards and constructing a collapsible wall table in our little kitchen. The Easter holiday soon came to an end and I had to return to my teaching job at Whitchurch. I could not countenance leaving in the middle of the school year, especially since my Headmaster had been brave enough to rescue me from Kingswood

Grammar without having references. So, with the new title of Mrs. Luther, I began a short period of commuting between Wales and Bristol.

During this time, I stayed at home with my family from Monday afternoon until Friday morning when I left for school in Whitchurch. After school on Friday, I took the train from Cardiff to Bristol where I was met by Archie. I returned to Whitchurch by train in time for school on Monday morning. We spent the weekend together working on the flat or shopping for furniture and other household necessities to embellish our new home. Naturally, I needed to look for a new job in Bristol for September. We searched through The Times Educational Supplement and the local papers for a suitable post.

There was very little going that year but I was called for interview for a post as teacher in charge of French in one of the new Secondary Modern Schools. The interview went quite well until my bright new wedding ring caught the eye of the Head.

"As a young married woman, are you contemplating starting a family in the next few years?" he questioned.

Although I assured him that a baby would not be on the cards for some years yet, he decided to offer the post to a single lady in her late thirties as a surer option. Secretly, I could not blame him, as my track record of only staying for one year in each of my first two posts did not augur well. Eventually, I was lucky to find that a temporary job for two terms in a direct grant convent school in Clifton was available from September. La Retraite could not have been more convenient for me. This time, my experience and the reference I had obtained from La Sainte Union in Bath stood me in good stead. I was offered the job to replace Sister Mary Theresa, a young novice, who was to spend two terms in Angers, France, where she would take her vows. She would then return to take up her post as French teacher at the school. This was ideal for me as it gave me time to find a permanent post while in full time teaching in the area. The school was well run, the staff were friendly and the pupils most amenable. I had landed on my feet. The school year in Wales coincided with the miners' holidays which were at the beginning of July that year. La Retraite started back later than the state schools at the end of September, so to top it all off I ended up with practically three months' paid summer holiday in the first year of my marriage. Everything in the garden was rosy.

* * * * *

None of Archie's family had been able to come over from Pakistan to attend our wedding although they had all sent their love and best wishes and were with us in their thoughts. Now that we were settled in our new home, his father decided to visit us. I looked forward to meeting my new father-in-law who had been so kind and generous to us. We made him comfortable in our spare room and tried our best to make his stay with us both happy and memorable. Archie had managed to change our old Popular for a swish Ford Consul so we could travel the country with him in style. We took him to visit all the pretty villages around Bristol and to stay with my family in Wales.

My parents were very pleased to entertain him and he got on well with everybody. He brought gifts with him for all the family from exotic Pakistan. He gave Mammy some typically Baluchistani hand-embroidered mirrored cushions. Made up in a rich golden silk, they took pride of place in her front room for the rest of her life. He attended church with us in Ynyshir as well as in Bristol and was delighted to visit such famous ruins as Tintern Abbey. He was well known in Anglican circles and was received by the Bishop of Bristol and asked to give some sermons in our local churches. He was very glad to see that his son had come through all his earlier problems and was now happily settled with a wife of whom he approved. Although our families were very different in terms of professional status and wealth, they could not have been more similar in their devotion to the Christian faith, their love of music and their ambition for their children to have the best educational opportunities.

My father-in-law stayed with us for about a month and returned home loaded with presents for the family. When watching me removing the carbon from the bottom of my new saucepans with Brillo, he was amazed to see the shine that resulted. I was most surprised when he bought a packet of Brillo to take back as one of his extra gifts for his sister, Aunty Lily! When the time came for him to return to Pakistan, we drove him to London airport to see him off, stopping off at Windsor Castle for a last visit together. We were sad to see him go but hoped that he would be able to come again soon to visit us or that we would make the trip to Quetta instead to meet the rest of the family.

Soon afterwards we decided to buy our own house. Archie had been promoted at work so was earning a reasonable salary and we had enough money left for the deposit from what Dr. Luther had given us. We found a nice three storey house in the corner of Whiteladies Road in Clifton. It was just off Whiteladies Hill which led directly to our familiar university area then down Park Street to the centre of Bristol. Our living section of the house was composed of the first and second floors consisting of a spacious lounge / dining room, a large kitchen and a toilet on the half landing between the two floors. There were two double bedrooms and a bathroom on the top floor. On the ground floor there was a small self-contained flat which was occupied by a young couple. We were happy to let them stay on as tenants to help pay the mortgage. Similarly, when I had started at La Retraite, I had met another new young teacher called Eileen Naylor from Liverpool. She was living in a bed and breakfast place and was looking for a room to let. Archie and I decided that we could let her have our spare room for the time being so she moved in with us. This extra rent boosted our income and the arrangement suited everyone.

After our marriage I had been quite prepared to put my salary into a joint account with Archie but he did not agree. He said that it was his duty to provide for his wife and that I should keep my own money in a separate account in my own name. He gave me a generous amount of housekeeping money and even insisted on my having a cleaning lady to come in once a week to do most of the housework. He said that as I was working full time, I needed to have help in the home. I had never been accustomed to such a luxury but I was more than happy to accept this new state of affairs. Most of my salary, however, went towards buying expensive appliances for the home, as I had a horror of buying anything on hire purchase. This stemmed from my early years when any little extras, and often essentials too, had to be bought by weekly instalments.

One day Archie appeared at the top of the stairs quite unexpectedly although I had been keeping a sharp look-out for his car to arrive in the street below our front window.

"I didn't see your car arrive," I said. "Where did you park it?"

"It's there in the usual place," he replied pointing to a sleek white Ford Zephyr at the curb-side. He had changed his Consul for this shiny new car without discussing it with me and having no ready money available, he had purchased it on H P. Immediately, I had insisted on using my savings to pay down for it. Although this emptied my personal account, I had no compunction in using it.

Life went on smoothly for us both. We had many friends still living in and around Bristol. We had attended Eileen and Andrew's wedding in the summer after ours and they had bought a house on the other side of Bristol where they both still worked. We saw them regularly as we did our friends Valerie and Fred who lived much closer in Aberdeen Road. We got back in contact with Archie's friend and fellow student, Bertrand Louis Quesnel du Quesnel (known as Bert in Bristol circles) with whom he had previously shared a flat. He was now married and living just around the corner from us with his wife, Dinah, who was not only Welsh but also a Bristol graduate and an ex-pupil of La Retraite. Archie and I played badminton together in a good club in Clifton. We also exchanged visits with my parents in Wales quite regularly.

Our social life was always quite full. We enjoyed meals out and often attended dinner dances with our friends. For such special occasions I would make a new dress, so I had fabricated a really glamorous dress and bolero for myself in exquisite black velvet to go to the Saint Valentine's Dance. We invited Eileen Naylor to join our group of friends. She was shy and didn't know anyone, so I asked Archie to dance with her. While they were dancing I was invited to dance. Without thinking, I accepted. Archie was not at all pleased and asked me not to dance with someone else when he was dancing with my friend at my request. In his Eastern culture, a wife would never dance with another man when accompanying her husband at a function. I was rather bemused but flattered by this little show of jealousy and was quick to do what I could to make it up to him. By the time we dropped off to sleep that night locked in each other's' arms, there was no sign of the little tiff. However, on 14 November nine months' later we would be happy to welcome the surprise result.

Archie had not been keen on starting a family immediately. He was happy to savour our free and easy life as a young couple able to do what we liked when we liked without any encumbrances. Apparently, like many young Asians, he had had his fortune told as a young man in Pakistan. Although the promise of new experiences, new friends and a happy marriage had delighted him, it was all spoilt when it was predicted that he would die young. Half-jokingly he said to me:

"Once you become a mother you will no longer be a wife. Our children will take my place in your heart."

"You don't believe that rubbish, do you?" I retorted. "These gypsies with their so-called crystal balls are just out to make money. Just forget it. We'll be just fine."

We never spoke of the subject again. I put it all totally out of my mind and life continued as before.

Archie applied for British citizenship and procured a new passport with the intention of going to Europe for holidays. We started to plan for a holiday in Italy during the school summer break. I began to feel sick in the mornings, but Archie was convinced that it could not possibly be *the* Morning Sickness heralding the imminent arrival of a new addition to the family. During the last two years Archie had frequent recurrences of the pains he had suffered when he had collapsed while playing a badminton match for the university. He consulted our doctor and underwent several X rays but nothing serious was diagnosed. Apart from a few short periods of sick leave, he soldiered on and we hoped things would soon clear up. Between bouts of "taking it easy" on doctor's orders, he continued to play sport and became captain of our local badminton club. As for me, when my bouts of morning sickness became severe, my pregnancy was soon confirmed and we reluctantly cancelled our planned trip to Italy for the summer holidays.

Archie's brother, Henry and his wife, Indira, had just completed further medical studies in America and decided to visit us before returning to

Pakistan. As Eileen had gone home for the holidays to Liverpool, we had a spare bedroom for them. Once more we embarked on day trips in the car to show them as much of the West Country as possible during their stay – this time with obligatory stops for me to be sick on the way. Apart from that, I was extremely fit and gave myself leave to eat for two. Archie, now accepting the coming birth of our first child, spoilt me dreadfully by pandering to my every whim, buying me boxes of strawberries, chocolates and anything I fancied. I put on far too much weight not realising how difficult it would be to shed it after the birth.

Out of the blue, one of Archie's work colleagues, who owned a caravan, was kind enough to lend it to us to take our guests for a week to Devon. Unfortunately the weather was most unkind. Rain and wind rocked the flimsy frame of the caravan and we were unable to take advantage of the lovely beaches or to swim in the sea. It became too uncomfortable for four adults to remain locked up in the constricted space while summer storms raged outside, so we packed up and returned home. Despite such problems, Heno and Indu thoroughly enjoyed staying with us. It was a unique opportunity for them to get to know us as a couple and for me to forge family bonds on Archie's side.

After my first two terms at La Retraite, I had worked as a supply teacher until the end of the school year. I had my first brief experience of teaching in a Junior School and ended with a stint in a Secondary Modern School where I introduced French. The Headmaster was delighted and offered me a permanent post but La Retraite was also happy to have me back. As they were actually making room for me, I was asked to teach some first year maths as well as my French assignment. I had accepted this offer without hesitation as I enjoyed teaching there and it was so close to my home. It was with mixed feelings therefore that I tended my resignation at the end of July after only one year. As soon as I was at home during the day, Archie bought a sweet little terrier as a pet. We were warned that spoilt dogs could become jealous of babies who usurped their place in their master's affections, but fortunately we had no problem with *Bijou*. We named him *Bijou* (meaning Jewel) because he was a beautifully-marked Jack Russell with diamond-shaped brown and black patterns on his smooth white coat.

I was very excited and threw myself into acquiring all the necessary paraphernalia for the coming birth. I also bought an electric sewing machine and set about making baby items like embroidered dresses, rompers, hats, cot and pram coverlets, while Mammy knitted mountains of pretty matinee coats, bootees and bonnets. Before long everything was ready and I became impatient awaiting the birth, especially as it appeared to be overdue. On meeting me, friends would say,

"Haven't you had the baby yet?"

Eventually, Dr Cowie admitted me to Clifton Maternity Hospital and set about encouraging the reluctant baby to make an appearance. Mammy had come to Bristol to be with us for the birth of her first grandchild and was with Archie and me at visiting time. I felt the first little twinges in mid-afternoon and by the time they left, the contractions were quite regular. I was so excited, but the nurse told Archie that there would be no news until the next morning. I was taken to the labour ward at about 9pm and after only approximately one hour of final stage labour, Mark was born safely at 1am on 14th November 1961. Archie was given the news when he rang at 6am before leaving for work. I was overjoyed with my beautiful, healthy baby boy. He fed immediately he was put to the breast and slept contentedly. The nurses said that he must have been here before.

Archie and Mammy had no problem in picking him out from amongst the row of babies in their cots, as he resembled his father so much. They were both bursting with pride as they walked into the ward, Mammy carrying the huge bouquet of flowers that Archie was too embarrassed to carry himself. Before the birth, Archie had warned me that I would still be a wife as well as a mother, but his own attitude changed completely as soon as his son was born. The first thing I would hear as he entered the house on returning from work, was his voice calling Mark's name and little endearments as he mounted the stairs. He bought a child's car seat which he placed next to the driver on the front bench seat of his car. He would prop his sturdy son up in it to take him out and show him off proudly to all and sundry, while I busied myself in the house.

Mark's cot was put into our bedroom and after a short period of colic he settled into a good routine. He was bright and lively during the day and slept well at night. I would feed him on going to bed late at night so he rarely woke us until about 7a.m. He made good progress and was a happy little soul who brought great joy to both his parents. He was christened in All Saints Church, Clifton, and the top tier of our wedding cake was brought out along with champagne for the toasts. Morfydd and Bernard and Eileen and Andrew were Godparents. All our family and friends were there to share in the celebrations and everything in the garden was, once again, rosy.

# Chapter 15
# A Bolt from the Blue

The third year of our married life saw us established as a small nuclear family well settled into a pleasant regular routine. Archie went out to work to provide for our needs while I organised the running of the house. I had everything I wanted out of life – a loving husband, a thriving baby, a comfortable home, lots of friends and Bijou, our cute little dog. To cap it all, a second baby was now on the way and we both hoped for a little girl to complete our pigeon pair. I would bath Mark, feed the dog, tidy the house, do any necessary light shopping, then take Mark and Bijou out for a walk, usually meeting up with friends and their young children. We would then return home and with a tasty meal prepared, await the return of the man of the house.

"Hudou, Hudou, Hudou," would ring out as Archie climbed the stairs two at a time to pick up his beloved son as he chanted one of his many Asian pet names for him. Mark was usually wide awake seeming to recognise the familiar voice and ready to respond with wide smiles and chuckles. Having been told that new born babies slept most of the day, I was surprised to see that Mark's eyes were usually wide open almost all of the time. He didn't seem to want to miss anything that was going on. Bijou was equally welcoming and would jump up and down excitedly around Archie's feet.

Life continued to be good. We were both young, optimistic and in the prime of life. We were invincible. Nothing bad could happen to us. Neither of us had heeded the warning signs, although they are plain to see in retrospect. Ever since that first frightening episode that had laid Archie low so suddenly while playing his badminton match as a student, he had experienced recurrent pains in his chest, left arm and shoulder. When these were severe, he had consulted the doctor and had occasionally been sent to the hospital for various X-rays and tests but nothing serious had been diagnosed. Like us, the medical team thought him to be young and intrinsically fit and attributed his pains to the fact that he was an athlete and was straining his muscles by overdoing things. He was given little medication and told to "take it easy" until he felt better. We were still blissfully unaware that catastrophe was looming. Then, out of the blue, lightning struck.

One evening without any warning Archie was struck down with exactly the same symptoms as he had suffered at the time of his collapse during the university badminton match. This time the incident did not occur during a period of strenuous activity but just before we were about to retire to bed after a normal stress-free day. He had excruciating pain in his chest, back

175

and particularly down his left shoulder and arm. He was soaked with sweat as though a bucket of cold water had been thrown over him. Of course the memory of that previous episode immediately flashed through my mind. I urged him to let me call the doctor, as he was obviously in great pain, shivering and had turned a very strange pasty colour.

"No, don't call him yet. It's very late now; we'll call him first thing in the morning. I'll be alright if I go straight to bed and rest," insisted Archie.

"I don't think we should wait. You are in too much pain and I don't like the look of you. He needs to see you now," I argued.

"No Pat, I'll be alright, really. I'll take some of those Phensics I still have left and we'll get him in the morning."

There was no arguing with him so we went to bed. He was very brave and did not moan and groan and complain about the agony he was in. We passed a very restless night and were up with the dawn. The sheets and Archie's pyjamas were ringing wet, so he took a bath and put on fresh pyjamas while I changed the sheets.

When Dr Cowie arrived, Archie recounted his symptoms in a calm, clear and professional manner. He was no longer sweating profusely and not wishing to frighten me, managed to hide the fact that he was in agonising pain. After carrying out a series of tests, Dr Cowie diagnosed "severe dorsal strain" and prescribed complete rest for two weeks with Phensics for the pain. As I saw the doctor out at the door, I told him that I was very worried about Archie and recounted to him the previous incident from Archie's student days. I described the symptoms in detail which were exactly similar in all respects to those experienced the night before. Dr Cowie reassured me, however, saying that "a little knowledge was a dangerous thing" and that Archie was not suffering from angina as he had suggested, but simply of a recurrence of over strain, such as occurred regularly in young athletes. He was confident that when Archie came to see him at the end of his fortnight's sick leave, he would be well on the way to recovery. With that, he left.

From then onwards, Archie continued to experience severe pain in his chest, back and left arm. He only kept to his bed for a few days. Shortly afterwards, he started to get up slowly, dress and sit around watching me bath little Mark and do the usual morning chores. He felt most frustrated, as he could not help me in any way, but he was very happy to dangle his son on his knee once I had placed him in his lap after his toilet and feed were over. He never spoke of his pain but when I enquired once about it he told me,

"I think that someone must have cursed me, darling. The pain is so excruciating."

I cuddled and comforted him as best I could but that did nothing to allay my fears. So we continued, sharing each precious minute of our day together, little thinking that there were so very few left to share. Later I remembered another little tell-tale sign that I had thoughtlessly disregarded. One evening when I had felt too tired to accompany Archie to our local pub for a drink, I had persuaded him to go alone to meet his friend, Gem. I became a little anxious when he was late coming home. Eventually, after the click of the front door, I heard Archie calling out softly as he mounted the stairs on his hands and knees,

"I'm sorry I'm late. Don't scold me, Baby. I haven't got long to live."

Naturally, I took it as a way of avoiding a little argument and replied,

"Don't think you can get around me like that. Where have you been until now?" and then I burst out laughing.

He then reminded me of what had had been foretold before he came to England. No long, happy life was predicted for him. He was told that he would marry and have children but that no sooner would his wife become a mother than she would no longer be a wife. Obviously, the practice of fortune telling, very prevalent in Asian countries, exerted a strong influence on Archie's way of thinking. That must have been the reason that he wanted to delay starting a family after we had set up home, as he believed that he would die soon after becoming a father. Such things were far from my thoughts at this time. I looked for any little signs of improvement in him and still had great hopes for a bright future together.

Since he was expecting to be better by the end of two weeks, Archie forced himself to try to go for short walks with us. Leaning heavily on the pram, he managed to accompany us as we went to meet our friends in the close locality. One afternoon, we were on our way to visit my friend, Valerie, who lived nearby, when a sudden shower forced me to run to avoid getting Mark and me drenched. Grabbing the handlebar, I had started off before I realised that Archie was panting hard and could in no way keep pace with a seven-month pregnant woman pushing a baby in a heavy pram. He lumbered after us with great difficulty and eventually arrived safely at our friends' house. It was now obvious that he was in no fit state to resume work after only two weeks' rest. When he attended his consultation with Dr Cowie, he was diagnosed with "slight pleurisy in the left lung" and prescribed antibiotics and Phensic for the pain. He was given another two weeks off work.

Recovery was much slower than we had hoped but now that the doctor had at last found out what was wrong and was treating it, we hoped that he would soon be better. Mammy was concerned to hear that Archie was not making good progress and was also pleased to know that a treatable illness had been finally diagnosed. She was really missing her only grandchild and wanted to come to Bristol to see us all. Ann was doing her Teacher Training year in Cardiff, so they decided to come up for the day together by train. I was very pleased to see them and we spent a lovely day with them, Mark taking full advantage of being spoiled by his Nanny and Aunty Ann. Archie managed to drive to the station to pick them up but was unable to suggest taking them on a trip anywhere. He did, however, run them back to catch their train, though Mammy wanted to go by bus, as she could see that Archie was totally exhausted. On the way home in the train she told Ann that she didn't like the look of Archie at all. His grey colour gave her great concern. On her return, neighbours and friends inquired,

"How are Pat and baby Mark doing?"

"Oh, they are both fine. It's Archie I'm worried about. I don't like the look of him at all," came the reply. My sister, Mary, with her boyfriend, Vince, decided to put off their planned visit to us until after their holiday in Scotland due to Archie's illness – a thing she bitterly regretted later.

Another week had passed and it was time to think about opening up the Badminton Club for the autumn season. Being captain, Archie felt that he was obliged to be there on the first night, although he was still very unwell and in no way fit to play. Nevertheless, he packed us all in the car with me and Mark comfortable in his carry cot on the back seat and Bijou on his lead, calmly sitting beside him. Everyone was so pleased to see us and made a great fuss of Mark and our very well-behaved puppy. Of course, they were sorry that Archie was unable to play and hoped that he would be his old energetic self by the following week. It was obvious that he was not quite his usual sociable self always ready to recount interesting and amusing anecdotes. We stayed for a while enjoying the pleasant company and then went home to bed.

By this time, the ground floor flat had become vacant and Eileen Naylor had moved in there so that we could convert her bedroom into a nursery for Mark. The end of the second fortnight was in sight and Archie thought that we ought to make an effort to go to choose the paint and paper to decorate the nursery before he was to return to work. We all climbed into the car and drove off to the centre of Bristol. After sauntering gently through several shops, we found what we wanted and made our choice. Archie was very keen that the expected new arrival should be a little girl "just like her mother" and must be called Patricia after her. I accepted this so long as it was to be her second name and we decided that she would be known by the pretty Welsh name of Sian. Thus the nursery was to be decorated in both blue and pink with the alphabet illustrated with pretty pictures in a border around the room.

Happy with our purchases, Archie wanted to take us out for a short ride in the country, as we seemed to have been stuck indoors for so long. He suggested going to visit Prinknash Abbey which was only a short distance away. It was a beautiful afternoon as we drove through the countryside. I was very happy sitting next to my husband with our chirpy son Mark between us in his car seat watching everything that was going on and Bijou jumping up and down on the back seat. We admired the beautiful abbey as we strolled through it and stopped to buy three porcelain mugs with our three initials A, P and M as souvenirs of our visit. On the way home, we talked about decorating the nursery and installing Mark in it well before the new baby was to be born. I couldn't wait to get it all done.

Once home, we unpacked and put a very tired baby down to sleep. Archie was to go to see Dr Cowie the next day hoping to be signed off to go back to work on Monday. After a light meal, Archie said that he thought he would go for a short walk with Bijou and call in at his local pub to say hello to his friends whom he had not seen for some time. Thinking that he must be feeling better and that it would do him good, I encouraged him in this and so he went out. When he entered the pub, he was warmly greeted by many friends who were surprised and happy to see him after so long. The barman placed a pint of his favourite Worthington in front of him. It had been paid for in advance by a friend to be given to Archie as soon as he showed his face in the pub. He was touched by this mark of friendship and though he did not really feel like drinking, he drank it down, enjoying the cheerful atmosphere surrounding him. It was with difficulty that he refused further drinks and then he left the pub, promising to see them all again soon, Bijou trotting at his heels.

He had scarcely walked a few yards from the pub before he collapsed and fell unconscious to the ground. No one came to help him as he lay alone on the pavement. Maybe passers-by took him for a drunk and simply went on their way. Bijou seemed to know that something was wrong and stayed by his side, barking and licking his face. This appeared to have brought Archie around and he staggered up and made his way slowly home.

I was shocked when I saw him. He looked all in. He sat slumped in his chair, his face a dreadful grey colour.

"We must get the doctor immediately," I insisted.

"Not at all. I have an appointment tomorrow morning so what's the point of getting him out at this time of night?"

I gave him a drink of water and left him to rest in front of the fire pretending to be going down to the toilet. Instead I went straight down to the bottom flat and asked Eileen if she would be kind enough to go and 'phone the doctor for us. There was a red telephone kiosk at the corner of our street. Before she could leave, Archie appeared in the doorway and totally forbade her to call the doctor on his behalf. He insisted that there was no need, since he was to see Dr Cowie in the morning and would be alright until then. Nothing more could be done so we went back upstairs and prepared to go to bed.

"Would you like some supper, love?" I asked.

"No thanks. I don't really feel like anything. I just want to go to bed and sleep."

"Well, I'll just make us both a nice hot drink of Horlicks in our brand new mugs. That will help you get off to sleep."

So we sat quietly together sipping our drinks in front of the fire and then went up to bed.

Archie seemed to drop off to sleep almost immediately but I tossed and turned for some time before eventually falling asleep too. My restless slumber was disturbed when I felt movement beside me. Archie was getting out of bed.

"What's the matter, love? Are you alright?"

"I'm OK. I just need to go to the toilet. You go back to sleep, darling."

He managed to descend the steep narrow stairway as far as the toilet on the half-landing with a slow, shambling gait and then to make his way up once more to the bedroom. I waited anxiously until he had returned and got back into bed. Archie reassured me once again that there was nothing wrong. I put my arms around him and snuggled up close.

"Go back to sleep then, love," and I kissed him.

Suddenly, I was fully awake. A rather strange loud noise was coming from the other side of the bed. I quickly switched on the light and started to shake Archie to wake him as he seemed to be fast asleep and snoring very loudly.

"Archie! Wake up! Please wake up, darling," I pleaded.

It had absolutely no effect and I realised in horror that he had completely lost consciousness. Unable to lift him, I stumbled down the stairs towards the ground floor calling,

"Eileen, Eileen! Please come and help me. I can't wake Archie and I want to give him a drink."

Eileen came up and helped me to get Archie into a sitting position and try to give him a drink of brandy. All this time, the harsh rattling sound was getting louder and louder. Eileen looked absolutely terrified and rushed away fast when I begged her to go to 'phone for the doctor. Disturbed by all the noise, Bijou started barking and scratching at the kitchen door. A loud wail came from the nursery next door.

In the midst of this mayhem, a sudden eyrie silence occurred back in the bedroom. I could no longer seem to hear my husband breathing. I took him in my arms and placed my head on his chest but could hear absolutely nothing.

"Hurry - hurry, Eileen! I think he's stopped breathing. Go quickly!" I shrieked.

Frantically, I ran to find Archie's stethoscope and placed it in my ears and on Archie's chest. An unearthly silence. It can't be working! It's not possible! I turned it on to my own chest. Bang, bang, bang. The noise was shattering. There was absolutely no doubt at all that my heart was thumping fast and furiously like a loud drum booming out and shattering the silence of the night with its relentless thunderous beat. I jerked the stethoscope away and placed it back on Archie's chest. Still nothing. Something must be wrong. I'm not on the right spot. The leads have got loose. It just can't be! The dreadful truth hit me and I let out a piercing scream. I had lost my dearest love. Sobbing, I took my beloved in my arms as my tears flowed over his still face.

"Eileen, Eileen. Has the doctor come?"

"I'm just going to 'phone now," was the incredible reply.

What to me seemed like an eternity could have been no more than a couple of minutes while Eileen was throwing on some clothes before going out into the night.

"Oh, please go now. Don't wait. Just put on your coat. Archie's not breathing at all!"

A loud wail broke into my consciousness – oh yes, Mark. Did I wake him? Have I frightened him? I could no longer ignore the baby who was now shouting at the top of his voice and weeping as though his heart would break. I dashed into his room. He was standing up in his cot, his little flushed face wet with tears, his hands held out to me. I gathered him up into my arms and tried to soothe him. I then ran downstairs and out into the street, the inconsolable baby still weeping in my arms, wildly shouting,

"Oh God, please help us. Please, please, don't let Archie die! Somebody help me. My husband is dying!" before running back upstairs and down again, Mark still clutched tight to my chest. Locked in the kitchen, Bijou's frantic barking and scratching added to the commotion. By this time, the noise had disturbed a number of people who were looking out of their bedroom windows or standing on their front doorsteps, clad only in their dressing gowns. One lady, who said she was a nurse, tried to calm me.

"You must sit down. You'll harm your unborn baby if you're not careful and you are really frightening your little boy. Try to calm down. The doctor will be here soon."

Dr Cowie eventually arrived after what seemed like hours to me. We went up to the bedroom together while someone took charge of little Mark.

"Can you do something, doctor? Oh, please do something!"

"Let me examine him. You just kneel down by the bed and pray," was his reply.

Hope flared once more. I prayed incoherently for a miracle, the jumbled words tumbling over one another in my desperation. The doctor proceeded to do all the necessary tests one after the other. Finally he sat me down on the edge of the bed.

"I'm afraid I can do nothing more. Archie has passed away. He is with God. We must pray for his soul," he said, trying to comfort me. I have little recollection of events after this. He must have contacted the hospital. It appears that he was unable to issue a death certificate, as he could not state the cause of this totally unexpected death in such a young, apparently fit man. Archie was thirty-two at the time of his death at 3am on 3 October 1962. I was left at twenty-seven years old, seven months pregnant, to bring up my ten and a half month old son and his yet unborn sibling alone.

The ambulance arrived and Archie was taken away for a post-mortem examination at the hospital. The cause of death was diagnosed as coronary thrombosis. Eileen must have informed my friends Valerie and Fred of what had happened, so they were soon by my side, well before dawn. They took charge of everything. Early that morning they phoned my parents' neighbour Rose Griffiths asking her to go to tell them of the tragedy that had occurred.

A loud knock sounded on the door of 7 William Street, Ynyshir. Mammy was already awake. She had a sort of premonition that something was wrong.

"I'm sorry to say that I have some bad news for you, Annie May. But don't worry. It's not Pat," said Rose quickly without taking a breath.

"No. It's Archie, isn't it?" replied Mammy.

"I'm afraid it is. Archie died suddenly at home at 3 o'clock this morning. Some friends are looking after Pat and the baby until you can get to Bristol."

"But there's a rail strike on today. There'll be no trains. How will we be able to get there?"

"Don't you worry, Annie May. Fred is on his way from Bristol by car to pick you and Tom up and take you both straight to Pat. You just get your things together and be ready to leave as soon as he arrives. Valerie is staying with Pat to look after her until you get there," said Rose.

Good friends are invaluable at a time like this. Thanks to Valerie and Fred, my parents arrived at my side by lunchtime. Mammy stayed with me until well after the birth of my second child. Michael went to stay with Bopa near Porth Sec and walked back-and-fore to school with Cousin Rosemary until Daddy returned to go back to work. They managed quite well together until Ann came home from Cardiff at the weekend to look after them and almost poisoned them by undercooking the pork she produced for Sunday dinner and mistaking daffodil bulbs for onions.

There was one thing, however, that nobody else could do for me. Archie's father had received a stark telegram telling him of the sudden, untimely death of his youngest son. Only I could tell his heartbroken father of the circumstances of Archie's death. I sat down and wrote a long letter to him explaining the exact circumstances of what had happened prior to the sudden death of his son. I told him that although Archie had been under the care of the doctor for about a month, he had failed to diagnose heart problems and that consequently Archie had died suddenly of a severe coronary thrombosis. He was relieved to know that Archie had taken Holy Communion shortly before his death but remained absolutely inconsolable. He kept repeating that he wished God had taken him, an old man, rather than his dearly loved young son.

As soon as word had got around that Archie had died, tributes and expressions of sympathy flooded in. They came from everywhere – our families, friends – people who knew us both, friends from Archie's student days, and even old friends from abroad who had somehow got to hear of our loss from somewhere or other – Archie's work colleagues from The National Smelting Company, members of the two churches we attended, members of the Clifton Badminton Club and, though I was no longer teaching there, staff and pupils of La Retraite Convent School. It spoke volumes for the great affection and respect in which Archie was held by all who knew him.

This knowledge gave me some measure of comfort but it is hard to understand how we manage to get through such devastating blows without totally collapsing under them. I remember that my dear friend, Vendla, told me that her mother, a committed and practising Catholic, always said that God never gave us more than we were able to bear. He would uphold us in our darkest days. Indeed, my greatest consolation came from my Christian faith. I seemed to know in my heart that Archie was at peace and in the bosom of God. Though none of us are perfect, Archie was an intrinsically good, kind, loving person who was always ready to help others. Though I was desolate at his loss, the hymn "I know that my Redeemer liveth" kept ringing in my head day and night. This gave me great comfort. I just knew without any doubt that Archie was in a better place, free from pain and that he had been taken suddenly, being spared the realisation that he was leaving me alone to bring up our children. Masses were said for him at the convent and when Reverend Mother came to pray at Archie's side in the chapel of rest, she was very touched to see how very young he looked. We lived very close to Christ Church, Clifton, so we had attended services there for some time. It was there that Mark had been christened. Nevertheless, we had always kept in close touch with Rev Vyvian Jones of Saint Michael's, Cotham, who was an invaluable support to me at this time. He took a full part in the funeral service which was held at Christ Church.

The church was packed full. My large family in particular rallied round in great numbers to support me. Aunties Florrie and Olwen came with their husbands from Bournemouth, Aunty Iris, though suffering from very painful rheumatoid arthritis, came from Nuneaton, while a large contingent of my father's brothers and sisters made their way to Bristol from Wattstown in the Rhondda. All were very shocked and sad at the death of my young husband. Archie's family could not arrange to be there in time for the funeral but were certainly with us in their prayers that day. Miss Stocken, Dr Luther's old friend from the Church Missionary Society, made the journey all the way from Kent to represent him and the family at the funeral. A young couple who lived just a few doors away and who had a son, Paul, just a month or so older than Mark, looked after him while we were all at the funeral. All I remember of the service was that it was very solemn and moving but I went through it as in a trance. One of my Catholic friends from La Retraite, loaned me her black mantilla to cover my head as I, alone, followed the coffin down the aisle, dressed all in black.

In those days, the widow usually stayed at home with the ladies of her family around her, but I was determined to follow my husband to his final resting place, in a family plot at Westbury Cemetery, Bristol. God gave me strength to go through all this without faltering. The grave was covered with floral wreaths from all our relatives and friends. In our early days together, I once taunted Archie, saying accusingly,

"I thought you didn't love me," to which he had replied,

"Love you? I adore you. I worship you."

Love as deep as that can never die. It remains in the heart to uphold and sustain the loved one throughout life. Thus I wrote on the card accompanying the flowers I placed on his grave:

"Dearest Archie,

Thank you for giving me a lifetime of happiness in the few short years we shared together. All my love, Pat."

I had managed to hold myself together throughout the church service and the committal at the graveside. However, back at home in the midst of my protective family, I dissolved into irrepressible tears. I nursed my little boy in my arms. Although so young, he seemed to know that I was sad and in need of comfort. He looked right up at me and put his tiny hand on my face in a soothing gesture. There was an inexplicable feeling of empathy between us which gave me some relief. My terrible grief was partially numbed in the atmosphere of love and support surrounding me.

In this strange atmosphere life began to take on some semblance of normality once again. The funeral now over, people returned to their homes promising to be there for me whenever I needed help. Even Daddy was forced most reluctantly to leave us in order to go back to work. Only Mammy stayed on in Bristol with me. Of course we had lost the sole breadwinner in the family. Fortunately, the house was on Archie's name alone and, as it was well insured, it became mine outright. This was a great financial relief, of course, as was the lump sum of more than £4,000 paid out to me from Archie's work. Archie had also started to pay insurance for Mark's education and that was paid out swiftly and without any hitches. This was due mainly to the help I received from our insurer, Phil Lewis, a fellow Welshman, who helped me enormously with all the complicated administration to be done following a death. He took me to register the death, dealt with probate for me and even advised me on how to invest the money I had received. He was a totally honest and trustworthy man and I relied on him utterly. He was a true friend to me and I am eternally grateful for all his help.

I received help too from an unexpected source. I had only met Pam and Les since Mark's birth, when we found ourselves attending the baby clinic together. Paul was just two months older than Mark and the two babies played happily together. This kind young couple decorated the nursery for me, using the paper and paint that Archie and I had bought for that purpose. They took Mammy and me shopping once a week to transport the heavy goods in their car. Les ordered the coal and then carried in the bags and emptied them into the store-room under the stairs for us. This was invaluable help during the big freeze of 1963 for Mammy and me.

Archie's car, his pride and joy, stood dejectedly outside our front door until a friend of his sold it at quite a good price for me. I had not yet passed my driving test at that stage. I had learnt to drive a couple of years before but I found our large cars difficult to manage. After circumnavigating Bristol through heavy Christmas traffic, I was failed for not adjusting my speed to other vehicles, pedestrians and cyclists and on gears. Our car at the time, a big Morris Oxford, had gears on the steering wheel. I was stopped on an incline to negotiate my reversing around a corner. Thinking that I had put the car into first gear, I rolled slowly down but the car did not react to the accelerator when I pressed it to mount the incline on the other side. I soon found out my mistake and changed from neutral to first gear and finished the manoeuvre successfully – but too late to pass that day! I retook it in February on a nasty rainy day. This time I was confident I would pass but failed for driving too fast. I was over confident. At the time, I was pregnant with Mark, so we decided to postpone the test for the time being. I eventually passed my test with no problem at all, having been well schooled by Uncle Ted, when it became absolutely essential for me to have transport to go to work and be able to get about with my two little children.

Mammy and I ran the home competently between us. We tried to get back into some sort of a routine so we took Mark and Bijou out for walks regularly in the autumn sunshine, often visiting Valerie and Fred and other friends in the vicinity. Mark slept in his cot in the nursery next door to me as I wanted him to get used to it before the new baby arrived. This room had to act as our guest room as well, so Mammy slept in the double bed there. However she found that more often than not she had company in her bed at night. Whenever she went to bed, Mark would be found wide awake, standing bolt upright with his hands held out to be taken in with her. He rarely failed to get his way and usually ended up *cwtching up* (cuddling up) to his Nanny all night long, his little hand always on her neck. It was understandable that he should miss his adoring father and he became quite clingy with his Nanny. With the security of the constant love and protection of his mother and grandmother though, he continued to be a very easy, happy child who slept through the night and began to speak at a very early age. The first word he spoke was "Biou, Biou" as he called out to his little dog. For his part, Bijou never snapped at him and allowed him to stroke him even when Mark proved less than gentle with him.

Mammy stayed with me permanently, though she worried a bit about how Daddy and Michael were coping without her. We were so glad to see them when they managed to come up to spend weekends with us. My sisters also visited us in turns whenever possible. The baby was expected in December but Christmas was approaching and there was no sign of an imminent arrival. It was therefore decided that the whole family would spend Christmas together in Bristol. By Christmas Eve we had all gathered in 20 Sunningdale to celebrate the joyous Christian festival together and hopefully the birth of the new addition to the family. Archie was sorely missed at this time, of course, but we concentrated on the hope of receiving a very special Christmas present for all of us. Since there was no sign of anything about to happen, the whole family went to Midnight Mass at Christ Church, leaving Michael and me at home. Christmas day passed too with turkey dinner, Christmas pud, crackers and all the trimmings – but no new baby joined us. The Reverend Vyvian Jones came to the house on Boxing Day morning to give Michael and me our Christmas communion. As I was taking it, I felt the first tiny twinges. Could the baby have decided to make an appearance today at last? Excited, I called out to Mammy as soon as Rev Jones had left,

"I think it's started, Mammy. We'd better have dinner *now*. I'll get the cot and blankets ready."

The baby was to be born at home, as I couldn't face being in a maternity hospital amongst all the mothers being visited by their husbands. Anyway, since I had experienced so little difficulty with Mark's birth, there was no reason why I shouldn't be quite alright under the care of a qualified midwife. Bernard, Morfydd's husband, who was a doctor, was staying with us. I also had Mammy and Mary, who was then a nurse and midwife in training, at hand in an emergency. There was certainly no lack of medical care should it be required. The midwife was sent for, lunch was eaten and everything made ready.

By mid afternoon, the midwife arrived accompanied by a young African nurse under training, so I was very well cared for indeed. It was none too soon either, as the little baby seemed determined to make an appearance before the aunts and uncles had to leave to return home. A strong, lusty little baby, my daughter, forced her way out into the world on 26th December 1962 within an hour or so of the midwife's arrival. The final stage of labour was over in less than ten minutes, as she pushed her way through without giving me time to catch my breath. It was all well worth it all the same as I gazed

186

in wonder at my beautiful little angel sent to comfort me. Weighing just over eight pounds, she was perfection itself. No red, wizened, little old person had entered the world but a sweet, rosy-cheeked, blue-eyed baby girl had come to bring us joy at last. She was the answer to her father's prayer – the little girl to be named after her mother to complete our "pigeon pair." She was the miracle child who had stayed curled up cosily in her mother's womb, not stirring despite all the grief and turmoil surrounding her, until she could emerge unscathed, to reintroduce joy and happiness into our lives at Christmas.

Much discussion as to what she was to be called had taken place before the birth. Finally, I had decided that a boy would be called Archie and a girl, Angie, a shortened form of Angela. Thus in deference to Archie's wishes, she was christened Angela Patricia. Everyone crowded round to admire the new- born child. Mark, not to be left out, put his index finger into her tiny hand and she grasped it firmly. Delighted, he sang out "Annie, Annie, Baby" as he stroked her face gently. He had quickly picked up the name and added it to his growing vocabulary at thirteen months old. My efforts to bring Angie into the world had not dulled my appetite in any way. Mammy had made a lovely trifle for tea and I was quite ready for it by five o'clock. With the new baby sleeping peacefully in her cot, we all trouped down for tea before some members of the family had to make tracks for home.

What a surprise was in store for us when looking out of the window; we were met with a winter wonderland. We had not noticed that during the excitement of the birth, heavy snow had laid a thick white blanket over the entire city. Bernard was on call at the hospital the next morning, so he and Morfydd made haste to pack up to leave. A blizzard was blowing and there was no way they would be able to drive to London that night, so they called a taxi to take them to the station and had to return to London by train. This was the beginning of the great freeze of 1963 when roads were impassable and pipes burst in the streets in every city, bringing large parts of the country to a virtual standstill. Little Angie, confined with Mammy, Mark, Bijou and me to the house for the first six weeks of her life, never put her nose outside the door in that bitter weather. However, as our kind neighbour Les had got in a good supply of coal for our back boiler, Mammy and I kept it going full blast so that the central heating kept every room in the house warm and cosy and prevented our pipes from freezing. The self-sacrifice and love of my parents had meant that we had got through these first difficult and painful months better than anyone could have expected and were now almost ready to face the world again and to make a new life together.

# Chapter 16
# Pakistan

Now that there was a glimmer of light at the end of the tunnel, it was time to make some decisions. Mammy could not stay on with us indefinitely. She needed to go back home to Wales to look after Daddy and Michael once more. On the other hand, my father-in-law wished to be able to do something to help us and invited us to come to stay with him, Henry and Indira in Quetta. At first it seemed to be too big an undertaking for me to even contemplate journeying to the other end of the world with my two tiny babies. However, I felt a great need to be with the one other person who had suffered a similar loss as I had and whose love for Archie was as deep. By mid-February, Angie was thriving despite the severe winter we had experienced. I told my parents that I was seriously considering taking the children to stay with their grandfather Luther in Pakistan. Naturally, they were worried about my undertaking such a long voyage alone with the babies. Nevertheless, they knew that once there, we would be in safe hands and well cared for at the mission hospital with our family. I consulted Dr Cowie who advised me to wait until Angie had had all the necessary vaccinations before leaving the country.

Our first short trial journey was to Wales. Mammy and I packed up all the necessary paraphernalia for the children and travelled home to the Rhondda to stay with Daddy and Michael for two or three weeks. Getting away from Bristol and its recent associated trauma, I managed to derive some pleasure from caring for the children and taking them round to see my aunts and uncles and all my old friends and neighbours. A great fuss was made of them everywhere. Of course, Bijou could not be left behind. He settled reasonably well in 7 William Street and loved being taken for long walks to accompany my father to his mountain allotment in Wattstown.

Unfortunately, there was one problem. When the postman dropped the letters through the front door, Bijou would rush along the passage as fast as his little legs could carry him barking fiercely all the time. One day the door was ajar and he defended his territory by nipping the postman's ankle. He was reported and Daddy was summoned to court for keeping a 'dangerous' dog. We were all terrified that Archie's beloved dog would be put down, but he was saved by pleading that he was grieving for his deceased master and had been taken away from his home. He was reprieved by an understanding judge and the article that appeared in the local paper that day was entitled:

"Curb that suffering dog!"

Bijou stayed on with my parents after that and was happy in Wales where he had more freedom to run. He was soon able to make his way home alone from the allotment if he got tired of waiting for Daddy.

The decision made, Mammy returned with us to Bristol to help prepare for our departure. We checked that both babies had been inoculated against all the usual infant diseases and started on the mammoth business of packing everything that they might need or that might not be available in Pakistan. We acquired a huge wooden packing case into which we stored a plastic baby bath and stand, terry towel and soft washable nappies, bottles of orange juice, cod liver oil, toys, clothes etc. and nailed it shut, secured by strong metal bands. A large cabin trunk was also packed full of clothes, shoes and necessities for the journey. Our passage was booked First Class on Anchor Line sailing from Liverpool to Karachi. The packing case and trunk were sent on in advance to the ship. I must admit to having a few misgivings as I watched our luggage being taken away to be loaded on to the huge van which was to convey it to the port. All the same, my resolve did not falter. At three months, Angie's vaccinations were complete and we three were ready to set out for the great unknown.

As for Mark, he had continued to make excellent progress except for one thing. Although his little playmate, Paul, was very mobile and crawled everywhere, Mark preferred to sit up straight like a little sultan, while his toys were brought to him. His vocabulary had increased by leaps and bounds so he had no difficulty in making us understand what he wanted. He got around in a baby walker in the house and had begun to attempt walking, holding on to the furniture as he went. Feeling more adventurous, he stated to walk alone but ended up falling down several stairs to the half landing. After that, he would only walk clinging to a hand or holding on to something solid and would not let go. Thus it was that I was setting out on a hazardous journey with two babies in arms, one of whom was quite a weight to carry. While I was making the preparations, Mammy would take them both out for a stroll with Angie lying down in the body of the pram, while Mark sat up on the top in a pram seat surveying all about him.

Our dear friends Eileen and Andrew offered to take us to Liverpool by car. We stayed overnight in Huyton, a leafy suburb east of Liverpool, where Eileen's parents lived. We were to sail in early April during the school Easter holidays so that our teacher friends were free to drive us up. As it happened, our lodger, Eileen Naylor, also lived in Liverpool so she took most of our luggage in her car.

After a restful night, we arrived safely at the port the next morning well before the ship was due to set sail. Eileen and Andrew saw us into our double cabin, Andrew carrying Angie in her carry cot and our overnight case, Eileen and I taking turns to carry Mark. Our trunk was awaiting us, sitting on one of the two single beds situated one each side of the small cabin. Andrew placed the suitcase next to it. The space between the beds was totally taken up by two large drop-side cots so that the dressing table and drawers on the back wall between the beds were totally inaccessible. We placed Mark in one cot with a packet of Smarties to keep him happy and Angie's cot in the adjacent drop side cot. Opposite these were wardrobes and a door into the en-suite taking up the whole of the last wall.

"I'll never manage like this," I said dolefully.

"You don't need two big cots. There'll be lots more space if you get them to take one of them away," suggested Eileen.

With that the ship's hooter sounded to warn visitors that it was time to leave. With warm hugs and kisses, we made our tearful farewells and suddenly my two friends had left and we three were alone in the claustrophobic cabin.

I looked across at Mark. He was sitting contentedly in his cot finishing off his packet of Smarties. His face and all the front of him was stained with the multicoloured sweets and smeared with chocolate, as was the pristine cot cover. He was still wearing the beautiful Fairisle top and white knitted trousers that Mammy had knitted for him to travel in. What was I going to do? How on earth was I going to manage? Had I bitten off more than I could chew this time? I felt like dissolving into tears but seeing Mark's cheerful face looking innocently up at me and Angie sleeping peacefully next to him, I managed to pull myself together. I opened my case and took out the photos of Archie and my family and called the cabin staff. Together we arranged the cabin so that it became more suited to our needs. One large cot was removed and the other placed up against the far single bed on which Angie's carry cot was put, leaving me adequate space to access the dressing table and drawers. The cabin attendant could not have been more helpful.

The ship set out on our long voyage which was to take us three weeks to reach Karachi. After we had unpacked everything that we needed our trunk was taken away and stored for us. Our pram magically appeared on deck and life became quite pleasant as we started to make full use of all the facilities and help on board for mothers with young babies. I was not the only mother with two small babies on board. I met a young Indian girl with two children of similar ages to Mark and Angie. She was in a pitiable position as her rich doctor husband was divorcing her and sending her back to her family in disgrace. It appeared that he had fallen in love with a British woman and wanted to get rid of her and the children. We made friends with each other, strolling over the decks pushing our prams and allowing the babies to play together throughout the voyage. Sometimes the two older children played in the ship's crèche enjoying the paddling pool under the supervision of trained staff while the three month-old babies took their afternoon naps in the cabins under the watchful eye of the cabin attendant. It was on the gently swaying ship's deck that Mark at sixteen months, finally decided to take his first steps alone and from then he never looked back. Thus it was that the two children continued to make good progress in the bracing sea air.

We passed through the Suez Canal where lots of passengers took advantage of the ship's excursion to see the pyramids of Egypt, but it was impossible for me to go with the children or to leave them on board for any length of time. However, I stayed out on deck and watched as we sailed slowly past many of the most famous sights of Egypt, marvelling at the wondrous pyramids. I did manage to get off the ship for a brief hour or so in Aden where one of Archie's friends had arranged to show me around the town. The cabin was now comfortable and convenient, the food, entertainment and facilities excellent and the voyage passed off very pleasantly indeed. The three weeks came to an end eventually and we docked in Karachi.

My father-in-law, Dr Samuel Luther, and Moses Kodot, my sister-in-law Eva's new husband, came on board to greet us. Mr Kodot was a successful businessman. Both he and Dr Luther were dressed in light westernised suits and hats to keep off the sun. It was wonderful to see them and I put myself entirely in their hands. Father-in-law and I had tears in our eyes as we greeted one another. It was not the reunion we had envisaged when he had left us in Britain. Unsure of his reception, he looked longingly at the two tiny children, the last link between him and his youngest son. I had prepared Mark for this meeting by talking to him constantly about the Grandfather who would be waiting for us so he went confidently into his outstretched arms. Angie too allowed herself to be kissed without making any fuss, so all was well.

With Mr Kodot in charge, we left the ship and made our way into the centre of the city. It was wonderful to be with them. I felt absolutely safe and secure in their care in the midst of this bustling, exotic city. Karachi was a huge teeming city and the traffic was absolutely chaotic. Buses painted in loud colours with passengers clinging to the roofs and sticking out through doors and windows swerved crazily past us, horns blaring and making a deafening din. Mr Kodot took charge of everything, including all our luggage from the hold of the ship. When we left the ship, we went to stay with Eva for a couple of days. Although we were given the warmest welcome and made most comfortable in their home, I couldn't wait to leave for our final destination in Quetta. I had never experienced such torrid heat and humidity. I wanted to be under the shower constantly, as no sooner was I dressed, than I was in a bath of perspiration once more. Father-in-law consoled me:

"You'll soon be in Quetta. It's a dry heat there and it's cooler too."

Arrangements were made for our packing case and trunk to be despatched direct from the ship to the hospital at Quetta. Two days later we left Karachi. Father-in-law accompanied us by train to Quetta. He had booked us berths in a sleeping carriage, as the journey took over twenty-four hours. The train was immensely long and crowded and our carriage absolutely full. I had never experienced such conditions. Fortunately, Mark was eating almost anything and, as I was breast feeding Angie, there was no real problem. To avoid any possibility of buying unhygienic food and drink we took our own picnics and drinks with us for the journey. The scenery on the way was stupendous. We passed through vibrant cities swarming with people, noisy with the incessant bustle of life. Then, in contrast, the train snaked through vast tracts of stony desert, a seemingly-endless wilderness, the only sign of life being the far-off glimpse of a caravan of camels. All the time, we were climbing slowly through mountains, magnificent in the sunshine, getting higher as the track became steeper as we approached Quetta. We went through narrow steep-sided ravines and looked over high, craggy mountains towering all around us as far as the eye could see. After a very long, dusty and tiring journey we had at last arrived at our final destination which stood at 5,500 feet above sea level amongst the mountains in the North West of Pakistan.

My brother-in-law, Henry, and his wife, Indira, were waiting to meet us at the station in Quetta. In the welcoming party were a number of servants ready to carry all our luggage and bags. I was relieved to discover that it was indeed pleasantly cool in comparison with the humid heat of Karachi. We set off by car to Henry's house through the wide avenues of the city, teeming with people. Men in smart western dress mingled with elegant ladies in bright colourful *saris* or *salwar kameez (*trousers and loose tops*)* as well as very poor people in white cotton *dhotis* (loose draped trousers) and bare chests, pushing carts or riding bicycles pulling customers in rickshaws. Dust swirled all around us and progress was slow as our driver used his horn constantly to force his way through the throng of humanity. The noise was deafening, mingled with the unaccustomed sounds of the braying of donkeys and the complaining of camels that met our ears, together with the shrill cries of the vendors selling their wares. I stared in wonder at the array of shiny, multicoloured, exotic fruit and vegetables piled high on the open market stalls. In some places beautiful, colourful flowers embellishing gardens of stylish houses gave off a sweet perfume, in others the pungent odour of spices wafted to our nostrils whilst elsewhere the whiff of animal smells met us as we passed. It was a totally different world to my western eyes.

We arrived safely at Henry's comfortable home surrounded by a large walled garden full of bright flowers and wide green lawns. A spacious bedroom had been prepared for us. The crisp cotton sheets and pillow cases on my bed were covered with a gorgeous silk coverlet and the children's cots were decorated with nursery figures. The cook had prepared a light refreshing meal for us and we thankfully relaxed with our obliging relatives administering to our every need. We were at home now, safe with our loved ones. Heno and Indu (pet names used by the family) did not have children of their own and were delighted to welcome my two little ones into their home. I would have to be careful to make sure that they did not get too spoiled by their doting aunt and uncle. Nikki, Archie's former *ayah* (Nanny), was also awaiting us, ready to spoil them too. Of course, my father-in-law was happiest of all to have his dear grandchildren with him. Although he did not actually live with his son, he came every day to see us and play with his sweet darlings of whom he was very proud. His home was a little distance away in an older house where he had lived with his sister, Lily, for many years. Her friend and colleague, Miss Davidson, the ex-missionary Head of the school where Lily had previously taught, also lived with them since her retirement.

At this time, The Mission Hospital was run jointly by Ronnie Holland, son of Sir Henry Holland who had worked with father-in-law previously, and Dr Henry Luther. Father-in-law had retired and was running a small private practice. I was soon invited to meet the Hollands and thereafter attended a Ladies' Sewing Group which met weekly in the gardens of their home. I quickly settled into a new pleasant routine. Our bathroom did not have hot running water, but this was no problem as a house servant would bring as much as I required. Having politely refused morning tea in bed, I would get up to feed Angie, then having received *garam paani* (hot water,) I would bath her and Mark using the plastic baby bath already set up in the bathroom. Nicky would then look after them while I showered.

Mark was now trotting about everywhere and would pop into Indu's bed to play with her if she had not already left for the hospital. He made a great friend of the cook too, who, I suspect, would give him titbits surreptitiously. He was soon conversing with him in Urdu as well as English and gained quite a reasonable vocabulary in this new language. Mark had so much constant attention that it was not surprising that he made immense progress in speaking. As I was feeding Angie, Indu took every opportunity to pick up Mark and play and talk with him. Though father-in-law took as much notice of Angie as of Mark, he was able to teach him to sing to his sister as he went about singing his favourite hymns. Mark had always reacted to music from a tiny baby by waving his hands about in time to the tune. His innate musicality also enabled him to pick up a tune in no time, so that he was soon singing the hymn "Stand up, stand up for Jesus" all the way through, and in tune, well before he was two years old.

Mark loved his little sister and sang and chatted to her all the time. He would pick up the soft toys that she hurled from her cot or her pram and give them back to her. He would bend over her cooing her name softly and stroking her cheek until one day a sharp cry of resentment came from the little girl. Mark had suddenly poked her in the eye. Was it curiosity, jealousy or simply an accident? Whatever the case, it was made clear to him that he was never to hurt her like that again and that he should always be gentle with his little sister. Amongst other interesting things, our big packing case contained Mark's old baby walker which proved invaluable for Angie as she grew. She learned to scoot around everywhere in it and was often helped to travel even faster when her big brother pushed her from behind.

The spicy food prepared by our cook was very much to my taste. Archie had introduced me to Indian meals in Bristol after getting recipes from his sister Eva. There was a wide variety of tasty meat and vegetable curries. Besides the usual lamb and beef, we also ate goat curry which was new to me. Living in the north, we often had *naans* or *chapattis* (delicious flat breads) to accompany our meals instead of rice. As we lived in a Muslim country, pork was never on the menu. There were mouth-watering but very sweet desserts too, but it was the fresh fruit that I appreciated most. As a doctor, Henry was often given large trays of delicious fruit such as mangos, as a token of gratitude by his patients. Pakistani mangos are reputed to be amongst the juiciest and tastiest in the world. I found it hard to limit myself to a sensible amount, as I enjoyed them so much. I had to be careful, however, as if I got an upset tummy then poor little Angie got it too. She continued to thrive in this foreign climate, benefitting from my healthy immune system, as she fed mainly on breast milk. Although Mark had had to be bottle fed after about four months old when I became pregnant with Angie, she refused to take anything from a bottle and went straight to a cup, continuing to be breast fed until our return to Wales at almost one year old.

My life in Quetta was an easy, luxurious one. I had absolutely no chores to do. All I had to do was to care for my children and even for this I had Nikki at my beck and call. She was a great help to me and we became good friends. She washed their nappies, laundered their clothes and could be trusted to see to their every need when left in sole charge when I was invited occasionally with Heno and Indu out to dinner with their friends. She still lived with her family in a small mud house just outside the garden wall and would come as soon as she was called. The caste system was prevalent throughout Pakistan, so she was not required to do the house work. A *sweeper* (of the *untouchable caste)* came every day to clean the floors and do all the dirty work.

There was also a gardener employed to cut the lawns and tend the flowers who also acted as a sort of guard to keep watch over the house and look after the two fierce Alsatian guard dogs. At first, I was frightened of these huge dogs but Mark showed no fear and was soon able to pat them on the head under the watchful eye of the gardener. The *dhobi* (washer man) was the final employee of the household. He collected all the dirty washing – clothes and bed linen – which he took away and washed in the running waters of the rivers and dried in the sun. He brought them back beautifully ironed and in pristine condition the very next day. We always had plenty of freshly laundered clothes to wear every day.

Besides the sewing circle with Joan Holland, we visited friends, attended children's birthday parties and entertained friends at home. On one such special occasion we were entertained by an American magician who astounded us all by his sleight of hand and party tricks. Heno also took the three of us to visit outlying eye camps where he operated on patients suffering from many prevalent eye diseases, restoring sight to people who had suffered from cataracts for many years. The Mission Hospital that he ran in Quetta was quite unlike our British hospitals. Patients were brought by their relatives who stayed with them to tend to them while they received medical attention from the doctors and nurses. Heno also did general surgery and allowed me to observe him operating in the theatre on a few occasions. Two operations stay in my memory in particular. One, a haemorrhoid operation horrified me by the amount of blood lost. The other, the amputation of a leg above the knee astounded me by the amount of pure physical strength needed to saw through the bone. I greatly admired the good work that was being done in the Mission hospital to treat so many patients.

As Christians living in a Muslim country, we experienced no problems of any sort. We were able to worship openly in our Anglican churches and our western dress was not frowned upon. This was probably chiefly due to the good work done in the hospital which was greatly appreciated by the community. We were reminded each day, however, that we were living in a Muslim country by the frequent calls to prayer chanted by the *Mullahs* (Islamic clerics) which rang out over the city from the mosques.

The month of Ramadan was faithfully observed in Quetta. For thirty days all practising Muslims fasted from daybreak to sundown until it ended in the Festival of Eid. During our stay, the religious practice of *Tatbir* (self-flagellation) took place in the streets of Quetta. This is a worldwide march which takes place every year on the Day of Ashura to commemorate the Battle of Karbala and the martyrdom of Imam Hussein. Devout Muslims march through the city in massive parades while hitting themselves on the chest or slashing themselves with chains called *Zeanjer-Zani*. It is a very frightening, bloody spectacle to behold and we were kept well away from the parade for fear of causing trouble by going to observe Muslims indulging in such fierce and extreme religious practices. Nevertheless, I was taken to a secluded spot where we could observe from afar what was going on and I would never wish to witness such a sight again.

Although Quetta had seemed quite green and cool on our arrival, as summer came on it became drier and hotter. Very regular watering was essential to maintain the green lawns around the house. There was the occasional dust storm which kept us shut up indoors to avoid the huge clouds of stinging sand. The constant clear blue sky and bright sun started to weigh on me and I scanned the sky every morning for any sign of clouds. When a shower eventually came down, I ran outside and, raising my face to the heavens, let the cooling water run all over me.

The family decided to take us all away on holiday for a couple of weeks. We were to go with another family to a hill station which had been a favourite holiday resort of the British when they ruled India. We set off over the mountains, through the stony desserts and high passes. On the way, we had seen tribesmen using a very primitive method to thresh their corn. They drove donkeys round and round pulling huge grinding stones over the corn that had been piled high. We also came across the odd camel caravan winding its way through the barren wilderness. These tribesmen, tall, strong, fine-looking men, carried guns openly and looked very fierce and proud in their traditional robes. Eventually, we arrived safe and sound at the spacious villa surrounded by trees and lovely gardens where we were to stay. It was a green oasis in the middle of a vast mountainous desert. We spent two pleasant weeks with family and friends. There were children of similar age for Mark and Angie to play with and the adults enjoyed relaxing and chatting together.

The highlight of our stay in Quetta was when Eva and her four teenage children came to spend their summer holidays with us. They were absolutely delighted to be able to get to know their new baby cousins and never tired of playing with them. Instead of one *ayah* to help me, I now had four willing nurse maids (though one, Reggie, was a young boy, of course) so I rarely got to carry my toddlers anywhere. Angie was very mobile by this time. She could make her way anywhere in her baby walker, sometimes a little too fast when aided by her brother. Reggie in particular was thrilled to find that Mark had already started to acquire some Urdu and did his best to teach him as much as possible by talking to him tirelessly and encouraging him. The oldest girl, Honey (Cynthia), was just a bit younger than my sister, Mary, and she too wanted to train to be a nurse. The twins, Baby and Bunny, were doing well in school and had ambitions to work in the Aviation Industry. The youngest, Reggie, wanted to become a pilot. Their ambitions were fulfilled later when the twins became air stewardesses and Reggie joined Pakistan Airways and flew all around the world. He later joined Singapore Airways and retired as a captain.

It was a very sad day when we had to say goodbye to them when they returned to Karachi at the end of the holidays. They were afraid that as their cousins were so young they would not remember them and that perhaps they would never see them again. They need not have worried as I kept in contact with all the family. Father-in-law spent holidays of up to three months with us, both in Bristol and later in Wales and we planned to live in Karachi for at least a year together when the children were still young. We had contact with Henry and Indira when they worked as registrars in the UK. Eva, Moses and Honey visited us in Bristol when Mark and Angie were in Infants' School and Reggie and his family spent a short holiday with us in Wales as well as attending a wedding and dropping in now and again when he had flown into Britain.

Angie and I were also welcomed by different members of the family on our frequent travels to Asia. As an adult, Angie was very happy to be able to spend a long holiday with her aunty Eva when she really got to know her and her grown-up cousins and their families. This was very important for Angie, as she was keen to find out as much as possible about the father she had never known. She got on exceptionally well with Eva who was happy to chat with her and answer all her questions.

"Let's have a chitty-chat," Eva would say as they settled down together over a nice cup of coffee.

The last few months in Quetta simply flew and it was soon time to prepare for the long trip back to Britain. This time, I did not dread the journey as I had on the way out. Although I knew that it would be long and tiring, I now knew exactly what to expect on each leg of the journey. We repacked the large packing case, this time discarding the baby bath and replacing it with the study toy car that Mark had been driving around everywhere since he had received it as a present. We also packed the many beautiful gifts that had been showered on us. These included a lamp made of exquisitely enamelled camel skin, a round brass table which sat upon three legs carved out of a single piece of wood, a wooden cake stand and tray inlaid with ivory as well as embroidered mirror work of all sorts. The gold and silver jewellery given to Angie and me was packed in the case we kept with us, of course. All this arrived safely with us and much of it is still cherished as mementos of our first happy stay amongst Archie's people.

As before, we made the long journey from Quetta to Karachi by train accompanied by Father-in law. We had a grand send-off from the station. A great crowd of well-wishers had assembled to see us off. There were many tears and hugs. We had all grown very close and we did not know when, or even if, we would ever meet each other again. The train left with us three leaning out of the window and waving to our loved ones until the group was out of sight. Excited by the thought of the long train journey, Mark happily called out his goodbyes in both English and Urdu while Angie clapped her hands and waved just as happily. They were completely unaware of the momentous nature of the parting. They then set about examining all the other passengers surrounding us in the carriage and the journey passed off

197

pleasantly enough. After a brief reunion with Eva and Moses in Karachi, it was time to set sail for Britain. The journey home had begun.

# PART 5

## Return to my roots

# Chapter 17
# A Happy Homecoming

The ship sailed from Karachi on 14 November 1963 – Mark's second birthday. We had already celebrated it with all the family in Quetta and again briefly with Eva before leaving for the port. Everything was set fair for a pleasant voyage home. We were happily strolling on the deck together when some earth shattering news was relayed throughout the ship. The assassination of the President of The United States of America was announced. John F Kennedy had been fatally shot at 12.30 pm on 22 November 1963 while riding with his wife, Jacqueline, and other dignitaries in a motorcade in the town of Dallas, Texas. This tragic news which caused consternation throughout the ship was to have worldwide repercussions. People were shocked by this dreadful assassination and many were openly weeping. It was almost the sole topic of conversation for the remainder of the voyage, as people listened avidly to the radio to glean any further news regarding the developments in America. All this naturally had little effect on the children who continued to enjoy the company of their playmates in the crèche as they splashed about in the paddling pool.

On arrival in Liverpool, it was wonderful to find my parents waiting to accompany us home to Wales by train. Back in The Rhondda of my childhood, we soon settled down together in 7 William Street. We had a fantastic family Christmas. Michael was home for the holidays and all four sisters couldn't wait to come to see their adorable nephew and niece again after so long an absence. They were totally spoilt. Mark was delighted to be reunited with Bijou and quickly made friends with the children living in the street. Angie, just a tranquil babe in arms when she left, was now a whirlwind whizzing around in her baby walker threatening to knock lumps out of her Nanny's well-cared-for furniture. Presiding in her high chair at the head of the table in the middle room, she celebrated her first birthday surrounded by several little Welsh infants of a similar age. We were now completely installed in my parents' cosy home where we were made very welcome. As we still had reliable tenants in both sections of our Bristol home, we decided to remain with my parents for the time being.

After a while, I began to think seriously about our future. Since Archie had died so young, having paid in only a few years national insurance, I only received a pittance as a widowed mother's allocation. I would therefore have to take up my teaching career as soon as possible to earn a living. Mammy was willing to help care for the children if I could find work in the Rhondda. As luck would have it, there was a vacancy for a full-time French teacher to start after half term in Porth Grammar Secondary School due to the long-term illness of the incumbent. All was in place for me to take over when he returned unexpectedly. What a disappointment. However the LEA wanted to retain my services so they sent me to take charge of a nursery class in the Rhondda Fawr.

I arrived quite confident of my ability to cope with this new task only to find that it was quite a different kettle of fish to run a class of three-year olds than to manage two toddlers. I clapped my hands and said with authority,

"We'll all sit down now and I'll read you a story."

Nobody took a bit of notice and carried on playing as before. I certainly had a lot to learn! However by the end of my three week stint, they all started to do my bidding and would even bed down docilely for their after lunch nap to allow me to catch my breath. The post in Porth was still not available, so I was transferred to Pentre Grammar School until the end of term to replace the Deputy Head who taught Latin to A Level. What a jump from teaching nursery children to preparing pupils for university entrance, and in Latin too which I had last studied in my second year at Bristol! Needless to say, I was glad to be able to start in Porth Grammar at the beginning of the summer term, as were the pupils, since their teacher had lasted less than two weeks before going off sick once more. We had to work very hard indeed to make up for all the time they had lost but the number of happy pupils who passed French O Level, sometimes at the third attempt, made it all worthwhile.

The tenants in 20 Sunningdale had been given notice to vacate the property at the beginning of the summer holidays. Michael, now studying at Bristol University, and I went to arrange the sale of our house in Clifton and the purchase of a roomy semidetached house on the Portway in Shirehampton, formally a village on the outskirts of Bristol now amalgamated with it. We were greatly helped in this by our solicitor friends, Bob and Helen Brandt, through whom Archie had bought our house in Sunningdale and who also lived in Shirehampton. We had let out our part of the house to a doctor and his wife while we were in Pakistan. The rent for that, together with that of the downstairs flat, had paid for our return passage to Pakistan and helped us buy the new house with the proceeds of the sale of 20 Sunningdale without taking out a mortgage. We were now ready to return to an independent life in Bristol.

# Chapter 18
## Resettled in Bristol – then itchy Feet!

The Portway is a wide main road running from Avonmouth through Shirehampton to the centre of Bristol and connecting the city to roads leading out towards the south west. Our home, no 421, had a small gated front garden and large lawns and flower beds at the back behind which were allotments, a single rail track and the river Avon flowing past towards Bristol docks. The children could safely watch a huge variety of vehicles roaring past at the front and trains and ships passing the bottom of the garden. There was also a large shed in excellent condition which was quickly converted into a room-sized Wendy house and toy store, complete with lights, carpeting and furniture. Inside, the house was roomy and comfortable so Michael came to occupy the third bedroom for the next two years while he finished his science degree at Bristol. This arrangement meant that the children had a young surrogate father, my brother Michael had a home from home and I had some adult company with whom to share my life while the children were tiny. In a small way, it also allowed me to re-enter student life by taking the children to watch the rugby matches where Uncle Michael played scrum half for Bristol University and sometimes to host the whole team after the match was over when Michael occasionally brought them back for supper.

Life settled into a pleasant routine once more. I saw a lot of my good friends, Eileen and Andrew, forged close bonds with Bob and Helen, who had four children of similar age to mine, and made new friends, Pam and Den, whom I met while attending Shirehampton Church. Our social life was full with children's birthday parties and outings with local friends together with theatre visits to Bristol Old Vic etc. for us adults. Another chance meeting at church had some unexpected consequences. I got to know a round, rosy, chatty Welsh lady who was the Domestic Science teacher at Portway Comprehensive School just over the road from where we lived. Mrs Williams had an innovative way of engendering interest in her subject amongst her most difficult pupils. She sent them out once a week into suitable families where there were children under school age. The idea was that during their lessons they discussed and planned nutritious menus, then armed with a list of ingredients, they went shopping in the morning before arriving at the children's homes to prepare lunch for the family and themselves. They fed the children then cleared the table and washed up before taking the little ones out for a walk, leaving the mother time to relax or to do the weekly shop.

For Mrs Williams we were the ideal family, as some mothers would have had difficulty dealing with stroppy girls but my experience as a teacher stood me in good stead. In fact the whole thing worked out very well for both the two girls and us. Mark chatted away to them and amused them when he actually corrected their English by saying,

"It's not 'I done it,' it's 'I did it,'" as he'd been told to say so many times before. One day, they assured me that they had permission to take the children to school that afternoon and asked me to pick them up at the school gate after I had finished shopping. They met me minus the children.

"Mrs Williams said that the Head would like to see you."

Rather embarrassed by my unsuitable attire for what looked like turning into an interview, I was forced to comply and was astounded when I was offered a job!

"I'm sorry, but it is impossible as I have two children under school age," I explained. However, the Bristol Education Authority offered free nursery places for teachers to get back into work. Mark was three while Angie was only two, but as she was clean and potty-trained already, they were both accepted. Thus it was that I spent a term teaching French in Portway Boys' Secondary Modern before moving to the mixed Comprehensive School when they amalgamated the following September. I was back in harness rather sooner than expected.

About to earn a salary once more and benefitting from Michael's contribution towards his keep, I felt that I could now accept Vendla's invitation to spend some time with her in Paris. I decided that we should take the opportunity to go to France before I was due to start my job after the Easter holidays, so we set off in spring. We went by train and ferry. After their recent travels, the children took it all in their stride. Vendla was living in Paliseau, a suburb in the south of Paris, where we were to spend a short holiday with her. She lived in a flat with her husband Yves on the third floor of a large apartment block where there was no lift. It was not easy to go up and down the stairs with toddlers and all the necessary paraphernalia and to lug up the heavy shopping, too. We had an emotional reunion and introduced the children to one another.

Vendla had four children – Cathy five years old, Eric six months older than Mark, Maureen about Angie's age and Diane a small baby. All Vendla's children were blonde and blue-eyed in contrast to Mark and Angie's brown eyes and dark hair. Rather than the girls, it was the two boys who had the curly hair. Amazingly, the toddlers got on like a house on fire, playing and chatting away together, each in his or her own language. They had no trouble at all in understanding one another. We all spent a fantastic week or so together in her welcoming home. Shortly, Vendla and I hit on a great idea: why not send Mark and Angie to the Ecole Maternelle (Nursery School) attended by her three older children? Arrangements were made and off the four of them trotted every afternoon while their grateful mothers relaxed with

205

a glass of wine while baby Diane went down for her nap. Needless to say the holiday was a great success.

On our return to Britain, we made preparations to be ready for the new term and the new life it would bring for all three. Angie had become very much attached to her dummy so we tried to tell her that she would not be able to take it to school with her as it was too babyish. When the time came, she left it behind like a "big girl" but the first thing she did on returning home was to grab it and stuff it straight in her mouth – that is, until Mark threw it out of the window onto the patio roof. We simply could not get hold of it and Angie cried herself to sleep. She grew up in one fell swoop and never had another dummy. I taught part-time in the Boys' School where I was the only female teacher, while the children went happily to nursery school. The only slight problem was that Mark picked up a wide new vocabulary of swear words (many of which I had never heard before) from his play mates, many of whom came from more disadvantaged backgrounds.

I initiated French in the new Comprehensive School when it opened in September 1965 and found myself the go-between between the male and female staff who occupied separate staff rooms. I settled down to teaching and enjoyed the challenge of introducing my subject and trying to engender an interest in a foreign language in my pupils. I taught three and a half days a week in Portway for two years. This was just across the road for me and so was very convenient while the children were so young. I was now on track to take up my career in teaching in earnest.

During this time, a birthday I shall never forget occurred on 22 October 1966. I was preparing to take the children to Wales to celebrate with my family when news of a catastrophic disaster was relayed throughout Britain and the world. At 9.15 am on 21 October 1966, just after morning assembly where the school children had been singing "All things bright and beautiful," 110,000 cubic metres of slurry had engulfed Pantglas Junior School, Aberfan, in South Wales covering it with a 10 metre mountain of mud and rocks.

There was nonstop coverage on the TV, as harrowing tales of courage and heroism followed heartrending scenes of the rescue attempts. Mothers who dashed to the school at the first alarm, clawed at the mud with their bare hands in the hope of finding their children alive. Almost immediately droves of miners from local collieries converged on the village to dig through the rubble for survivors. Within 24 hours 2,000 emergency workers and volunteers were working night and day in a futile effort to rescue the victims. In all, 116 children, mostly between the ages of seven and ten, and 28 adults lost their lives in the tragedy. Mr Beynon, Deputy Head of the school, was discovered dead in the debris clasping five small children in his arms in an effort to protect them.

The slip had occurred after exceptionally heavy rain had destabilised the No7 Tip which had been built on top of natural springs on the hillsides. The National Coal Board had previously remained deaf to repeated requests for the removal of the tip by Myrthyr Tydfyl Council and was soundly blamed for the tragedy by the tribunal established to ascertain the causes of the disaster. The Aberfan Memorial Fund, set up on the very day of the tragedy, received contributions from all over the world and soon reached £1.75 million. However, the NCB was reluctant to remove the remaining tips until a contribution of £150,000 was made from the Memorial fund. This scandalous wrong was eventually put right when the British Government repaid the money and the newly established Welsh Assembly donated £1.5 million to the fund in 2007 along with £500,000 to the Aberfan Education Charity.

That birthday in 1966 turned out to be one of great sorrow and weeping as the full scale of the horrific tragedy unfolded throughout the morning. There must have been few dry eyes throughout the world that day as the pitiably tiny bodies were pulled out from the mud and slime. This was doubly poignant for those of us with a close connection with the mining communities of the South Wales Coalface where constant danger and fatal mining accidents had been part of life over the years. Now, the totally heartless and indifferent attitude of those in authority had resulted in the destruction of a whole generation of precious children in one of our most deprived villages. The treatment of Aberfan remains a huge blot on the government of the time and the whole capitalist system in general.

Meanwhile, Father-in-law was missing his grandchildren and was keen to do whatever was possible to help us. We had talked of the possibility of my finding a post in Pakistan when we were out with the family. Meanwhile, he had made inquiries about a post in Karachi Grammar School where the teaching was all in English. They also followed the British syllabus and exam system. I sent out my qualifications and applied for a post to teach French and other subjects to a lower standard if necessary to fill up my time table. I was offered the post to start in September1967, so I handed in my resignation at Portway and was hoping to leave for Pakistan at the end of July to holiday in Quetta before starting work. For the second time, an event of worldwide significance occurred which was to disrupt our plans completely. On 5th June 1967, a Six-Day War broke out between Israel and Palestine which ratcheted up the tension throughout the Middle East and had repercussions on relations between The West and all Muslim countries. At once, Father-in-law wrote to tell me that it would be far too dangerous for me to travel with the children to Pakistan and I was forced to cancel our trip immediately. This left me without a job and very little time to find one. Since I needed to work near home, there was not much choice.

Fortunately, there was a part-time post going in Shirehampton Junior School for a support teacher to take charge of pupils with learning difficulties. These were taken out of the main class and given special help. I explained that I did not feel qualified for this but as French was beginning to be taught in junior schools in Bristol, I was taken on to teach French to each class while the class teacher gave help to the slow learners. In the summer term, I was also put in charge of a group of trainee teachers coming to do a project on Roman Britain. This turned out to be most interesting, entailing as it did exciting visits to a Roman dig which was taking place in the vicinity and many linked projects. We made togas to wear, models of Roman centurions and cross sections of Roman roads. One project nearly ended up as a disaster for us. I persuaded a male teacher to make me a shallow, square, wooden recipient into which I wished to put wax in order to make a wax tablet on which to write. Watched by the children, I was trying to melt wax candles under the grill in this contraption when it all caught fire. Shooing the children away with shouts and screams, I grabbed the flaming grill pan, rushed outside and put it on the floor on the path until the flames subsided. The candles had all melted and I had my wax tablet. A disaster had been averted, but only just!

After the pleasant experience of teaching in Shirehampton, I was quite happy to accept a post in Sea Mills Junior School where both Mark and Angie had started in the infants' class. My good friend, Helen Brandt, took them to school with her children until I took up my post there. This proved to be another most rewarding experience for me. I taught four and a half days a week and had charge of my own class as well as teaching French throughout the school. The Headmaster was very modern and go-ahead and all the teaching was centred around a new project each year. When I arrived, it was "Greece." My English and drama lessons were built around the myths and plays of ancient Greece with their dramatic masks, religious studies around Paul's letters, Geography and History around the Trojan wars, Maths around Pythagoras's theorems and Art around the making of models of the Trojan horse and all the Heroes. Finally, Music and Movement centred on the story of Orpheus playing his lute to charm three-headed Cerberus while Eurydice attempted to escape from the underworld.

Although very interesting, it was extremely hard work. My class contained forty-three ten-year-olds of mixed ability, so it took all a teacher's ingenuity to keep the brightest pupils working while coping with the slower learners. One mother thanked me profusely for teaching her son to tell the time after everyone had failed to do so. I had succeeded by teaching him to tell the time in French first using brightly-coloured charts. These had caught his attention and he was at the same stage as all the others learning French, so the block was removed and he had succeeded. I also taught them to sing simple French songs with actions and in two parts. The Head happened to be in charge of the joint choirs of all the Bristol Junior Schools and got my class to sing in front of the whole school during assembly to encourage others to do likewise. I began a second year in Sea Mills when the project was "Canada".

By now, having finished his degree in Bristol and completed a year combining Teacher training and sport in Loughborough, Michael had set sail for Canada. On the boat, he had met an attractive redhead, Carol, and one year later they were planning to wed. The National Colliery, Wattstown, had closed and Daddy had been made redundant at the age of sixty-four and had been given early retirement. Neither he nor Mammy had ever set foot outside Britain in their lives but they wanted to attend their only son's wedding. Daddy had already walked all three of my sisters down the aisle on their wedding days. Mark and Angie had recently been page boy and flower girl at Ann's wedding and were both invited to take part similarly in Michael's wedding. It was agreed that all five of us should go to Canada for the summer holidays and that I would organise the whole trip.

Meanwhile, since our plans to go to Pakistan had floundered, father-in-law had decided to make an extended stay with us in Bristol. While it was great to be together again and for him to be with his grandchildren, it became more and more difficult for me to cope. I was doing an almost full-time job for which I had not really been trained and had two small children to look after alone. Father-in-law did his best to fit in and not make extra work for me but he was another adult to cater for who had never done anything to help in the house. I fell ill with influenza and after antibiotics and a week off, I found I could not cope when I returned to school. The doctor put me on a week's supply of anti-depressants but when they finished I was no better, so he gave me stronger ones. I dissolved into tears when telling Helen that I was afraid of becoming hooked on them.

"Don't take them, then" she said. "Just bring the children here tomorrow morning and I'll take them to school. You'll go straight to bed here and rest until they come back. You can take the children home at the usual time and your father-in-law will be none the wiser. I'll ring the school and say you won't be in for a week and you will soon be better."

I was only too glad to accept Helen's advice and sure enough at the end of a week I had recovered sufficiently to enable me to cope at home and at school once more. We had a short break in Wales with my parents and eventually Father-in-law's visit came to an end and he returned reluctantly to Pakistan. He even expressed a wish to return permanently to live with us one day but his elder son Henry and I decided that it would be far too much for me to take on and that he would be better looked after with him in Pakistan. The parting was sad and, as it turned out, it was our final parting.

209

Nevertheless, we had managed to spend some good quality time together and the children, nearly five and six, would always be able to remember their grandfather Luther.

The time to set out for Michael's wedding in Canada was fast approaching. Passports had been purchased for my parents and tickets bought. Mark was slightly off colour.

"Why are you scratching your face, Mark? Let me see."

Sure enough a couple of marks had appeared on his face. It couldn't be the start of a rash. Not now! The doctor confirmed that it was indeed chicken pox which had been rife in school recently. This highly contagious children's disease looked likely to put an end to our plans for attending Michael's wedding. Fortunately, Mark recovered quickly. The rash disappeared except for one or two faded marks which would hopefully pass unnoticed. We scanned Angie's face for any tell-tale signs, but all seemed fine so we left for Canada as planned.

We were met at Toronto airport and taken to New Sarum where Carol's family lived. We were there in time for the shower parties (an American tradition, a party where guests bring gifts for the soon-to-be married couple) one of which we had to host as the groom's family. We were introduced to all Carol's relatives and friends and given a warm welcome everywhere. Leaving the children with my parents, I made a quick dash to Ottawa to visit my Polish friend, Josefa, now married and happily reunited with her family. On my return, a cloud suddenly appeared to darken the horizon. Angie started to come out in spots and was soon covered with a typical chicken pox rash. There was consternation in the house – someone actually saying that it looked like small pox! We were isolated from the main party and put into a summer house in the garden where we nursed Angie, trying to break her fever by administering cold bed baths constantly to keep her as cool as possible in the hot summer. However, panic was soon over and it was only poor little Angie who had to suffer a bad dose of chicken pox in the humid heat. Although she was feeling better by the time the wedding was to take place, she could not walk down the aisle covered in a rash and so, dressed in her pretty white dress and green-blue sash, she had to sit at the back of the church and watch her brother basking in all the limelight.

All went well with the wedding and the bride and groom set out on their honeymoon. Their destination was a small island on Doe Lake in Northern Ontario where we were to join them a week later to holiday together before returning home. Meanwhile, we went to spend a week in an apartment on the twentieth floor of a tall block in central Toronto kindly loaned to us by some friends of Michael. On arrival, Mammy and I set about familiarising ourselves with the flat and preparing something to eat. As there was no fresh milk, I asked Daddy to go down to buy some. When he returned to the flats, he had forgotten how to get back to our apartment and spent over half an hour travelling up and down in the lifts, totally lost in this huge rabbit warren of a building that was so alien to him. Mammy was panic stricken,

"You shouldn't have sent him out on his own, Pat," she complained. "You know he's not used to big cities. He's only ever lived in Wattstown and Ynyshir. Now what will we do?"

With that, there was a knock on the door and an apologetic Daddy was standing there, milk in hand, so all was well again. We did the usual tourist things, including climbing to the top of the CN Tower with its vertiginous panoramic view over the whole city. Then we left to join Michael and Carol on their private island.

What a contrast it was to the teeming city we had just left. All was peace and tranquillity. We spent our time swimming, boating, relaxing and getting to know the new addition to the family. The children's swimming improved by leaps and bounds. All too soon the fortnight was over and we headed back to New Sarum. During this last period of our trip, we visited my cousin Jane, now living in Harrow just near the US border and the town of Detroit, and had our first stupendous experience of the magnificent Niagara Falls. Bright blue plastic hooded capes were purchased to keep us dry as we were tossed about on the swirling waters passing beneath the horse-shoe falls in the tourist boat, Maid of the Mist. That didn't stop Mark and Angie from getting merrily drenched as they capered about on the little boat. Another unforgettable trip was over and we left for home.

Back in the UK, now that the children were older, I wanted to get back into teaching French full time. Junior schools had proved to be an interesting interlude and I had been happy trying my hand at teaching younger pupils but that was not where I wanted to go in my career. I began applying for full-time French posts in the Bristol area but was dismayed to find how difficult travel would be. Then an offer of a term's full-time post in Pentre Grammar in the Rhondda turned up. It was certainly worth considering.

# Chapter 19
# A welcome in the hillsides

The vacancy in Pentre Secondary Grammar had arisen because a student had previously obtained the post at interview on the understanding that she would be released from her Teacher Training course early to take it up for the summer term. However, she was not released and the school was desperate for someone to hold the fort until September. This was tempting, as Mammy was prepared to look after any sick child to enable me to keep teaching and though both children were sturdy, I felt that they had sometimes gone to school when a day or two off was really called for. I decided to take the post as a taster to see how we three would like living in Wales. Once again we were afforded the warm Welsh welcome typified in the well-known song *"We'll keep a welcome in the hillsides, we'll keep a welcome in the vales, we'll keep a welcome in the hillsides when you come home again to Wales."*

As it happened, it worked out very well indeed for everybody. The children loved their school and made friends easily with their fellows and enjoyed playing safely in the street, the park and on the mountainsides as we had done before them. My parents spoiled them rotten, had lots of time for them and loved having them at home in 7 William Street. The staff at Pentre was a jolly lot and I found going back to my specialised subject most rewarding after having to turn my hand to almost anything in Sea Mills. I made a very good friend there. Pat Williams and I had lots of things in common besides our Christian names and we were both young and without a partner. She introduced me to all the lively night spots in Porth, Pontypridd and Cardiff and, with a built-in baby sitter, I was able to make the most of them, as well as of the theatre, opera and musicals in the area. Everyone was happy. What a pity the job was for one term only.

One day, Mr Howells, Deputy Head and Head of French, called me to him and asked if I would be interested in applying for a permanent post in the school. It appeared that since the young lady had not taken up the post as agreed, they were obliged to re-advertise. He was happy with my work so I decided to apply, without much hope, as the student who had previously been appointed had influential contacts on the Board of Governors. Nepotism was rife in the Rhondda. Nevertheless I was offered the job. Once again, I found myself in a school which was soon to become a brand new Comprehensive amalgamating all the grammar and secondary modern schools in the area. Thus it was that I took over the bulk of the French teaching for a year in Pentre Grammar while the Deputy Head, Mr Howells, was busy with the reorganisation and I subsequently became Head of French and eventually Head of Languages in Treorchy Comprehensive School. Consequently, I sold our house in Bristol and purchased a spacious detached house on a large corner plot in Graigwen, a sought-after area of Pontypridd, less than thirty minutes by car from my parents. 18 Whiterock Close was where I brought up my children until they left home to continue their education in Music College or University.

Graigwen was an ideal area to bring up young children. Situated as it was overlooking the old market town of Pontypridd, our chalet bungalow was surrounded by a large garden where Mark and his friends could play football and cricket on the lawns. The house next door had been on the market at the same time and I would have bought it in preference to No.18, as its garden was much smaller and more manageable but it was more expensive and not so well set out inside. Daddy, although keener on vegetables than on flowers, undertook to create a rock garden and small flower beds and mow the lawns until Mark was old enough to take over the mowing. There were lots of children of their age to play with and they could run free over the mountains as I had as a child. We passed many happy years together in Whiterock Close.

During this time, I appreciated the enormous support we received from my parents. We were kept provided with as much fresh garden produce as we could eat by Daddy and when we spent weekends with them, Mammy spoiled us with her delicious home cooking. Whatever we were doing, we always met without fail for Sunday lunch, and afternoon tea, at 7 William Street until the children left home. Of course, the children were happy and well cared for when I pursued my social life with my friend Pat Williams. I also found a *treasure* in Mrs Moon, whom I employed for many years when the children were young to clean the house and to be there each afternoon when they arrived back from school long before I got home from Treorchy.

I remained in Treorchy Comprehensive, this huge school of approximately two thousand pupils, for rest of my working life. The Languages Department expanded to include German and Spanish as well as a flourishing Welsh Department. At first, money was available to equip the new school. We acquired a brand new language laboratory and were allocated foreign language assistants to help with individual oral work while perfecting their English. Due to the difficulty in finding suitable accommodation for these young foreign students, I took several into my own home, three of whom – Rémi, Marguerite and Michelle - became lifelong friends. While Marguerite was with us, Mark won a scholarship at the age of seven to the Cathedral School in Llandaff, Cardiff, and became a boarder there. At this time, Treorchy, situated in the widest and most affluent part of the Rhondda, now received a large proportion of pupils who had hitherto gone to Porth County and soon acquired an excellent reputation. Quite by chance, I had landed in what soon became one of the most reputable schools in South Wales.

My career flourished during this period. I trained pupils from First to Sixth Form levels to participate successfully in competitions in drama and French song held in The Sherman Theatre, Cardiff, for all the schools in Mid and South Glamorgan. I embraced the new challenge of technology and invented ways of using computers as a teaching aid which I shared with others in teacher-training courses. Through a useful contact with a teacher in Evian on the lake of Geneva, I organised the first pupil exchange from the Rhondda when we spent two weeks at Easter in this beautiful part of France close to the Swiss border. My two young children went with us and we stayed in a convent there. Some of my pupils had the opportunity to try skiing when their exchange family took them off for a weekend. Maybe it would turn out to be the only chance she ever got to participate in this sport, but Beryl Bundock was highly delighted, even though she returned home with her leg in plaster of Paris signed by almost all the group.

Shortly afterwards I was contacted by a Madame Michèle Grèze in France and together we organised a most successful exchange with the Dordogne which continued for many years. My own children also took part and stayed alone in French homes well before they were of secondary school age. Educational and social outings were organised and both Welsh and French benefitted greatly from their experiences. The Welsh learned what life was like in the country, especially on farms. This included sometimes earth toilets at the bottom of the garden, no running hot water and food liberally laced with garlic. The attitude towards animals in this rural area was totally foreign to our young Welsh visitors. Angie got to love the fluffy white "bunnies" kept by her exchange partner, Corrine, and when she was asked to choose which one was her favourite, she chose the prettiest and the cuddliest. Imagine her horror to find that this cute bunny was served up at dinner the next day! Horse meat was another no-go area for the Welsh visitors. On the other hand, they received a very warm welcome, lots of interesting visits to châteaux and prehistoric caves etc. and lively parties and discos as well as attending a few classes at school with their French exchange partners.

The French pupils, on the other hand, had an ingrained horror of *English food* "boiled beef and cabbage." However, they soon changed their opinion when they tasted Welsh cuisine. They enjoyed it so much, especially the Welsh cakes, *Cawl* and fish and chips eaten out of newspaper, that many of them had gained a little extra weight by the time they returned home instead of wasting away as they had feared! They revelled in the freedom to meet up with friends and attend Youth Clubs so often impossible in France due to the long distances involved between their homes and the lack of transport in the country. Trips to the sea side, the mountains and places of interest were also really appreciated as much as the parties and dances given in their honour. Mostly everything went off smoothly once they had settled down and become accustomed to the strange ways of their hosts.

Of course there are inevitably one or two incidents that stick in the memory. One boy in particular stands out. An over-enthusiastic fifth former, he wanted to sample all aspects of French life. Cheating his age, Clive over indulged in French wine so easily available during the day in cafés for those who managed to convince the proprietor that they were old enough to buy alcohol. Later that day, I was informed that one of my pupils was ill in the sick bay of the school. He was suffering from a very severe hangover and was violently sick. No serious problem resulted from this incident but he and the rest of the pupils were taught a salutatory lesson.

This same ingenious pupil, however, caused us all a great deal of anxiety on the return journey. Travelling by rail necessitated a change of train in Paris entailing a wait of over half an hour in the station. Pupils were divided into small groups in the charge of Sixth Form pupils while being allowed to visit the toilets or shops while they waited. Graham Davies reported that Clive was missing and had not been seen for some time. Enquiries were made and it transpired that Clive had confided in one of his friends,

"I'm going to see the Eiffel Tower while we are in Paris. There'll be plenty of time to go by metro there and back before the train is due in."

His friend refused to accompany him on this hazardous expedition but was forced to break his confidence and tell us where Clive had gone when he failed to return. Consternation reigned. Graham blamed himself for not supervising Clive more closely. My colleague Don Morgan would now have to stay behind to search for the errant pupil while I returned home with the bulk of the party alone. At the same moment that the train chugged into the station, a shout went up,

"There's Clive! He's back."

Indeed he was, calm as a cucumber wondering what all the fuss was about. He soon found out when Graham swooped on him, beside himself with anger, and had to be prevented from almost murdering the culprit before he was bundled into the train. Incredibly Clive proved to be a serious pupil and went on to study French with me in the Sixth Form.

# Chapter 20
# Back at university in Swansea

During one of the school exchange visits I organised to France, I took the opportunity to do some research for my M.Ed. The previous year I had managed to obtain permission to get a year's secondment to study for a master's degree at Swansea University. My Headmaster was not keen to let me go and said,

"You know, Mrs Luther, just because you go on a course, it's not given that you will get a degree. Candidates are often unsuccessful."

I was furious with this negative remark and was determined to prove him wrong. This was not the first little *contretemps* between the Head and me. Some time previously the female staff had been up in arms because they were forbidden to wear trousers to school. I personally rarely wore trousers but, like everyone else, I was very annoyed at the Head's intractable attitude. I did possess one very smart trouser suit, so one morning I appeared in morning assembly wearing it. Suddenly the Head caught sight of me and steam seemed to be coming out of his ears. I was summoned immediately to his room where a confrontation took place. In the end, he had no answer to my statement that:

"Women staff do not wear uniforms and as long as the attire is smart and decent, there could be no valid objection."

Shortly afterwards smart trousers were deemed to be acceptable wear for female members of staff, though jeans were still banned.

A replacement Head of Department was appointed for the whole school year. Mark was already boarding in Llandaff Cathedral School and Angie went to live with my parents and was about to start at my old grammar school, Porth County, recently turned comprehensive. So, with my children happy and secure, I left for Swansea. I studied for a master's degree in comparative education comparing the British system with those of France and the USA. I let my house to an American couple on a year's exchange in my school and rented an attractive semi-detached house just above Caswell Bay in Mumbles. We holidayed there for the month of August along with my parents, before two other mature students joined me for the academic year. I would regularly make the pleasant journey over the mountains to spend the weekend with Angie and my parents and take them down to Llandaff to see Mark and visit the school Tuck Shop which was a must for all the little boys to stock up for the week.

The M.Ed. course was very demanding including, as it did a course in Sociology, a subject totally new to me, as well as in-depth study of different methods of education. Having been able to make very concise notes as a student, I now found that I was writing reams of notes at the age of forty. I worried that I might succumb once more to the sort of panic attacks and depression I had experienced previously when teaching in Sea Mills Junior School. However, my tutor was most supportive and encouraging, so I managed to carry on without the need for tranquilizers. Once my nervousness subsided, I enjoyed the course and made good friends. When revising towards the end of the year, I found that a brisk walk down to the sea and a stroll along the beach in Caswell Bay did wonders in sweeping away all the cobwebs and refreshing me to continue with my work. The written exams at the end of the year went off well and I was left with my master's dissertation to complete my degree after returning to school.

My dissertation entitled *A study of secondary education in a rural area of France,* was to be based entirely on primary data collection in two secondary schools in the Dordogne. The first was a CES (11-16 years of age) in Lanouaille and the second a Lycée in Exideuil (11-19 years of age) where Michèle Grèze taught. During our exchange visit I busied myself making taped interviews with pupils and staff of both schools, even managing to secure an interview with the Director of Education in Bordeaux. I returned to stay with Michèle Grèze in the following August to complete my research before writing up my thesis. When the next exchange pupils arrived at Easter, I was juggling a responsible full-time job, the organisation of the exchange visit, running my home, caring for my children and writing my dissertation. It was truly exhausting but I was eventually recompensed by obtaining my M.Ed. in almost record time to prove my Headmaster wrong in his negative predictions.

I took up my teaching duties in Treorchy once more while also tutoring on weekly courses for pupils and teachers at Ogmore in The Vale of Glamorgan and Dyffryn House, Cardiff, at the same time. Hoping to further my career, I aspired to become an inspector of schools (French). At the interview I was asked how I would manage when needing to be away from home with two teenage children to care for. Although I assured them that my parents were available to supervise them in my absence, I was passed over in favour of a male colleague who was the father of four children. He was not asked whether he was not afraid of "a teenage rampage in [his] absence" as I was! Men and women were certainly not on a level playing field when it came to career advancement at that time.

At about this time, Mark became Dean's Scholar in the Cathedral School and made us all proud, leading the treble choir and singing solos in the Christmas services. When his voice broke, we thought of putting him in for further music scholarships to enable him to continue his education in such prestigious schools as Brecon, Monmouth or Taunton. Mark, however, wanted to come home, so he started at Pontypridd Comprehensive which

Angie was already attending. They both continued there until they left for higher education, Mark in The Welsh College of Music and Drama, Cardiff and Angie at Swansea University to study languages.

Mark took lead parts in all the college productions from the first year then went on to Opera School in the Guild Hall, London. After finishing his training at the internationally-renowned Opera Studio in London, Mark married Julie Unwin, a fellow opera singer, on 26 July 1992. All the family came from Canada, California and all over Britain to attend their spectacular wedding where all their friends (future operatic stars) produced music of the highest quality. To follow this, they gave a wonderful charity concert and a fantastic birthday party for Mammy where she performed such old-time music hall songs as "Berlington Bertie" leaning on her son, Michael's arm. Mark went on to perform lead tenor roles in many of the big opera houses in Britain and worldwide. Mammy and Daddy were very happy indeed to see their grandson become a successful operatic tenor of whom we were all proud.

Angie was equally successful in her chosen career. When she had applied to do joint honours in French and German at Swansea, she wanted to take up Italian from scratch, having already exchanged with an Italian pen friend she had contacted through Ann. After signing up for the French and German courses, she was dismayed to find that all the places on the Italian course were full. I then rang my former tutor who suggested she signed up for any other course until students who had started the Italian from scratch course, dropped out, as they invariably did when they found the course too difficult. I persuaded her to opt for Russian meanwhile. After a while she liked Russian so much that she decided to continue it for the whole of her first year instead of taking up Italian. At the end of the year, she was offered an Honours Russian course or a Joint Honours course with another language. Following a fascinating visit to the Soviet Union, accompanied by me, she was very tempted by this offer, but finally decided to continue with the French/German Degree that she had originally chosen.

Having successfully completed her first two years at university, she spent the third year in Germany as an English language assistant in a secondary school as part of her degree course. Mark and I visited her during the Easter holidays and were welcomed daily to the beautiful homes of her German friends and colleagues for 'Kaffee und Kuchen' (coffee and cakes) and other delicious home-made foods. In the early summer she left for Paris to study French at the University of the Sorbonne for a few months and then had a stint working as an au pair on the Brittany coast just before she returned to Swansea in the autumn to complete her final year.

Towards the end of her postgraduate studies the following year, she spotted an advert on the University notice board for a language graduate to teach English in a Mining, Geology and Engineering University in central China.

Intrigued, she applied and, to her delight, was offered the job. She accepted it and set off on a momentous adventure to a 'closed city' in communist China to start her first job at the tender age of twenty-three. She worked there for two years and met and married David Bohua Tann, a brilliant Chinese academic in 1988. They eventually returned to the UK to pursue careers as University lecturers, and Angie dedicated her PhD thesis to her beloved grandmother Annie May for whom education was everything. Both my fledglings had flown the nest at approximately the same time and I was left to my own devices back home in the Rhondda.

There followed a period of hectic social life interspersed with my normal teaching commitment and tutoring on courses. My friend Pat Williams took me on the rounds of all the night clubs in Cardiff and surrounding areas. We regularly attended all the best concerts together and went on various holidays abroad. We became "Friends of the Opera" and were later rewarded by seeing Mark perform on the stage of The New Theatre, Cardiff, as well as such famous actors as Ian McKellan in our favourite Shakespearean plays. I joined various clubs for single people, such as Coffee Pot, where I met my friend Jean Coslett and which I attended with Michelle Bonifacio, my French Assistant, who lived with me for two years. These clubs offered varied social activities, such as lectures, outings, theatre visits, jazz and parties, where we met up with a wide variety of people. I socialised with a number of different men some of whom I went out with for a year or so. Bill Berry, a lively, pleasant man who was kind and helpful, did some necessary decoration for my parents. Mike Coles from Cardiff was a divorcee who moved to Pontypridd to be near me, but I could not envisage spending the rest of my life with either of them.

I had met a mature student from Algeria called Mahi, who was studying for a Master's Degree in Maritime Law and we had a close relationship for over two years although he was seventeen years younger than me. He invited me to stay with his family in Algiers where I was given lavish hospitality. We travelled extensively visiting the Sahara and coming up close to Arab nomads and their disagreeable camels. We came across other famous places, such as Tipaza with its interesting Roman remains and also visited Tizi Ouzou, where Mahi secured his first lecturing post. We also spent some time with our friends, Mohammed and Fuzia Miliani, both English graduates, who lived in Oran. Mohammed had obtained his Ph.D. in English from Cardiff University and was then lecturing in the University of Oran. I had earlier managed to help Fuzia obtain a post as French Assistant in a good Cardiff school so that the family spent a very happy year with their young children in Wales while Mohammed completed his studies. While in Oran, we visited Michelle Bonifacio's brother who still lived in their elegant former home which the family had been forced to leave after the troubles when Algeria had become independent of France.

Meanwhile my sister Ann had met a peripatetic music teacher called Terry Cregan and decided to get married. I took my parents to their engagement party in Tamworth in 1989. The party was held in a large house and unknown to me, Terry's best friend, Ray Mellor, had brought his seriously ill wife Mavis and their two teenage children to the celebration. They were unable to stay long so I never met them and could have had no idea that my future life would be linked with people who lived in Dunstable, so far away at the end of the M4 and M1 motorways.

1 Proud parents with newborn son Mark

2 Archie, Pat & Mark with grandparents

3 Pat with Mark at Angie's birth

4 Pat with babies on the boat to Pakistan

5 Pat, Mark, Angie with Nikki

6 Pat, Mark & Angie with Indu & Grandpa Luther

7 Pat & children at Quetta sign

8 Family group L to R - Grandpa with Angie, Pat, Honey, Baby, Bunny, Reggie, Indu with Mark

9 visit to Uncle Heno & Auntie Indu for morning spoiling

10 Mark pushing Angie in her walker

11 A stop en route for Hill Station

12 Camel caravan in Pakinstan

13 Tribesmen with donkeys

14 Pat's first ski holiday in the Alps

227

15 Mark at the start of his singing career        16 Angie as young graduate

17 Mammy's 80th speaking with Mary

18 Pat & Ray, Heritage Park Trehafod, 2.8.93

19 Pat's family wedding Group

20 Annie May with her children and Ray

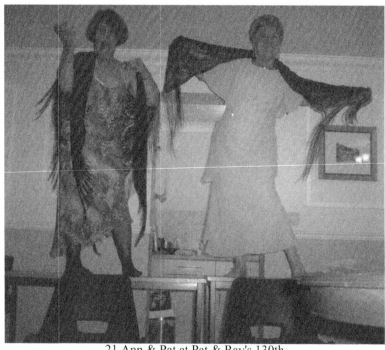

21 Ann & Pat at Pat & Ray's 130th

22 Ray planting as cows look on

23 Harvest at La Rivière

24 Fun with Tegan in the pool, La Rivière

25 La Rivière, our home in the Vendée

26 In the lavender fields of Provence

27 On the Esterel overlooking the Mediterranean

28 Roses round the door at our home in Provence

# PART 6

# A New Chance of Happiness

# Chapter 21
# A New Start

Ann and Terry were married in Yoxall in 1989 and all the family members living in Britain assembled to wish them well. I attended the wedding with my parents, Mark, Angie and David and Mike Coles. They were wed in the Registry Office in Litchfield and were blessed in Saint Peter's Church, Yoxall, where Ann was the organist. As the Matron of Honour, I read the first lesson and Terry's friend Ray Mellor read the second lesson. He also made the best man's speech at the reception where he recounted his long-standing friendship with the groom. He had only recently lost his wife of nineteen years to cancer, as Terry had done some time earlier, but was determined to be there to wish him happiness in his new life. Owing to the circumstances, we had little contact at that time but an introduction had been made.

Gradually, I continued to meet up with Ray through Ann and Terry and when I arranged to go to visit Morfydd in Harpenden, Ray invited me to stay with him later to show me around Dunstable. After a pleasant weekend in London with my friend Eileen, slotting in as many museums, musicals and theatres as time would allow, I spent a day or two sampling the delights of historic Dunstable with Ray as guide. At this time, his daughter Rachel was at Winchester Teacher Training College but his son Tim was still at school. He was heavily involved with Dunstable Dramatic Society which was producing "Under Milk Wood," so I was quite useful in helping Tim to acquire a genuine Welsh accent.

The visit went off well and I reciprocated by inviting Ray to spend a weekend in Pontypridd with me. Drives around our green hills, now almost recovered since the coal mines had closed, trips to the Brecon Beacons, the Wye Valley and Cardiff parks together with outings to Sophia Gardens to see an international netball match and to meet my friends in our Jazz Club, ensured the success of his introduction to my home area. We found that we had much in common, including the loss of a dearly- loved spouse. With Ray, still raw from the loss of his wife Mavis, I was able to empathise with him and encourage him to let the tears flow for the first time since his bereavement. Naturally, this brought back the pain of losing Archie, so a bond of sympathy began to be forged between us and from then on we stayed in contact by telephone and started to wear out our car tyres whizzing up and down the M4.

Ray was a keen skier and had been organising school skiing trips for some years. When he mentioned that they would soon be going to Flaine, I immediately said how much I regretted not ever having had the chance to try this exciting sport. He offered to try to get me a place on the trip and, convinced that he would succeed, I got my friend and colleague Jennifer Hughes to show me the ropes on the Cardiff dry ski slopes. Sure enough a seat on the plane was found and I set off for the Alps with hand-me-downs and borrowed equipment on my first of many ski holidays. Being a sunny Easter, the snow was not ideal for a beginner, being icy in the morning and slushy in the afternoon, but I persevered and by my third holiday I was proud to be the second fastest of our group in the slalom at the end of the course, although I was by far the oldest.

Our friendship gradually matured into a full-blown romance and by this time I had developed a deep respect for this Head of Science who held down a responsible job, at the same time juggling the duties of bringing up two teenagers devastated by the loss of their mother, and work for the Teachers' Union. These feelings were fully reciprocated by Ray and we decided to become engaged. Rachel found it hard to accept the fact that her father was contemplating marriage, rather too soon in her opinion, after the death of her mother, but we consoled her by saying that we intended waiting a year or so before actually getting wed.

A few years before meeting Ray, I had become a carer for my parents. Mammy had been suffering from osteoarthritis, and chronic bronchial asthma for many years and had become progressively more physically unfit while Daddy showed strong signs of succumbing to senile dementia. At some periods in life, problems seem to pile up one on top of another. I also began to suffer from painfully swollen joints and all the signs of the onset of severe osteoarthritis. Mark was in London pursuing his musical studies and Angie in China where she had just married David Bohua Tann. She needed me to contact the Foreign Office so that they could return to Britain together and Mike Coles was finding it difficult to accept that we were not suited and wanted me to go to Relate with him. Often the only escape I had from my problems was to immerse myself in my teaching, but all these issues eventually got the better of me and I was unable to enter my classroom after getting my A Level results in school. I collapsed in tears in my Deputy Head's room and he advised me to see my doctor and take at least a month off school. I was on the verge of a nervous breakdown. Although I soldiered on for another couple of years, I was eventually forced to take early retirement on the grounds of ill health in 1990 at the age of fifty-six. My teaching career was over and I became an almost full time carer about the time that I met Ray.

One positive, though, was that Mammy and Ray got on like a house on fire from the start and she approved wholeheartedly of our decision to marry. She had always confidently said:

"There'll be someone for you one day, Pat."

However, she had never actively encouraged me to embark on a serious and permanent relationship with any of my previous men friends, although she had not openly criticised them either.

Shortly before meeting Ray, I had embarked upon a rather hefty project. I had decided to build a chalet bungalow in the ample grounds of my home at 18 Whiterock Close. The garden had always been too big for me to handle and now that Mark had left home and Daddy was no longer able to help keep it in shape, I thought that it would be a good idea to cover up a significant part of it by building a modern bungalow to suit my new situation. I had noticed new buildings pop up in gardens where there was a lot less space than I had on my corner plot. If others could do it then so could I. Firstly I had to obtain permission to build from my local council, so I made application and was surprised and shocked when it was refused. Undaunted, I appealed and arrived at the meeting, supported by my son-in-law David, when it was to be heard with lots of photographs of houses already built in the vicinity where there was clearly much less space available than there was around my house. Having listened to my arguments and studied the photographs, the decision was overturned and I was given permission to build. I was all set to start.

To begin with, I set out my ideas for what sort of house I wanted. It should have three bedrooms, one with an en-suite, an open plan lounge/dining room, with patio doors leading to the garden, a modern kitchen and a garage. I then found an architect to draw up plans to my specifications and ended up with my ideal home. When Mammy heard what I was about to undertake, she said,

"Don't do it, Pat. You know nothing about building and you could easily get your fingers burnt and lose lots of money."

Nevertheless I was determined to carry on and went about finding out how to tackle the project. I opened an account with a local builders' merchant and started by employing some brickies to dig the foundations and put up the walls. I had excellent advice from David, who was a civil engineer at that time and who kept an eye on the progress of the work. I sought out well qualified and well known artisans in the area and employed in turn roofers, plumbers, electricians, double glazing installers, painters and decorators. As Ray had come on the scene just as the first spade was put into the ground to dig the foundations, he offered to use his DIY skills to tile and put up shelves etc. and was always there to help me choose things like the shower screens, ceramic tiles and carpets. He was as skilful as the professionals I employed and the bungalow was finished to a very high standard. I was delighted and Mammy very relieved indeed.

In no.18A there was one bedroom downstairs with its adjoining en-suite, a very roomy master bedroom with a huge bathroom upstairs and a second double bedroom with a sloping ceiling. The dining room opened out onto a sunny patio at the back with an enclosed, private, established garden with flowers, bushes and trees and a drive up to the garage. I moved in immediately and put no.18 on the market. Mammy really enjoyed her en-suite bedroom when she came to visit. As it turned out, I only lived there for about two years before I got married to Ray.

Daddy died on 7 December1991 after a short period in care. I was very sad, and sad also that he would not be present at my marriage to Ray. Mammy too was denied the sixtieth wedding anniversary she had been eagerly anticipating for some time. He would have been eighty-eight just one month later on 7 January. He had deteriorated slowly over some years and seemed to revert to his childhood. On his way back from Day Care, he would ask to be taken "home" to Bailey Street to see 'Mam', his mother, not to William Street to his wife. He was always reciting the scouts' pledge with the appropriate salute as he had in his youth. He became incapable of finding his way home if he strayed out by himself.

Eventually, a crisis was reached when Mammy became very ill with pneumonia. She was taken to hospital in Pontypridd while I took Daddy to live with me and we visited her together. He became very disorientated with this change and much more confused and anxious about Mammy. When she was allowed home from hospital, I stayed with them both in Ynyshir, but Mammy soon had a relapse and was again diagnosed with pneumonia. This time, she refused to be admitted to hospital so, under instructions from the doctor, I undertook to nurse her at home. I had to learn to use a nebuliser to relieve her chest and found it increasingly difficult to cope with Daddy at the same time. I sent an S.O.S. to my two sisters who both immediately came down to help. Ann took care of Daddy, Morfydd ran the house, while I concentrated on nursing Mammy, so we managed to cope for the time being

Daddy was visited regularly by a male nurse who, on seeing our predicament, suggested taking him for a week's respite care to the new George Thomas Hospital in Treorchy. While he was there, a permanent place became available and Mammy very reluctantly agreed that Daddy should take it up, as she had to accept that she was no longer fit enough to care for him herself. Mammy gradually recovered but could not be persuaded to go with me to visit Daddy in hospital. She felt guilty about having to put him into care. I kept telling Daddy that she was still very poorly and that she would be up to see him the next time I came to visit until one day he said to me:

"Don't bring Mammy up here. It's not nice for her here. Let her stay home."
I was very moved by the concern he obviously felt for her welfare and the deep love for her he still had in his heart, despite his own personal problems. On the other hand he accepted that he himself had to remain in hospital.

While there, he was regularly taken out for days by his daughters and by Angie. Sometimes we took him home and he loved to sit in his old comfortable easy chair watching the television and looking out of his window. It was often quite difficult to persuade him to get into the car to go back to hospital. When we left him there, he would sing:

"*Goodbye, don't cry. Wipe the tears baby dear from your eyes.*" He never forgot any of his songs, as he proved when I took him to a church service when we sang hymns requested by the congregation and Daddy sang every one of them without the hymn book and perfectly in tune.

Though Daddy was well cared for in the hospital, he lived less than a year there. A strong healthy man all his life, never troubled with arthritis or respiratory problems, he eventually succumbed to a deep vein thrombosis in his leg and was sent to Llwynypia Hospital for treatment. Mary had come over from California to nurse him in hospital for some weeks before he died. Mammy and his three daughters kept vigil at his bedside during his last weekend. After my sisters had returned home for work, I remained alone with him during his last night, feeding him his favourite grapes and ice-cream and holding him in my arms. Several times, I felt he was slipping away, but he hung on. The following morning, the nurses came to care for him and suggested I went for breakfast. Instead, I left to fetch Mammy and bring her to the hospital. As I entered her house, the phone rang. Daddy had passed peacefully away. I am convinced that he waited until I was home with Mammy before he finally let go. His love protected her to the end.

Daddy's funeral took place in mid-December and, sadly, was very sparsely attended, as he had outlived most of his friends and relatives. Mary was unable to return for his funeral, having spent almost a month nursing him earlier. She was forced to return to work. Michael, who had been devastated when Daddy had failed to recognise him on his last visit home, gave a poignant eulogy at the service. Ann played the organ while the rest of us, including two of his nieces, Ivy May and Rosemary, sang his favourite hymns. Mammy remained quietly dignified in her grief.

Having lost Daddy on 7 December 1992, Ray and I were married in Saint Catherine's Church, Pontypridd, on 2nd August 1993. This time the bans were called as both of us were widowed and could be married in the Church in Wales. Mark came back from Vienna where he was appearing in Mozart's *Don Giovanni* to walk me down the aisle to where Ray was waiting with his best man Terry. Angie attended me as matron of honour together with Ray's two little nieces Betsy and Amy, as flower girls. The music was special once more as Ray's brother Gordon played the clarinet during the signing of the register, Ann played the organ, her step-son Richard the trumpet, Julie sang Cherubino's solo from *The Marriage of Figaro* while the choir, made up of friends and family, sang "Jesus Joy of Man's Desiring" with Morfydd as soloist. Rachel read the lesson and Tim was chief usher. We were surrounded by all our family and friends from many countries and all over Britain. Reggie had flown over with his young family to represent the Luther side of the family. Mammy was the proud matriarch once again, content to see her eldest daughter happily united with her new husband to support each other through the rest of their lives.

The entertainment at the reception was exceptional too, in that nearly all the guests participated to make it unforgettable. Wonderful operatic solos and duets were sung by Mark, Julie and a Russian baritone, and Olga, Angie's friend from the Ukraine, led us all in some lively Russian/Ukrainian dances. Besides the usual speeches from the best man and groom, both my children spoke to express their special wishes for our future happiness, Angie recounting incidents of support from the past and Mark wishing us a second chance of happiness. Reggie was delighted to reconnect with his cousins, first seen as babies in Pakistan, and expressed how proud he was that Mark had become such an excellent singer and Angie a wonderful orator.

After honeymooning in Vienna where we met up with Angie, Ann and Terry to see Mark in *Don Giovanni*, Ray and I left to continue our honeymoon in the beautiful Lake District. We ended the month by visiting Ray's old haunts in Scotland where he had studied at university. The Tattoo at Edinburgh Castle was spectacular, as were the craggy mountains in the Highlands and the mysterious Loch Ness where we failed to catch a glimpse of the renowned monster. We also managed to fit in a brief visit to my cousin Rona, (Mammy's niece and daughter of uncle Davie) and friend Margaret before finally returning to find that Michael had closed the deal for us to sell on 18 Whiterock Close. Now we could go off to start our new life in Dunstable where Ray was still teaching while Mammy had gone off to stay with Mary and Vince in California.

# Chapter 22
# The call of France: La Rivière

Mammy had become very ill during her stay with Mary and Vince, so her return was delayed. As soon as she began to improve, she insisted on coming back to Britain. Mary made use of her insurance to travel to London with her as her accompanying nurse, while Ray and I picked them up at Heathrow Airport. Mammy stayed with us for Christmas and until she felt well enough to return home to Ynyshir. We took her back to Wales and I stayed with her for a week or so to get her settled in and all arrangements made for her to be able to cope alone in 7 William Street. We had found a very nice young lady who had been coming weekly to do the cleaning. Mammy got on well with her so she took over my caring responsibilities along with the Home Help who came every morning to get Mammy up and help her to bed in the evenings. Megan always did the cleaning in the mornings then stayed for company during lunch, leaving after washing up and settling Mammy down for the afternoon.

Neighbours, Mair Howells in particular who lived next door, called regularly to chat with her and we children rang daily to reassure ourselves that all was well. Mary rang almost daily too from California at tea time and Mammy looked forward to a good chat with her at a regular time. Morfydd, Ann and I took turns to visit her, so she was never lonely and she came to stay with us for long periods in Dunstable. She never locked her front door, so regular callers like the carers, neighbours, the baker, the milkman, the ice cream man, the fish man and the greengrocer, Peter, delivering the order already telephoned to him, simply knocked at the door, called out and entered. Though she missed Daddy, she led a happy, comfortable life, independent in her own home and was often taken on outings, especially by Angie who was now lecturing in Cardiff and was devoted to her grandmother. She also telephoned her daily, did her heavy shopping and visited her every week, often staying over. She was also free now to travel to all parts of England and Wales to hear her grandson sing in many famous opera houses.

Soon after moving to Dunstable I joined the Bedfordshire NASUWT teachers' union of which Ray was President at the time. The national body of the NASUWT was starting to form an association for retired members. Having already retired, this was something in which I could participate. I became involved in the inaugural meetings and was given the task of initiating a newsletter for the new national association. I became the editor, ably assisted by Ray, and in 1993 published the first edition of FORMAT (the Federation of Retired Members' Association Times) which is still distributed to all retired members of our Teachers' Union today. Ray continued to work for the Beds NASUWT in several capacities and has become an Honorary Life Member of the Union. He also served for four years on Bedfordshire County Council during this period as a Labour Councillor.

Now that we were satisfied that Mammy was secure and well cared for, Ray and I took on a new venture. Both Francophiles, we decided to look for a second home in France now that both my houses in Graigwen had been sold. After attending French Property Exhibitions in London and devouring numerous house agents' catalogues, we became very excited about the vast number of French properties available all over France at seemingly bargain prices. We decided to concentrate our search on the west of France slightly inland from the coast. Armed with brochures, we visited countless houses of various shapes and sizes and greatly differing states of repair until we found our dream home.

Once, as we visited properties from tumble-down two-roomed cottages to spacious houses surrounded by acres of land, we found ourselves parked outside a little house in the village of La Villette in Deux Sèvres. Wary of the barking of huge guard dogs, I waited in the car while Ray returned the keys of the property just visited to the neighbouring farmer. A lady emerged from the house and started talking to me. It transpired that she and her husband had recently come from Paris to spend their retirement in the area where she had found refuge as a child when her family had fled from the Ardennes before the German invasion during the war. She invited me in and, when Ray had joined us, insisted we stay and share a simple meal with them as they assured us that we would not find restaurants open at that time on a Sunday evening. We were not to know then that Jeanine and Zephirin Okal were to become lifelong friends after we settled just twenty minutes' drive away from them.

Before starting visiting properties, we had drawn up a list of requirements: the house should not be too big, it should be situated in a village close to shops and all facilities, be in a reasonable state of repair with not too much work to make it habitable, should have all living rooms, bedrooms, bathrooms etc. on the ground floor and have a manageable garden. When we set eyes on La Rivière we ripped up our list and threw it to the winds. It was a huge, rambling two-storied farm house with enormous, high-ceilinged rooms, several dilapidated outbuildings, situated in the middle of nowhere and surrounded by fields with no sign of a garden. The roof leaked and the floors consisted of bricks laid on earth. It was quiet, though, about 2 km. from the village and shops. Well, you can't always get a perfect match! It would certainly need a great deal of work to bring it up to an acceptable standard. Mr. Poisbelaud, the French estate agent, assured us that these few items would be put right.

"*Bien sûr. Pas de problème. Ce n'est pas grave.*" His reassuring tone allayed all our fears.

"It's a long way from the village and the shops. We'll have no neighbours," I said doubtfully.

"It's only a few minutes in the car and I can see one farm over there on the hill and another on the other side just around the corner," Ray replied.

"There's loads of work needing doing and it will cost a bomb to decorate those high walls and ceilings."

"That's no trouble and look at the space we have. After all, it does have more than adequate living rooms, bedrooms, kitchen and bathroom all on the ground floor and it has no end of possibilities," enthused Ray.

We had experienced what the French term as "*le coup de cœur.*" We had fallen for it hook, line and sinker. We were hooked. I needed little persuading, so the decision was made. La Rivière was to become the first home we would make together. On the day of purchase, we arrived with a car loaded with everything two people could possibly need for a week in a new home with rather basic facilities, which is a lot! The "Clampetts" had arrived in the Vendée. At the house the estate agent met us, together with the farmer who rented and worked the fields round about our new house, his wife, his brother and his wife, the electrician, and the plumber. It seemed that we had unwittingly walked in on some strange kind of French custom, yet we were clearly key players!

"First there will be an inspection of the house." Mr Poisbelaud announced, and he kindly came round with us........ and so did the farmer, and his wife, and his brother and his wife, and the electrician, and the plumber! Half way round, this caravan of inspectors took a break and Ray was able to point out that the leak in the roof had not yet been fixed. Louis Poisbelaud beamed his enormous smile and reminded us that it was not a problem:

"Ce n'est pas grave."

After the ceremonial walk round La Rivière, the whole party boarded their various vehicles, we in our still overloaded car creaking under the weight, the artisans to go to their work, the rest of us to the office of the solicitor who was to do the conveyance. I don't know how we all managed to squeeze into his tiny office, but somehow we did. M. le Maître took his work gently but carefully. Each of us, I, Ray, the farmer, the farmer's brother, the estate agent and the Maître all having to initial each page of the deed of transfer. After this long procedure, we all added our full signatures duly dated and La Rivière at last became ours. In the Maître's lobby afterwards, we invited the whole group back for a glass of bubbly at the house. So off we all trooped to our new abode, and out came the champagne, still a little warm from our long journey. The ice was broken and we spent the rest of that week enjoying the warm hospitality of the brothers Bisleau and spouses, Jean-Paul and Chantal, and Michel and Paulette, later to become firm friends.

The next day we looked around at our vast domain. One ancient oak tree whose luscious green branches stretched high into the sky affording welcome shade in the midst of our bare fields, painted an artistic picture standing tall against the impressive barn belonging to Michel just over our border. Apart from the trees lining the edge of our property along the little road leading past our house and ending at Le Puy Ardouin just a bit further along, all we could see were fields of pasture land with not a tree, bush or flower in sight. Curious cows stared at us over the electric fences that bordered our lands. Undismayed, we set up our tiny table and folding chairs in front of our door and enjoyed our first open-air meal washed down with a glass of the local wine as we basked in glorious sunshine. We were full of optimistic plans to create our perfect home and we were not afraid of the hard work that lay before us.

While all this work was about to begin, we had unexpected guests. Ray's brother Gordon was holidaying in the Vendée with his wife and daughters. They spent a day with us and we managed to produce a real party. The Bisleau family lent us some trestle tables which we heaped with salads, fruit, meats, cheeses and delicious French patisseries and French and British sat down to feast together on the quiet little road running in front of our new abode. We toasted our new life and established an *Entente Cordiale* with our French neighbours.

We offered Michel the greater part of our fields as extra pasture for his large herd of beef cattle, but kept a considerable patch in front of the house to make into a lawn with some flower beds. We camped out in the massive reception room on the right of the entrance door while we tackled the forty-five square metre room on the left. We were glad of the farmers' help in transporting the floor tiles, which weighed a ton, purchased from *Le Moulin Des Affaires*. Recommended by a friend in the village, the *Le Moulin Des Affaires* was an enormous enterprise which, amongst other things sold building and DIY materials and new and second-hand appliances and furniture. We became faithful customers of this establishment as the years rolled on.

New drains were dug, plasterboard panels erected to combat the rising damp that threatened to destroy our walls and oil-fired central heating was installed. We tackled the bulk of the work ourselves with occasional help from our children, relatives and friends but we had to employ professional artisans to repair the roof, rewire the electricity as well as to sandblast our oak beams and doors. Even our beautiful sandstone fireplaces and the antique *potager*# had been covered in thick white paint and had to be sand blasted too. Ann and Terry proved invaluable in the early days. Terry helped Ray with the enormous amount of tiling needed to cover all the floors and Ann helped me scraping off old wall paper, filling up holes and painting and decorating in general.

Directly behind the house was our *fosse septique* into which all the sewage and waste water from the house flowed. This was well hidden by a jungle of nettles and overgrown weeds. The septic tank outflow of cleansed water emptied into a ditch about ten metres from our patio doors. Mademoiselle Marie Thérèse Thomas de la Barte, the aristocratic owner of all the surrounding lands who had sold La Rivière to us, was unwilling to provide *buses* (huge concrete pipes) to drain the water from the surrounding fields into which the outflow from our septic tank could be directed. These could then be placed in the bottom of the ditch and covered over.

Since we had been sold an *assurance juridique** we were able to persuade her to pay half the cost of laying these massive pipes as long as Ray did the work himself. Fortunately, Pierrot, one of the Bisleau brothers, not only helped Ray with this heavy work but also showed him how to lay a huge twelve metre wide patio covering all our land behind the house and replacing the tangle of brambles and weeds previously there. Ray also erected a pergola there over which he planted climbing *vignes vierges* and pink and white flowering clematis giving us much needed shade in summer. We planted sweet juicy white and black grapes to grow at the corners and along the walls completing the fairytale setting where we could relax with our guests over a barbeque and admire the stupendous sunsets over the years we spent in La Rivière.

We would spend sixteen happy years living in the beautiful Vendéen *bocage* country while, with hard work and enthusiasm, we transformed our ancient farmhouse into our dream home, complete with swimming pool, jacuzzi, orchard and garden. Our swimming pool, 10m. by 5m., became a real godsend in the hot summers, allowing us to cool down several times a day as we continued the work. It was top of the list for our family and friends too as we relaxed on the patio with a refreshing drink, enjoying the perfume of the roses and lavender surrounding us. It was particularly good to swim in the cool of night when the pool was all lit up. The jacuzzi was a great favourite at night too when, all the lights turned off, we sat and admired the

---

# an ancient "cooker" made of the unique pink and grey *pierre de plocher* only to be found in our village, Saint Pierre du Chemin. Glowing embers were taken from the open fire and placed in three cast-iron grills set into a granite slab allowing the heat to warm the earthen vessels above. The ash from the embers fell through to another granite shelf below.

* *assurance juridique:* Insurance which would cover our legal costs to take someone to court.

dazzling wonders of the firmament in a sky unpolluted by the lights of huge cities.

We kept in touch with Mammy throughout the summer. Jean Paul and Chantal Bisleau were kind enough to allow us to receive phone calls from Mammy. Although they spoke no English and Mammy no French, they managed to understand each other enough to make the system work.

"Hallo. Bonjour, I am the Maman of Pat," an increasingly familiar voice would announce.

"Bonjour. Elle n'est pas ici en ce moment. Pourriez-vous rappeler vers cinq heures – err, five hours?"

"OK. I'll ring at five o'clock then. Merci beaucoup."

Then we would recount all the progress we were making, especially with regard to *Mammy's room,* the room just opposite the entrance door which she had chosen as her bedroom from the photos we had shown her.

We had allowed ourselves a short break to go to Vienna to see Mark once more performing in Don Giovanni at the Schönbrunn Palace, so off we went promising to ring as soon as we got back to tell her all about it. However, on our return to La Rivière, there was no reply when we phoned whatever time of the day we tried. Becoming anxious, we phoned her next-door neighbour, Mair Howells.

"Your mother's had a fall. She has been taken to hospital" was all she could tell us. After frantic calls to find out where she had been admitted and what condition she was in, we packed our bags, locked up the house and left for Wales the following day.

# Chapter 23
# A Death and a Birth

The journey home seemed never-ending but eventually we arrived and went straight to East Glamorgan Hospital. I was worried to see Mammy's bed empty but as I looked up, I saw her entering the ward wheeled in by a nurse. Her eyes lit up when she caught sight of me. I dashed up to her and took her in my arms weeping with relief. Her always indomitable spirit revived and she was instantly full of life, asking how we had got there so quickly, wanting to know all about the progress in the house and how Mark had sung in the opera. It appeared that after the visit of the chiropodist, she had got up to put away the card with her next appointment on when she had slipped and fallen against the radiator. This had resulted in a nasty compound fracture of the upper arm and had put her shoulder out of joint. She was in great pain and was unable to get up from the floor but knowing that her carer would come to help her get ready for bed, she did not press the emergency button that she wore around her neck. When her carer arrived she immediately summoned the doctor who phoned for an ambulance and sent her off to hospital.

Because of her bad chest and asthma it was decided not to operate but to treat the fracture through traction, so she had her right arm bandaged and held in a sling over her chest. Recovery would be slow and painful but she was in good spirits and was happy to receive frequent visits from her children and grandchildren who spoilt her with gifts of fruit and boxes of chocolates. Morfydd's daughter Elizabeth was over from Australia preparing for her wedding in September so seeing her was an extra treat. She was like a queen sitting up in bed to receive her loved ones and she later regaled her fellow patients with accounts of what everyone was doing and where they lived.

Ray and I visited her every day and spent many hours poring over photos of La Rivière discussing our plans and Mammy's intended stays with us. She even enthused about wanting to learn a smattering of French so that she would be able to communicate better with our farmer friends. Now that Mark and Julie had been married for two years she was eager to know when they would be producing a second great grandchild for her. She had already recently held Isobel, her first great grandchild, in her arms at her christening. She was confidently looking forward to a full recovery and an exciting future life even if she would have to miss Elizabeth's wedding on 1 September. All was set to have a happy outcome.

When Ray and I went to Harpenden to attend Elizabeth's wedding, we left Mammy in hospital. Angie decided not to attend the wedding so that she could visit her grandmother regularly during our absence. Most of the family were at the celebration, including Mary and Vince who had flown over from California and Mark who was back from Vienna to sing at his cousin's wedding. In the middle of the reception I was summoned for an urgent phone call. It was Angie:

"Nanny's been dropped by a nurse and she's in dreadful pain. She has broken her femur and she will have to be operated."

"Oh! How could they! They were not supposed to try to mobilise her without adequate support on each side," I gasped. "I'll come back immediately."

An auxiliary nurse had previously attempted to mobilise Mammy with the sole support of a walking aid intended for use in the right hand for her to use in her left hand. For some years Mammy had needed to grasp a walking frame with both hands to enable her to get around in the house and feeling very unsafe, she had refused to move. When she had told me, I had spoken to the sister in charge, who turned out to be a former pupil of mine, and we agreed that it was to be written in her report that Mammy was not to be mobilised without sufficient support on both sides. However, in the absence of the sister, a young charge nurse had taken it upon herself to ignore this instruction and had insisted on mobilising Mammy unaided, consequently letting her fall.

Ray had to stay in Dunstable as term had started, so I drove down to Wales with Mary and Vince who were both horrified at what had happened. We three confronted the charge nurse who had dropped Mammy.

"How did this happen? Who was helping you support the patient?" I inquired.

"I was on my own," admitted the nurse. "I gave Mrs Stevens the tripod to hold in her left hand and I held her by her back and right shoulder to steady her."

Mary was aghast:

"You actually held her by her injured shoulder with no-one on her good side and asked a patient who needed both hands to support herself on a walking frame to walk with virtually no secure aid! It's no wonder that she fell. I deal with disabled patients and know that there are secure methods of mobilising them which you have obviously ignored with the result that my mother has to now undergo a dangerous operation which should have been avoidable."

"We'll sue the hospital for negligence," Vince threatened.

Angie had also strongly criticised the lack of proper care when she had rushed to her grandmother's bedside having been informed of the accident only at 5pm as she was getting ready to leave Cardiff to visit Mammy in hospital. From what another patient told her, Angie learned that after the fall, which had occurred in the morning, Mammy had been bundled into bed and left for eight hours in agony without further attention until she had asked for her granddaughter to be called.

On inquiring whether Mammy had been X-rayed, Angie became very angry when told that it had not yet been done and said that she was leaving instantly for the hospital. When she arrived at the hospital at 6pm there was no sign of Mammy on the ward as only then was she being X-rayed. The lady in the next bed said she'd only just been taken to X-ray as they knew Angie was on way up and very angry. Angie dissolved into tears when the consultant told her that an operation was now inevitable, even though a general anaesthetic had been deemed too dangerous earlier to fix her shoulder. After that, the hospital authorities could not do enough to try to rectify the situation. The chief orthopaedic surgeon was called in to perform an emergency operation on a Sunday. When he had finished explaining what he was about to do, he asked Mammy,

"Is there anything else you would like to know?"

"No thank you. Just do a good job," she said brightly.

Having done everything possible to avoid operating on her arm, we now had to accept that an operation was now unavoidable. Nevertheless she appeared to have come through it all unscathed once more. Was the creaking door going to hold good again? At first it appeared so. The wedding over, the beloved matriarch was surrounded by her family and we were all hopeful that she would pull through yet again. Once she had recovered from the anaesthetic, she asked me to bring her reading glasses so that she could enjoy the novels, magazines and newspapers she had accumulated.

"These aren't my glasses," she told me.

"Yes they are, Mammy," I assured her.

However, she could not read anything with them. This was the first indication we had that something was seriously wrong. Another indication that she could not see very well was that she was unable to feed herself properly and swallowing became more and more difficult. After work, Angie would take her home-made soup and feed her as her meals were just left in front of her and she was not getting enough nutrition. True enough she had suffered a stroke and gradually she declined until she was unable to swallow anything at all and had to be fed via a drip. It became obvious that she would need to spend a considerable time in hospital before she would be fit to return home, so she was moved to the Graig Hospital, which specialised in geriatric care, where she had a private room.

We were all heartbroken. I stayed by her side almost all day moistening her dry mouth with medical swabs, talking to her and playing her Mark's CDs. Angie, too, came regularly to keep us company and Morfydd and Ann often relieved me at weekends. Although she could no longer talk, it was obvious that she appreciated our care and did not appear to be in too much distress. I was to become sixty on 22 October and planned to celebrate this milestone birthday with Mammy and Angie in the hospital. A former fellow patient, who was a hairdresser, came to cut and set Mammy's hair and she looked almost her old self again. We had tea and cake in the ward with her but it was so distressing that Mammy was only allowed to moisten her mouth once more. Showing her my birthday cards, I said:

"I'm sixty today, Mammy. I'm an old age pensioner like you now."

Mammy looked at me with understanding and somehow I felt that she decided that it was time for her to let go at last. It was half term, so Ray and I needed to return to France to put things right in La Rivière during that week. Reluctantly I said to Mammy:

"I have to go to France for a few days but I'll be back soon. Morfydd and Ann will look after you while I'm away and Angie will be up to see you every day as usual."

We had left France in a great hurry so there was much to do. We finished off jobs left half done and stored away all the paint, tiles and other building materials that were strewn all over the place then locked everything up securely. Our few days flew by and it was soon time to say goodbye to our farmer friends and set off for Britain. Rachel was about to graduate at Winchester so we intended to travel back on Friday to attend her graduation on Saturday 29 October. When we arrived in Winchester, there was a message awaiting us to say that Mammy was dying and that we should get to the hospital without delay. We left immediately, Ray promising to return to Winchester for his daughter's graduation the next day.

At the hospital Mammy was still hanging on surrounded by most of the family members living in Britain. On Sunday 30 October 1994, the Vicar of Ynyshir came to give her the last rites and we all crowded around her bed to say our last fond farewells. We held her hands and sang her favourite hymns, including psalm 100 "The Lord's my shepherd, I shall not want." We wanted her to pass on peacefully surrounded by those who loved her, but Angie could not let her go. Holding her in her arms, she clung on to her hand quietly begging her to fight on until finally we calmed her down and, accepting the inevitable, let her beloved Nanny slip away to be reunited with Tom in peace eternal.

At the funeral in Saint Anne's Church the incumbent was joined by the former vicar who had known Mammy well and he was able to speak of Mammy's strong, bright personality and her faithfulness to the church over many years. The church was full with worshippers from Saint Anne's, Mammy's friends and neighbours and my friends and ex-colleagues from all over the Rhondda. Michael, who was still teaching, was the only one of Mammy's children who was unable to be present. He had come over to stay for a week shortly before and had said his goodbyes when she had still been able to recognise him and listen to all the news about his family. All four daughters took part in the service. Ann helped to choose the hymns and played the organ, Morfydd sang "I give thanks for you" in tribute to Mammy, Mary read a passage from "Embraced by the Light" describing an uplifting post-death experience, and I gave a poignant eulogy recounting Mammy's life of love and service, caring through prayer and donations for Christian work both home and worldwide.

Heartbroken as we all were to lose our seemingly invincible mother, who had directed and supported us all from early childhood right up to the present day, we all managed to keep our composure and carry out our various tasks. Angie also gave a moving tribute to her "best friend" and Mark, although sobbing uncontrollably shortly before, managed to produce a professional rendering of a song Mammy often used to sing and which summed up her life for us:

*"If I can help somebody as I pass along,*
*Then my living shall not be in vain."*

Thus Annie May Stevens was laid to rest at the age of eighty-six after a lifetime of love, self-sacrifice and devotion to her family.

Life had to go on but a huge hole was left by Mammy. I, nor either of my children, could face the prospect of Christmas without her, so Ray and I invited our four children and their spouses to join us on a Christmas cruise with Brittany Ferries. This not only alleviated some of the pain but was a good opportunity for them to get to know one another. The cruise helped a little to take our minds off our loss as we enjoyed excellent food, entertainment and sightseeing tours in historic towns such as Rouen along the River Seine. A scrumptious cake resplendent with candles was offered to celebrate Angie's birthday on Boxing Day. It was a bitter-sweet time for us all.

After Christmas, Ray and I returned to Dunstable for his work but we were eager to be in France to get on with the work in La Rivière. We spent every holiday there, often with Ann and Terry, and good progress was made. A stroke of luck allowed Ray to take early retirement unexpectedly at the age of fifty and we were joined by Michael and Carol in the summer of 1995. They rolled up their sleeves and pitched in too, notably throwing out the rotten beams that Michel Clochard, the builder, was replacing in the roof. Following his father, Michael's gardening prowess was also put to good use as he got us all digging and planting both flowering plants and vegetables. He was utterly amazed to see how huge our lettuces grew in next to no time due to the fact that the field was rich with manure, having been used as pasture land for years. Over the years we gradually exploited this richness until we ended up cultivating most of our own fruit and vegetables.

Of course, it wasn't all work. We explored the nearby Atlantic coast, the pretty villages with their massive ancient churches and the unique Marais Poitevin where we sailed beneath a canopy of greenery along the meandering River Sèvre. One evening, as we were relaxing within the metre thick walls of our house which, together with the fans, provided us with respite from the hot sun, we watched three little mice make their way across the floor and disappear into the empty fireplace. Although I normally have a horror of mice, these looked so sweet and jaunty as they strutted past that I joined in the singing of "Three blind mice" and the laughter that followed. The following morning Carol placed a beautifully-constructed and decorated "Château des souris" edifice in front of our fireplace.

At this time, both Julie and Nicola, Morfydd's youngest daughter, were expecting their first babies. Nicola gave birth to Megan prematurely on 28 July, Mammy's birthday, but we were still anxiously awaiting news of our first grandchild. One day as we relaxed in the late sunshine, the phone rang. It was Mark:

"Julie has given birth to a beautiful baby girl. We have called her Tegan."

This charming and unusual Welsh name means "pretty toy" or "fair one." We were absolutely delighted and broke open a bottle of champagne to wet the baby's head. Born on 14 August 1995, Tegan grew to be a pleasant, healthy and easy child who was very adaptable and happy in any environment. This was just as well as her parents were away from home so often singing in operas that we played a considerable part in caring for her in her early years. This situation brought us much joy and forged a deep bond of affection between us.

# Chapter 24
# Round the World in less than 80 Days

With Ray now happily retired with a suitable financial package, we were free to travel the world. A fantastic opportunity offered itself immediately and we didn't pass it up. Mark was to sing in Beethoven's *Fidelio* in the Wellington Music Festival in New Zealand in the autumn. His daughter Tegan started travelling at the age of three months when she flew off with her mother to join her father there for her first holiday abroad. We wanted to arrive there just in time for the first night of the opera, so we planned a jam-packed itinerary entailing stops in Thailand, Indonesia, Singapore and Australia on the way.

This nine week trip was unforgettable on many counts. In Bangkok we were stunned by the vibrant colours of the floating flower market where vendors sitting in hundreds of little bobbing wooden boats toted their wares, and by the elegant golden-topped temples with their diverse statues of all shapes and sizes, including the massive Golden Buddha. We rode in tiny tuc-tucs which slipped easily in and out of the teeming traffic taking us all over the city, making our hearts miss a beat. It was a wonderful place to shop so we bought many gifts of crisp Thai cotton and gorgeous Thai silk in various colours and designs. Prices were very reasonable so we ordered a made-to-measure silk dress in light green for me, two suits (one black, one grey) and a white Egyptian cotton shirt for Ray. All was ready in record time and each was an excellent fit. In all, Bangkok was a fantastic first experience of the Orient for Ray. The friendly Thai people had given us a very warm welcome to their colourful country.

Our stay in Bali coincided with the time when Indonesian currency hit rock bottom. For the first time in our lives we felt like rich Americans able to afford anything and to buy whatever caught our eye. Our hotel was luxurious. We had our own little detached air-conditioned bungalow. However, when we left it to walk a few yards to the restaurant, we were bathed in perspiration. We certainly made good use of the swimming pool and the cool drinks constantly available in its bar. We hired a taxi for a whole day to take us to the most interesting sights on the beautiful, lush island.

At one stage the taxi driver stopped at the foot of a most impressive temple. Hundreds of steps led up to it. Although we were daunted by the thought of climbing up in the humid heat, we were persuaded to make the effort, having first bought a small offering to take with us on the advice of the driver. Having arrived exhausted at the top, we found that the ornate interior and the splendid view amply repaid us for our efforts. The downside of this situation was the desperate poverty of the charming Indonesian people. They constantly clamoured around us begging us to buy fans, expertly carved figures or pictures, lowering the price each time we refused until, once their desperate situation dawned on us, we finally gave in and bought numerous articles we didn't want.

The contrast with Singapore was stark. Hosted by Reggie who was a captain in Singapore Airlines, we found the island modern and pristine. Full use was made of the bargains to be had in this thriving metropolis. Reggie took us to buy a video camera of which we made good use throughout the rest of the trip. I bought a dark green trouser suit in heavy silk with an extra matching skirt and a white silk blouse embroidered with an elephant motif. I also ordered a second made-to-measure silk dress in a light cream colour with a metal grey geometrical design on it. The silk was much finer and the design more sophisticated than that of the Thai dress, so it could not be finished before we left. However, it was sent on after us and arrived safely in New Zealand in time for me to wear it for Mark's opening night. In the botanical gardens we marvelled at the stunning orchids of diverse hues that we were told were used to decorate Buckingham Palace on occasion. The cruise along the coast was truly unforgettable as we enjoyed a romantic dinner watching a spectacular pink, purple and blue sunset over a silver sea. We experienced the inevitable gin sling in the famous Raffles Club, but were dismayed to be told that it still retained some relics of racial discrimination from old colonial days.

Next, we flew off to spend some time with Reggie's wife Winnie and their children in their home in Perth, Australia. We were given a warm family welcome and advised about all the must-see sights in Perth. In our hire car we visited King's Park and the Botanical Gardens on Mont Eliza which offered sweeping views over the city. Going south we drove through extensive *outback* country where tall, thin *black boys* (skeletal remains of trees that had been destroyed in previous bush fires) raised their burnt heads over the parched brown landscape devoid of all green vegetation. On our way to the Harris River State Forest we were awed by coming across one of Australia's huge *road trains,* a common sight in remote areas, as it swept past us heading in the opposite direction. It seemed to take forever to pass us and must have been over a hundred feet long.

Our next port of call was Cairns on the east coast, necessitating a stopover at Australia's iconic Alice Springs. It afforded us a superb view of Ayers Rock (*Uluru*) - a yellowy red sandstone rock in the shape of an upturned basin dominating the flat arid plain surrounding it. It is a sacred place for the indigenous Aboriginal Australians, but the flies swarming around us made us glad to escape back into the aeroplane for the second leg of our journey. Cairns was fabulous. There was so much to explore. Not only does it boast tropical rain forest, but its coast lies next to the Great Barrier Reef. After a train journey into the middle of the area, we walked round a large section of rain forest using an elevated walkway, an almost frightening experience as we swayed high up near the tops of the lofty trees, enabling us to see much more than if we had simply walked along the ground, many feet below. We also took a trip out to the Great Barrier Reef in a large trimaran. We beached on a massive sandbank out on the actual reef and were able to swim with our snorkels to our heart's content in and under the amazing coral reef teeming with multicoloured fish of all sizes flashing past us in the crystal clear blue-green water, before heading back.

Moving on to Sydney, we had arranged to stay with my cousin Elizabeth, Uncle Glan's daughter, who lived in one of the city's suburbs. However, since her in-laws were visiting at that time, Elizabeth kindly arranged for us to stay for the first week with a friend of hers, who was on his own and was happy to have the company. He lived in a comfortable house on the outskirts of Sydney, a short distance from the centre. He led an open-air lifestyle and had the habit of feeding the blue parakeets, dozens of which would flock squawking to the lawns every evening around the same time of day. During our stay, we climbed up to the top of Sydney Harbour Bridge and strolled across the elevated walkway admiring the stupendous vistas over the harbour. We were thrilled to see Verdi's "Macbeth" in Sydney's iconic Opera House overlooking the ocean. Its unique sails gave it the appearance of being about to take off over the surrounding sea. Before leaving the city, a relaxing dip in the sea at the famous Manley beach was not to be missed.

We decided to take our host out for a meal in a local restaurant to thank him for his generous hospitality at the end of our stay. A rich Frenchman and his German girl friend were amongst the party. We were a little nonplussed when our host brought along a bottle of expensive wine. He then explained that in Australia, restaurants were banned from selling alcohol of any kind. So it was a case of BYO (Bring Your Own.) Having opened the bottle, a glass of wine was passed to the Frenchman for his expert opinion.

"This wine is undrinkable" was his disdainful judgement. "It is nothing but vinegar."

To save our host's blushes, Ray dashed off to a local off-licence to buy another bottle to take back to the restaurant. We later found out that our host stored his wine on open shelves in his drawing room – in all that heat! We ended our Australian adventure by visiting the Blue Mountains. It appears that the *Mie* light-scattering phenomenon causes this range of mountains to take on a bluish tinge when viewed from a distance giving it a quite unique colour. We were taken to see these mountains during our stay with Elizabeth and family who were always ready to drive us to visit other further-off touristic sights before we had to move off to resume our journey.

The next leg of our round-the-world sojourn saw us flying from Sydney to Christchurch in the South Island of New Zealand. There, after the heat and humidity of Australia, we appreciated the markedly cooler temperatures, just pleasantly warm like our UK summers. We did the typical tourist thing and were welcomed by a very lively and colourful Maori spectacle show-casing all the traditional Maori songs and dances ending with the spectacular Hakka. We drove through wild empty country in our hire car encountering more sheep than human beings. We were entranced by Milford Sound, on the south-west of South Island, cruising around the fjords of the magnificent Fjordland National Park, where we watched countless seals and dolphins basking and playing together in the sunshine.

On the equally beautiful east coast, we were able to go whale-watching and were lucky enough to encounter a shoal of Humpback Whales spouting and cavorting in the sea around our ship, a truly exciting experience. On our journey north through the island we came across the famous Fox Glacier which can only be visited easily by helicopter and so, up we went. Eight miles long, fed by four Alpine glaciers, it finally ends amidst lush rain forest almost 300m above sea level. The trip was fascinating, if a little on the chilly side! Finally, we took the ferry to North Island.

Having picked up a new hire car after getting off the ferry, we drove straight to Wellington where Mark had been allocated a flat. He, of course, was rehearsing his role in the opera and had only a day off here and there so we were often left to our own devices. However, we took the opportunity to visit the thermal spa town of Rotorua close to the north-east bay of North Island together. This highly volcanic area was quite amazing with its acres of steaming-hot, sulphurous, mud pools, water-spouts and the 30m-tall spectacular Pohutu Geyser. Then it was on to Napier, a popular tourist city, with a unique concentration of 1930s Art Deco architecture, built after much of the city was razed in the 1931 Hawke's Bay earthquake.

After all these visits, the date of Mark's opera performance was fast approaching. It was to be staged on the opening day of the Wellington Arts Festival. After the successful first night performance, we were invited to a special Champagne Reception held in a smart restaurant overlooking Wellington Bay. In his opening address, the master of ceremonies made mention of all the special guests including the Prime Minister and other dignitaries, and we were staggered to hear our names called out as Mark's parents who had flown all the way to New Zealand to support him! The evening concluded with a colourful fireworks display with all the guests gathered around the picture windows watching the changing play of sound and light over the bay.

At the end of our New Zealand trip, we made our way to Auckland on the northernmost tip of the island from where we flew off to Los Angeles. As usual, Mary and Vince were the best of hosts. They lived in the comparatively cooler hills above L.A. Vince kindly allowed us to borrow his large, comfortable BMW to drive over the state line to visit the Hoover Dam, the Grand Canyon, Las Vegas and San Francisco along the way. The massive Hoover dam was awe-inspiring. Built in the1930s and named after President Hoover, it provides hydroelectric power and water for Nevada, Arizona and California and is paramount in the control of floods in the area. Our flight in a tiny Cessna over the steep-sided Grand Canyon carved out by the Colorado River, over a mile deep in places, was a once-in-a-life-time experience, as our tiny seven-seater craft battled through the turbulence.

Unfortunately, our car broke down before we got to Las Vegas but Vince organised its repair whilst we stayed in a Vegas hotel. We had stopped off at a typical Best Western hotel just outside the casino city. Ray was somewhat of an expert card player and I encouraged him to have a little flutter playing *vingt-et-un* at the tables. Never a gambler after being stung at university, he was very cautious. However, he won enough to pay for a few nights in a luxurious suite in the Hilton Grand Hotel just off The Strip in Las Vegas. We dabbled a bit on the various gambling machines without losing too much money or making a killing before limping off in a temporally repaired car to San Francisco. There we stayed with my nephew Steven and his wife Harley who gave us a good welcome.

Harley kindly lent us her car while the BMW waited for the piece necessary to repair it permanently, so we went off to the Sequoia National Park. There we were amazed to see the stupendous Sequoia trees which not only grow to an unbelievable height, but in some cases are wide enough to allow a car to drive through their massive trunks. After sampling the delights of China Town, a visit to the infamous Alcatraz prison and crossing the Golden Gate Bridge, we said goodbye to San Francisco and took the well-known State Route 101 Highway along the beautiful Pacific coast and through wine country all the way to LA. After spending a most enjoyable Christmas with Mary, Vince and all their family, we finally made tracks for home. Our great adventure was over for the time being.

This round-the-world trip had whetted our appetites for travelling and there were so many places on the globe that tempted us and which we wanted to see before we were compelled to hang up our boots. In the years that followed we went on two long trips and several exciting cruises taking in such faraway places as the Panama Canal, Alaska, China, Egypt and South Africa. We saw Panamanian Indians, sloths and banana plantations on our luxurious Christmas Caribbean cruise which was in stark contrast to the reports of the horrific tsunami of Boxing Day 2004 which devastated huge areas of Thailand with a tremendous loss of life. We watched bears and whales and the spectacular crash of towering blue icebergs falling into the sea as they melted in Alaska, an ominous warning of the effects of global warming. The ancient wonders of Egypt astonished us on our river and land tour. So many human beings must have spent their lives toiling to construct the impressive pyramids to house the tombs of the great pharaohs and all their riches. All along the fertile Nile we marvelled at the Valley of the Kings, Luxor Temple and countless other fabulous palaces right up to the immense Aswan High Dam and colossal figures carved out of rock on the relocated Abu Simbel Temples.

After the fall of apartheid in South Africa, we stayed with Ray's cousin Pauline just outside Johannesburg and went on some remarkable safaris in Swaziland and Kruger National Park getting up close to such wild animals as elephants, crocodiles, hippopotamuses, giraffes and lions. Safety was of paramount importance in proximity to wild animals. A terrible tale was told us of the fate of an unwary Japanese tourist. It appeared that he had got down from his high four wheeled-drive vehicle to take close-up pictures of a pride of lions snoozing as their young played alongside them. The seemingly lazy lions immediately pounced and began to devour him as some of his fellow tourists continued to film the whole scene! We also toured the Garden Route and the surrounding wine area, looked out over the Indian Ocean from Table Mountain in Cape Town and made a short trip to Zimbabwe revelling in the cooling spray of the impressive Victoria Falls before flying over the imposing Zambezi River in a tiny helicopter.

Before venturing to China we consulted Angie and made a wish list which we managed to fulfil on a three week tour by plane, coach and train. Fortunately I was still able to climb up the gigantic steps of the ancient Great Wall of China although often I had to be hauled up by Ray. This unique and massive edifice is, it seems, the only man-made construction which can be seen from space. We toured the enormous enclosed Forbidden City, the former abode of China's emperors. Bicycles and people thronged the crowded streets and parks peppered with hexagonal pagodas with their upward sweeping roofs. We visited the Summer Palace, the Ming Tombs and Tiananmen Square where I gave thanks once more that Angie had been safely back home before the dreadful events that took place there soon afterwards when tanks rolled in on the student demonstrators.

Different provinces of China have different cuisines all of which we sampled as we made our way through this vast country. The strange sound of Chinese Opera is totally foreign to our western ears, as Angie had found out when she was persuaded into singing a duet with a male opera singer just because her brother was an opera singer. The interesting result was then broadcast on her province's Chinese New Year to many millions of Chinese. Angie still has the old VHS video which was presented to her as a souvenir. When we went to see a Chinese opera, the main protagonists, such as the

261

Monkey King, were explained to us and we were allowed to watch the singers putting on their traditional garish make up before taking our seats to see the performance.

We also attended other spectacular shows where beautiful girls performed exotic songs and dances dressed in brilliantly coloured silk costumes as we dined. Gifts of jade jewellery were purchased when we visited a jade factory. The very colourful and intricate embroidery on silk was almost beyond belief. From the silk factory we visited, we brought home many souvenirs and gifts as well as a beautiful silk duvet and cover which makes me feel as though I am experiencing the ultimate luxury when I snuggle down under it.

The dramatic landscape of scenic hills and lakes of Guilin charmed us as we sailed gently up the wide, meandering river and over the silver lake surrounded by tall conical mountains reminiscent of camel humps. The tops of these lush, green mountains were lost in the mist, creating a fairy-like atmosphere. Massive water buffaloes ambled lazily on the shores of the lake while the whole calm ambiance evoked images of the ancient Chinese fairy tales recounted by our guide. In contrast, the bright neon lights and modern shopping centres of Shanghai astounded us with its bustling avenues and shops full of all the latest fashions. Hong Kong too was amazing with its sky scrapers, Kowloon Park, stupendous views and an unforgettable night sail in a sampan to see fishing with cormorants. The night was clear and a bright moon shone over a shimmering sea. We watched, fascinated, as the huge birds dived into the water returning to the boat stuffed with fish. As their necks had previously been tightly ringed, they were unable to swallow their catch which they were made to re-gorge by the fishermen before being thrown a fish as a recompense for their efforts.

Two parts of our Chinese trip remain most vivid in my memory. The first was the visit to the historic city of Xian and the famous Terracotta Army unearthed originally by farmers in a rural area as they were digging a well. An army of over eight thousand warriors has been excavated in recent times. These buried battalions were meant to accompany and protect Emperor Qin, the first emperor of China, in his afterlife. These magnificent statues of soldiers are life-sized. Each one appeared to have been individually sculpted and no face looks the same as the next. The attention to detail is remarkable. Even the sole of an archer's foot as he knelt down to draw his bow, has been intricately sculpted. Chariots drawn by horses four abreast were also found and excavation is still going on so that this incredible site is constantly being enlarged.

The second was the cruise down the Yangtze River which is etched in my mind for ever. We were fortunate that we were amongst the last to sail through the huge steep-sided gorges before they were flooded to make the Three Gorges Hydro Electric Dam which is the world's largest power station in terms of capacity. We sailed sedately down the river which flowed through the bottom of the towering rocky gorges, a scene immortalised in countless ancient Chinese poems and scroll paintings. On each side were marks indicating the eventual level of the water once the gorges were flooded. Whole villages would have to be moved and roofs, being the most expensive parts of the houses, had already been removed and taken to higher ground leaving the rest of the homes to fall into disrepair.

We watched sampans and larger flat boats transporting coal and other commodities wending their way slowly up and down the majestic river. At one point we were to be taken to a typical peasant village on the bank of a tributary of the Yangtze. This necessitated navigating some fast-flowing narrow sections of water in small boats. Here the Chinese coolies got down into the water and placing strong ropes around their bodies, chanted and sang as they pulled the boats, loaded with their occupants, against the currents as they made their way to the isolated village. There, we all got out and purchased traditional Chinese metal objects and postcards on sale on the shore. It was a quite exceptional experience. Back on the cruise ship we enjoyed first class western food and Chinese entertainment and even participated in a show in a small way.

Our life had become very pleasant now that we were retired and could divide our time between Britain and France and travel. We also enjoyed caring for Tegan while her parents were away singing and we gained two more beautiful grandchildren when Rachel produced Ellie in 1997 and Mia four years later. Tegan came to visit us on her own in La Rivière when she was nine years old and Ellie and Mia also spent many happy holidays with us and their parents in France especially after we had installed a pool and Jacuzzi.

# Chapter 25
## Our Life in La Rivière

As the years rolled by, life took on an impetus of its own in La Rivière. The house exuded a good ambiance and we were certainly very happy there. Although in a quite isolated spot, we had many unexpected visitors knocking at our front door. The first was Pratiksha, our nearest neighbour, calling to welcome us. She was a very tall friendly Dutch lady who hosted many of her giant Dutch friends in her farmhouse just down the road in Le Puy Ardouin. One evening a little time later, as we were preparing to return to Dunstable the next day, there was a loud rap on the door. On opening it Ray found himself dwarfed by a group of strange young Dutch people towering over him:

"We've just arrived from Holland. We are alcoholics and we have no wine. Can you lend us some until we can buy some tomorrow?" We were dumbfounded. However we weren't going to argue, so we gave them the few bottles we had left and we returned months later to find a box of wine hidden in our dilapidated out-house awaiting us.

La Rivière stayed in the hearts of those who had lived there over the years. One day a jovial gentleman came walking up informing us that he and his family had lived in the house for very many years. René Bonnet was one of nine children brought up in La Rivière when it was a working farm. Through René we invited the whole family to come to see the changes we were making in their old home. More than twenty of them arrived headed by the matriarch of ninety-seven who even managed to clamber up the rickety narrow stairs so as not to miss anything. They pointed out where the old bread oven had stood before it was demolished with as many "coups de vin" (toasts to celebrate the progress) as blows with the hammer.

Previous to the Bonnets, only one other family had occupied the farm since its construction using the granite from the walls of a crumbling castle nearby in the mid eighteen hundreds. Sometime later a car drew up in front of the house. Monsieur Chatelier, now a very old gentleman, had been brought by his granddaughter to revisit the house where he had been born and brought up before his parents had moved away. He too had happy memories of La Rivière and asked if he could take away a bottle of the pure spring water that fed our lovely old granite well from which we still drank.

During our early days too we were astounded to see a strange Parisian arrive at our door shooing a young calf before him:

"I found your calf wandering on the main road. He must have escaped from your field and would have soon been run over if I hadn't stopped to rescue him."

"Actually it's not ours," we explained. "It belongs to our farmer friend whose fields surround our house. It must have escaped under the wire of the electric fence. We'll put it back and call the farmer."

Hearing us converse in English, Guy eagerly informed us that he was on his way to Saint Hermine in the south of the Vendée to help his English friends finish off tiling around their new pool. He brought out of his boot some delicious Charentais melons and a *vin d'arrivée* to celebrate our meeting. He insisted on my telephoning his English friend Richard, speaking in French. This ended in a burst of laughter when we both realised that English was the mother tongue of us both and it was not long before we were invited for an *apéritif* with Richard and Marion and a dip in their new pool. Our unusual first contact soon blossomed into a firm friendship. They were our only real British friends with the exception of Frank and Doreen Farmery from Saint Marsault, the neighbouring village where our farmer friend Michel Bislaud lived and where Frank had become an influential councillor.

Soon afterwards another unexpected character arrived at the door, sporting a crash helmet and asking Ray for directions to *Le Breuil-Barret.* Ray knew the village well, as we purchased our wine from the *cave* (local wine shop) there. Whilst he was giving him directions, carefully explaining where to turn at the crossroads in our village, Ray was puzzled that there was no sign of the stranger's motorbike or scooter.

"Non, non", the newcomer exclaimed, and went off into a long and very fast explanation, asking it appeared, for directions to get there across the fields! So, quite flummoxed, Ray fetched me. I quickly discovered that the young man had landed in one of the nearby fields in his microlight and needed help to turn it round before he could take off again. He really did want directions as the crow flies! After watching him fly off successfully over our fields, we walked back to our house.

In the fields behind the house, we could see from our back patio the black and white cows which formed the milking herd of the Massé family, a well-established farming family who also ran the château which we could glimpse behind their fields. The aristocratic Duplessy family, close relatives of the former proprietor of La Rivière, had renovated the little castle for a dual purpose – they enjoyed family holidays there and let it out in the summer as a *gîte de France*. Annie Massé acted as their agent. One day, Annie and her husband Yves called on us and introduced themselves as retired farmers who still did a lot of work to help out their son Christian who had taken over their farm. They invited us to their home in Saint Pierre which was just opposite the home of our very first unannounced caller, René Bonnet, and his wife, Thérèse, who were their close friends. We struck up a firm friendship with them all. They taught us to play the French card game of *belotte* and we passed many pleasant hours playing cards together in one another's houses, women versus men. Their son Christian Massé also became a very good friend, helping us regularly to cut down the jungle that invaded our *parc* in our absence each year. His eldest daughter Anaïse spent many hours playing with Tegan when she visited us as a nine-year-old.

Another close friend of the Massés was Louis Renaud, Mayor of Saint Pierre. He was a retired teacher of Spanish and was pleased to learn that I had taught French, as there was quite a large contingent of British people in the village who spoke very little French. He said that he might call on me occasionally to translate if necessary. Just before the planned celebration of the armistice of World War One, I was pleased to receive an official invitation from the *Mairie* (town hall). We mingled with a number of British people, some of whom had served in World War Two. After the ceremony we were all invited into the Town Hall for the usual *vin d'honneur* and the speeches began. The Mayor made a long speech recounting the part that Saint Pierre and its inhabitants had played in the war. When he had finished, he turned to me and, without any warning whatsoever, said,

"Now, Madame Mellor will translate for our English friends and allies."

For a moment I was dumbstruck then I recovered my composure.

"Of course, but could you kindly begin again and stop occasionally for me to translate, as I cannot remember such a long speech all at once," I explained in French. Thus I became the official translator and was called upon to translate the Mayor's message to the villagers at the beginning of *Le Bulletin Municipal* (the village newsletter) whenever it was published.

I must not forget to mention the most important interloper who took up residence with us at La Rivière. A feral cat was attracted by the smell of our barbeques. She was tiny with a pretty face and attractive tabby markings on her delicate body. In fact she looked more like a kitten than a full-grown cat. She was brave too and would prowl around until someone flung her a titbit, then would dash up and grab it before running off to a safe distance to enjoy it. It took some time to persuade her to eat out of our hands but eventually she adopted us. Mimi became our much-loved pet who brought us six little kittens to play on our patio each year before chasing them away when they were old enough to fend for themselves. It was always hard to leave her whenever we returned to Britain. One year she was determined to go with us. Having packed our car ready for the off, we looked behind and saw a cute little tabby cat perched on the back seat waiting to accompany us. It was heart-breaking to have to turf her out and watch her running after the car until we were out of sight. However, we had left plenty of cat food for her during our absence which Michel undertook to put out for her each day until our return whenever he came to tend to his herd.

The work done on our property had necessitated a good deal of investment, so we decided to go into the Bed and Breakfast business to defray our costs.

Although it was quite hard work it was very rewarding. We met some very interesting people some of whom were also letting out their properties and others who came to stay with us. Amongst the latter group were some members of a cycling club who had come to take part in a race in the area. They consumed large quantities of pasta on our patio to ensure good stamina for the race. We went along to support them and were invited to the bun fight to celebrate their victory after the race. As we were registered as providers of Chambres d'Hôtes, we were invited to meals at good restaurants and given reductions to visit local attractions by the local Tourist Office. *Le Puy du Fou*, the biggest and most prestigious theme park in Europe, was only a stone's throw away, so we had no difficulty in filling our rooms. Thus we built up a wide circle of friends and entertained them in our turn in our home and at the poolside once we had constructed our swimming pool. We were proud of what we had managed to achieve since arriving in the Vendée. We had renovated the whole house, created a park out of a wilderness, incorporating rose gardens, a productive vegetable plot and an orchard, and installed a swimming pool and a Jacuzzi.

Our children and lots of other relatives enjoyed summer holidays with us every year, but gradually we realised that we still had to work pretty hard just to keep it running smoothly. It took Ray a whole day to cut the lawns perched on a tractor. I had to have help to keep the huge house clean, the pool had to be cleaned daily and there was always something extra to be done around the house and garden – and we were not getting any younger.

Regretfully, we began to consider downsizing. I had experienced health problems for the first time in my seventies when I had contracted the very painful polymyalgia, a rheumatic disease. This hit me very hard and I ended up scarcely able to move or do anything for myself. The pain was so severe that I was eventually confined to a wheelchair until it was finally correctly diagnosed and treated with cortisone. It took me almost three years to recover enough to be able to do without the cortisone. We decided to look for an even warmer climate than that of the Vendée and hit on Provence in the south of France. Our good friends Michelle and Gerard Girel lived in Marseilles while our English friends Imelda and Martyn Cooke had a mobile home in Fréjus, so we would not be totally devoid of friends when we moved. We had spent sixteen very happy years in La Rivière but now it was time to leave, we reluctantly decided. We set about looking for a suitable home in *La Provence Verte.*

# Chapter 26
# Golden Years in Provence

A few years previously we had been burgled during our absence both in Dunstable and in La Rivière within a short time of one another. As we had been thinking of downsizing, we thought that this would be a good time to make a move. It was also a good time to consider the possibility of returning to my beloved Wales. We decided to sell our detached house in Dunstable and purchase a flat suitable for older people while we were still fit enough to make all the arrangements ourselves without needing help from our children. Of course, it would have to be convenient for travelling to France, in a big city with all the best facilities and near an airport. Penarth, a dormer town for Cardiff, fitted all these criteria. We bought a spacious two bed-roomed flat at 26 Cwrt Jubilee in 2004.

The flats were supervised by a resident manager and the CCTV system ensured security while we were away. It was only a pleasant ten minute walk down to the sea with its smart renovated pier, and there were numerous other walks including one around a lake inhabited by stately swans, ducks and other wild life. There was a bus (free for seniors) every ten minutes into the centre of Cardiff for shops, restaurants, museums and entertainment. To cap it all, it was within easy reach of my beloved Rhondda valley where I had grown up. I still had several good friends in the area and we acquired two more the day we arrived. We were in the middle of unpacking and supervising the removers when the bell rang. Bernard Stevens, a member of our church in Dunstable had forewarned his daughter Rosemary, who lived in Penarth, of our move and she had come with her husband John, bringing a beautiful bouquet of flowers to welcome us to our new home. What a wonderful surprise!

Almost the first thing we did was to organise a *130 years' Birthday Party* to celebrate my seventieth and Ray's sixtieth both falling at the end of our first year in Cwrt Jubilee. We booked the residents' lounge for a private party to which all our family and friends came from far and wide – the second of our reunions bringing most of my family back to their roots in Wales. I was still quite spritely and ended up dancing on the table and encouraging our little grand-daughters to do the same! My brother Michael stepped in for Mary to sing the obligatory "Three little sisters." She was not with us that time, as we were soon to be off to the Caribbean with her and Vince to celebrate their fortieth wedding anniversary shortly afterwards. We were very glad to have found a perfect place to live while in the UK. We made many new friends in Cwrt Jubilee, three of whom, Margaret, Sheila and Jean, visited our home in France at various times.

Having decided to downsize in France too, we started to look in earnest for a smaller house in the south of France in 2009. We visited over twenty properties between Avignon and Nice, before finally deciding on a three bed-roomed villa in *Les Machottes* (Provençal for "*The Owls*") just outside the medieval village of Le Val about forty kilometres north of Toulon on the Riviera. It was with a heavy heart that we left our home and friends in the Vendée. However, a manageable bungalow with plenty of neighbours all around was so much more suitable for us at this stage of our life. Le Val means "the valley" and 383 Avenue du Roi René nestles amongst similar houses on the *restanques* (terraces) on the sides of the valley so that although we have close neighbours, we are not overlooked at all and have stunning views over the wooded hills.

The bungalow itself was clean and tastefully decorated with a spacious veranda and a large *sous sol* (basement) which opens onto the established garden. Small in comparison with the land surrounding La Rivière, our garden still has four olive trees, a fig tree, a pomegranate tree and, in the middle of our lawn, a huge black cherry tree, all of which produce luscious fruit every year. The *potager* (vegetable plot) has been a great disappointment to us. With all that sunshine we had anticipated growing mounds of flourishing Mediterranean produce – shiny multicoloured tomatoes, green and yellow courgettes, purple aubergines, red, yellow, orange and green peppers, juicy pale green melons, etc. However, the poor soil and dry climate dashed all our hopes and we could only look back on our prolific harvests in the Vendée with regret. All that could withstand the dry, hot climate were the vines, olive trees and established fruit trees and even so one of our vines withered and died one particularly hot dry summer. Nevertheless, highly fragrant red, pink and yellow roses bloom everywhere along with spring flowers of every hue and flowering shrubs and climbers such as vivid pink-purple bougainvilleas. In a protected corner of the garden, we could live outdoors in the hot weather on our spacious patio complete with summer kitchen, comfortable garden furniture and a roof and curtains to shade us from the fierce sun.

It took us no time at all to settle down and be accepted fully by our neighbours in Les Machottes. Babou, a young Senegalese who lives opposite us, put his telephone and internet at our service and everyone offered us a *coup de main (*help) whenever needed. Having moved in towards the end of May, we were immediately invited on 1 June to the *Fête des Voisins,* a street party get-together of neighbours which also warmly welcomed new arrivals. There were trestle tables laden with plentiful food and drink, almost all home-made, including the wide selection of *apéritifs* and *digestifs,* and there was music and dancing to round off the evening. We found ourselves sitting next to a lady from Paris called Maryse Fleury who lived next door but one to us. She had moved in a few years earlier and had installed a swimming pool. As we fully intended doing likewise, we asked her advice. She invited us to try out her pool and somehow we ended up using her pool with her and helping her with any little practical tasks in return, so we ourselves never invested in a pool in Provence. Thus we kept our back garden with its lawn and shady cherry tree while still being able to swim daily in pleasant company.

The polymyalgia I had suffered had been finally cured after two and a half years and I wanted to put anything else right before moving to Provence as French residents. I had arthritis in both knees but exercises had kept me mobile. I decided to get them both operated simultaneously while I still had my private health care policy on 15 December 2010. I recovered quickly and astounded my surgeon by dispensing with my crutches on 4 January, my first post-operative consultation. I had put my little patch of poor health behind me and was ready to make the most of my new life in Provence, or so I thought.

However, life has often a few surprises in store for the unwary. In June 2013 at our *Fête des Voisins*, I was dancing with a tall stalwart neighbour, Jean, after imbibing rather too many of the tempting homemade apéritifs, wines and digestifs available, when I "gave a twirl," stuck my hand out to be caught and found myself full length on the hard tarmac of the road. I was rushed by the *pompiers* (ambulance men) to Brignoles hospital where a fractured pelvis was diagnosed. Several weeks of bed rest with regular injections into my stomach followed before I could sally forth in a wheelchair. Since then it was found that over many years I had developed a massive inward growing goitre covered in nodules on my thyroid. This had given rise to atrial fibrillation so, in order to remove the thyroid, I had to have a pacemaker fitted.

Both operations went off smoothly and I was very impressed with the French Health system. Finally, I hope, after a nasty fall on my front drive (am I not quite as steady as I was?), the X-ray revealed that I needed a hip operation. I told the surgeon:

"I get very little pain with my hip and it does not seem to have got any worse for the last year. Will I really need an operation?"

"There is definite wear and tear there and it will deteriorate, so you will need a new hip before long," he assured me.

I decided to get it done while I was still in good health, so I had the operation early in 2018. This took place in the *Renée Sablon* hospital in Hyères, where I had a private room overlooking the Mediterranean. Ray stayed with me on a put-u-up bed in my room which saved him a long daily journey and gave him a nice break at the sea-side. I'm becoming quite the bionic woman and clear ringing tones testified to this as I passed through the metal detectors at the airport. Until recently this has not been a problem but now that I have a pacemaker I have to remember to keep my medical papers with me at all times to avoid going through the usual scanners.

These little setbacks have not curtailed my travelling or the undertaking of new ventures. During this period we have embarked on several Viking River Cruises all over Europe and two MSC Mediterranean cruises taking in Italy, Spain and North Africa. On occasion, I have joined Ray on ski trips with our family and friends. As I no longer ski, I have been tutored on these occasions by my artist friend Dinah and have produced one or two reasonably acceptable snowscapes to adorn our walls. At other times, I have swanned off on my own with Dinah to Tunisia or to the Canary Islands. Just before last Christmas we paid a visit to Tim in Germany where we were entranced by the fantastic Christmas markets. The roaring log fires and the hot *Gluhwein* (spiced wine) did wonders in warming us up in the bitter weather.

As in the Vendée, we entered fully into the life of our village. In Le Val there are more than thirty associations of all sorts to which one can belong from *Boules* (often known as *pétanque* - French bowls played on rough ground) to the *Association Culturelle Valoise* (Cultural Association of Le Val). One of the Associations which appealed most to us both was the *Club de Loisirs* (Leisure Club). This was first set up to provide leisure-time occupations for the retired of the village. Originally called *Club des Anciens*, our friend Marcelle, President of the club at that time, changed its name to a more inclusive and politically correct one. It is open each weekday afternoon for various activities. We joined the card club which meets on Tuesdays and Fridays to play *belotte* and *tarot* but soon introduced contract bridge which quickly became popular with certain members.

At the end of our first year we were impressed by the Christmas concert given in the church by our local *Vent des Collines* (Breeze of the Hills) choir. The mixed choir, about forty strong at that time, were looking for new members, in particular men, so, fired with enthusiasm, Ray joined. Unfortunately, I was unable to sing as my goitre had displaced my trachea leaving me hoarse, but I joined the supporters group and attended faithfully all the concerts and participated in all the outings. Music had always played a prominent part in both our lives. Ray's father had established a dance orchestra which played regularly in the Belle Vue dancehall in Manchester while his mother was a competent pianist.

When Mark first visited Provence, he was delighted to come across the *Jardin Théâtre,* Le Val's open air theatre. With me to translate, he approached the Mayor and offered to produce a music festival in the village. He planned to bring over a troop of professional debutants supported by a few established singers to put on operas and concerts in Provence. He envisaged a two-week music course in which intense rehearsals under the

271

direction of professional coaches and *répetiteurs* prepared the young singers to perform at the end of the course. The British participants paid for the course which took place in the south of France in elegant accommodation with cool swimming pools, tasty French cuisine and included trips to places of interest, but there was not a moment to spare! At the end they would have had an unforgettable, though hectic, working holiday culminating in invaluable experience for their future careers. Young French singers were encouraged to participate free of charge by sending video clips and/or CDs to audition to Mark in Britain. British singers also auditioned early to give themselves time to familiarise themselves with their roles well in advance and members of the chorus were also recruited from local French choirs. The aim was to gather British and French singers to work together to create a production of high quality in a friendly and convivial atmosphere.

Naturally we were enraptured with the idea and immersed ourselves immediately into helping with all the organisational tasks involved in such a complex project. It was soon suggested that I create a new Association to launch the festival. I was told that it would take months to get an Association up and running but we only had a few weeks. Incredibly, by going down personally to the *Préfecture* in Brignoles, filling in all the forms and taking them back myself the same day we astounded everyone by creating the association before the first festival was due to take place in July 2015. I became President and Ray, Secretary, and we managed to persuade our local friends to fill the posts of the other officers needed. Corinna became Vice-President, Guy was Treasurer while Chantal, Thierry, Christina and Henri made up the rest of the first *Bureau* or committee of our *Les Amis du Festi'Val de Musique* (Friends of the Music Festival).

We had no idea of the amount of work that was involved in organising such a big undertaking. It took over our lives. The first thing we needed to do was to find venues where we could put on the performances. This was not easy as there was very little money available for supporting new cultural ventures. However, we did make an extremely useful contact in Carcès, a neighbouring village. While visiting the ancient *château* which dominated the centre of Carcès, we got into conversation with Kate, an English lady married to a Frenchman. She taught in the Junior School, helped in the *médiatheque* (library) and was in charge of running the castle which boasted a stunning open air theatre on its flat roof. Kate managed to persuade the Mayor of Carcès to book Mark's company to stage the Opera *Carmen,* and a concert of classical music at the château for a fee of 1000 euros per performance on the understanding that ticket money went to the Mairie. Madame Patricia Ingrassia, deputy mayor in charge of culture in Le Val, gave them free use of the Jardin Théâtre and other rehearsal rooms for the duration of the course and promised to provide sound and lighting for the performances.  The Mayor also provided a welcome meal.  We found an excellent young French Mezzo, Marie Pons, to take the part of Carmen and all the other main roles were filled by competent young debutant singers supported by a few professionals from Britain.  The festival was off to a good start.

However that was only a portion of the work involved.  We also had to provide transfers between Marignane Airport, Marseilles, and Le Val and transport for the whole two weeks to take them where they needed to be.  This entailed booking coaches for the transfers and excursions and cars and minibuses for the two weeks, with all the paperwork (passports and driving licences for the drivers etc) that was involved.  We had to find attractive accommodation which could host large groups and provide a relaxing environment with pools and spacious grounds.  The first year, we were obliged to book rooms in *Lou Valen,* the little tourist hotel in Le Val for 2015 but thereafter we acquired two large summer *gîtes* which housed most of the troop while the few remaining participants stayed in Bed and Breakfast accommodation nearby.

One of the *gîtes*, although walking distance from the centre of the village, stood apart and high up surrounded by hectares of lawns and well-kept parkland.  *La Bastide de Fontenelle* was absolutely ideal.  There was room to rehearse and eat outdoors in the shade so it became the headquarters of the course throughout the fortnight.  Food was organised sometimes at *Le Paracol,* a local restaurant which gave us a good discount, sometimes using a *traiteur* (caterer) at the Jardin Théâtre or the Bastide, sometimes making barbeques etc. in the grounds of the Bastide or post performance meals provided at the different venues.  At least two excursions took place each year for the troop to such tourist attractions as *Les Gorges du Verdon* where they sailed through the steep, narrow gorges and swam in the lakes before visiting the pretty village of *Moustier Sainte Marie* and passing through the magnificent gorges themselves in the coach.  The famous Mediterranean resort of Saint Tropez also proved to be a firm favourite.

There was important work to be done well in advance to ensure the success of the festival.  Sponsors had to be found and publicity needed to be organised.  Ray soon took over the design and production of posters, fliers and programmes.  I contacted our bank, *Le Crédit Agricole,* which became our main sponsor and paid for hundreds of eye-catching posters and fliers to be printed.  Before and during the festival, props had to be found and scenery to be made.  This task largely fell to Ray once more ably helped by Kate, Guy and Corinna and practical members of the cast.  Our friend, Michelle Girel, volunteered to act as official translator, so that took a load off my shoulders.  Thierry, Chantal and Christina took responsibility for the buying and selling of refreshments during the performances and the recruiting of volunteers to help. I had also to apply for permission to sell alcoholic drinks and for special parking arrangements during performances from *La Police Municipale.* Finally, Ray and other members of our committee together with some singers from *Vent des Collines* took small parts and sang in the choir and the chorus of the operas as well. Josianne in particular was most enthusiastic and played a part in all performances of the festivals while Henri introduced the items in the concerts. In 2017 Agnes also took a small part in Suor Angelica while Arlette and Keith Childs joined and made invaluable contributions in the sale of tickets and the making of excellent publicity videos.

From its inception in 2015, "Love to Sing Opera," produced several successful operas in various villages of *La Provence Verte,*" as well as classical concerts. In 2015, Purcell's *Didon et Enée* (Dido and Aneas*)* was performed in Le Val and Bizet's *Carmen* in Carcès. In 2016, Massenet's *Cendrillon* (Cinderella) was performed in Le Val, Carcès and Saint Maximin. On the day of the performance scheduled for Château Nestuby, Cotignac, a fire broke out in the nearby woods. Nevertheless, the dress rehearsal took place and while the cast were having a light meal, the smell of smoke became overpowering.

"Look over there. You can see the flames clearly. The fire is approaching fast. It's getting dangerous."

"Nothing to worry about! The fire fighters have it well under control. The helicopters are zooming overhead all the time. The show must go on!"

With that there was a loud clanging noise and the proprietors of the vineyard were announcing urgently that this was a *Police Announcement* and that *The fire is encroaching fast. Leave everything and evacuate without delay.*

Already very concerned, there was no need to tell us twice. Meals were left half eaten, drinks were left on the tables and everyone made a beeline for the minibuses without giving a second thought to the new piano and the props and costumes left behind. We scrambled into the vehicles on top of one another and off we roared anxiously eyeing the darkening skies and coughing in the thick smoke. We wondered whether Le Val would still be unscathed when we arrived. Fortunately it was untouched and the efficient police and firemen got everything back under control by the next day. Great swathes of woodland were left smoking, blackened ruins but no one was hurt. The authorities are always well prepared for such emergencies during the long hot summers. The panic was over, although the performance was cancelled. Eventually we were able to put on an extra performance in Le Val for those who had booked for Nestuby.

In 2017 we staged two short operas, Puccini's *Suor Angelica* and Leoncavollo's *Pagliacci* in Le Val, Correns, Le Château de Vins and Le Château de Carcès. Mark also conducted a classical concert in the church featuring an acclaimed performance of Fauré's *Requiem* and other choral works interspersed with brilliant solo performances from members of the cast. The beautiful voices of the troop combined to produce a quite spectacular sound. A second concert featured a mixture of solos, duets and trios and a bit of comic relief was introduced by a rendering of *The Policeman's Song* from Gilbert and Sullivan's *The Pirates of Penzance* featuring a small group with Ray as the sergeant. Each half of this concert which took place in the Jardin Theatre was closed by a choral piece conducted by Mark, the *Seal Lullaby* in the first half and the anthem from *Chess* which made a rousing finale.

The festival weeks engendered a great deal of excitement, pleasure, joy and camaraderie for us all but inevitably much stress was also involved. On the morning of the last opera performance I dashed out to speak to Mark before he left home and fell flat on my face on our drive. I let out a shrill shriek hoping to prevent Mark from driving off leaving me marooned and helpless on the drive. I need not have worried. My cry was loud enough to get everyone running towards me! I was soon surrounded by Mark, Ray, Tegan and the neighbours living opposite, Danielle and Jean-Luc.

"What's happened?"

"Where does it hurt? Don't move" and such like rang out as I lay there.

Ray fetched a pillow and a blanket to put over me while Jean-Luc summoned the *pompiers* to come and take me off to hospital in the ambulance.

"I hope this is not going to become a habit," I muttered, trying to smile.

Before I knew it, I was whisked off to Brignoles examined, X-rayed and cleaned up. Miraculously no bones were broken but there were grazes, cuts and bruises everywhere. My face in particular looked a real mess. However I was now ready to return home to have breakfast and get on with my busy day. Checking on my medication the doctor said:

"You are on Ribaroxaban which is a blood thinner. You must have a scan to make sure there is no haemorrhage in the brain and we must keep you here for some hours to be sure there is no problem."

The fall had occurred at about 7am and I was kept in hospital until almost 5.30pm without food or drink until the doctor was happy that it was safe to discharge me. I was more than ready for the nice meal Ray had ready for me when I got home! After resting up, I insisted on going to the final performance in Carcès but I did ask Michelle to introduce the show in my place. Thus ended the "*Festi'Val de Musique en Provence Verte.*" I was then persuaded that, at the age of 83, it was rather too much for me to undertake again in the future. I could not find anyone else ready to take on all the work involved with the presidency and secretariat of the Association. We left the *Festi'Val de Musique* in abeyance for a year but in 2018 when Mark, too, had other commitments which prevented him from resurrecting the festival, we regretfully decided to dissolve the association. All past and current members were invited to celebrate together what had been achieved during the lifetime of the association with an excellent meal at *Le Paracol* restaurant which had provided us with a much appreciated service throughout the festivals. Finally we gathered together for the very last time for an *apéritif dinatoire* in the Club de Loisirs. We hope that one day *Love to Sing Opera* will return to delight audiences with their splendid performances once more.

Now Ray and I will be able to make the most of our twilight years in travelling to far off places yet unseen while we are still fit enough to do so. We will have more time for our family and friends, too, and this past year I have even found time to write my memoirs, started at Mark's behest so he could learn more about his paternal antecedents. We are very much looking forward to more great family reunions to take place in our beloved Rhondda Valley. This summer sees the fiftieth wedding anniversary of my youngest brother Michael and his wife Carol, as well as our twenty-fifth wedding anniversary. Great plans are afoot to entice all five Stevens siblings to return with their families to the Rhondda to reminisce together once more over their happy upbringing in the valley. When eventually we will become too infirm to continue living in Provence, Ray and I hope to end our days in our flat in Wales. We feel very blessed indeed that the entire family is still able to meet up and can all make the journey back to their roots in the Rhondda to pay homage to the valley that formed them and helped to make them what they are today.

\* \* \* \* \*

# Epilogue

The return to our roots began with my marriage to Ray in 1993 when all my siblings made the journey back to the Rhondda with their children for our wedding. It continued with our 130th (joint) birthday celebration in 2004 just after our move to Penarth. 2014 saw the whole of the family return in force for two further big celebrations: Mary and Vince's fiftieth wedding anniversary in the summer and our 150th birthday celebration in the autumn.

Angie helped Mary and Vince organise a massive reunion in the Rhondda in July 2014. Having put them in touch with Reverend Paul Bigmore, the vicar of Ynyshir, a renewal of their marriage vows took place in Saint Anne's Church, where all four sisters had married many years before. We were all delighted to meet old friends again – Joyce Arthur, who had played the organ at Mary's wedding, was still organist at Saint Anne's in her mid nineties! However, it was a bitter sweet occasion as we were very sad to hear that our lovely old church was doomed to close permanently in the near future.

A small reception was held after the service in the church hall attended by all Mary and Vince's guests mingling with churchgoers with whom we had worshipped more than fifty years ago. We then all retired to the Heritage Park Hotel for a celebratory evening and dinner-dance together. People travelled from all over the world and all parts of Britain to surround the nucleus of the Stevens family swollen by the first full gathering of the Williams family. Returning from California, Mary and Vince's children, Steven and Sian, were thrilled to revisit old haunts still fondly remembered, with their own children, Emily and Evan and Annie May and Emma Rose. The following day, close family members gathered together in the Brynffynon Arms, Llanwonno, to round off the reunion with a typical Welsh pub lunch in an old familiar place. It was a very emotional get-together as we hugged one another happily breathing in the fresh mountain air of our youth and reminiscing.

Four months later our 150th birthday celebration also took place in the Heritage Park Hotel where we had held our wedding reception twenty-five years earlier. With my 80th birthday falling in October and Ray's 70th in December, we chose to celebrate them both in November, a month which also included Mark's and Mia's birthdays, so there was much to celebrate. Mark and Angie had suggested giving a party to celebrate my Big 80 and were joined by Rachel and Tim to make it a joint celebration for their father's Big 70. Top class entertainment was provided by Mark and Julie and a little jazz group played background music while we dined and danced later. Angie gave a lively speech and read out Mary's congratulations and Jane's poem before proposing the toast and lighting the multitude of candles on the special birthday cake while the strains of Happy Birthday rang out. Towards the end of a perfect evening our competent pianists, Ann and Nicola, struck up to accompany us singing all our favourite Welsh folk songs handed down to us by our grandparents and parents. Our hearts were bursting with joy.

To carry on the tradition and to show his love for his homeland, Michael, although having lived most of his life in Australia and Canada, brought his entire family back to Wales in his turn. He and Carol celebrated fifty years together by holidaying with their children and grandchildren in Wales culminating in a party in our familiar venue once more. It was held on 28 July, Mammy's birthday. We had hoped that all the Stevens siblings would be reunited as usual but, unfortunately, Morfydd was unable to attend as her husband Bernard was too poorly to travel. Arms around one another, Michael and Mark led the choral singing and everyone joined in. Rhys had brought his two girls from Alberta and Rheanne, her two boys from Vancouver while Gareth brought the star of the show, little eighteen-month-old Maya from Majorca to meet up with all their cousins in the old country. It was yet another jubilant international gathering.

Not wanting to intrude on Michael's party, we invited everyone to celebrate our twenty-fifth wedding anniversary with a champagne reception given in the lounge in Cwrt Jubilee on the following day. Tegan had flown over from Jersey where she is tasting the world of work in her first job as a paralegal. Together with Angie, she was invaluable in helping us organise our celebration. It was every bit as jolly as the earlier dos and included my little contribution of a limerick written to tell of Michael and Carol's meeting and life together. Of course it ended with a rendition of the unmissable "Three Little Sisters" performed by Ann, Mary and me. Not to be left out, Michael stepped in afterwards to take Morfydd's place and caused quite a sensation! Tearful farewells were avoided by the fact that everyone had planes or trains to catch and things to do, so suddenly the majority had disappeared and a few of us were left chatting about how certain family members had changed or grown up or had not changed at all!

Two more exciting trips are planned before the end of 2018. Ray, Angie and I will take a two week cruise in October visiting five beautiful cities in the Baltic, including the fascinating Saint Petersburg, while Mark plans a three week tour of Pakistan in December, hoping to become re-acquainted with the cousins he has not seen since his infancy.

Naturally, whenever we are together in the Rhondda, a pilgrimage to Trealaw cemetery is a must. We take flowers – pink roses especially – and prayers to the old cemetery on the side of the green valley where our ancestors are laid to rest. Great-granddaughter Annie May from California reads the name of the great Welsh lady after whom she was named and Angie arranges on her grandparents' grave the fresh long-stemmed pink-purple orchids she has brought back from Singapore especially for them. A prayer of thanks is said for Annie May and Tom as all their descendants bow their heads whilst keeping their eyes fixed on the black marble grave stone set against the green mountains of their beloved Rhondda Valley. They know their roots are here.

Although everyone has returned home temporarily for the reunion, the family is in fact scattered all over the world. At different periods in our lives, one or other of us has lived in Pakistan, China, Japan, Australia, USA, Canada, Mexico, Ukraine, Germany, Italy, Majorca, France and Jersey. Nevertheless we remain a close knit family keeping in regular contact by phone and internet. The desire for education and the love of music are themes which run through our lives. So many of us have passed part or the whole of our working lives in education, either as teachers or lecturers, and many have brought much joy by making music and performing in an amateur or professional capacity. Others have embraced the medical profession becoming doctors, nurses and dentists. Still others have dabbled in the cut throat world of business or entered the law profession. All this diversity stems from the courage, determination and drive of one tiny but infinitely strong woman. Imbued with the Spirit of the Rhondda, Annie May Stevens, together with her ever loyal partner Tom, built a secure foundation with love and sacrifice, inspiring in their children a deep respect for education. They also endowed them with a sense of adventure and the confidence to sally forth from their tiny mining village in the Rhondda into the wide world and carve out places for themselves.

Most of my siblings have spent large parts of their lives away from the land where they were born. Morfydd began teaching in London and has spent the rest of her life with her family in the Home Counties of England although one of her children now lives in Australia. After obtaining her BMus in Cardiff University, Ann spent two years living in Italy before returning to take up her career again as a music teacher in the Midlands where she still lives since her retirement. She continues to train her church choir and plays the organ at church on occasion.

After qualifying as a nurse in King's College Hospital, Mary accompanied her husband to California where she obtained all the necessary qualifications to enable her to nurse in America. There she carved out an excellent career in some of the top hospitals nursing such famous people as Richard Burton, Elizabeth Taylor and President Reagan before taking on a ground-breaking project. She became the first person in the world to rescue quadriplegic patients from wards where they were left to simply vegetate and care for them in her New Start Homes. This entailed a great struggle, including the making of new laws, and culminated in her being honoured by the President for changing the face of rehabilitation for severely disabled individuals in the USA. She lives in California with her family where she is still very much involved with charities supporting disabled people.

279

Michael, the youngest sibling, after taking his degree at Bristol, qualified in Sport and Education at Loughborough before emigrating to Canada to teach in Toronto. Shortly afterwards, he emigrated to Australia where all his three children were born. He had a wide and varied career running departments in Science and Maths while always taking charge of rugby training in all his schools. He brought his teams to compete against our Welsh rugby sides as well as playing himself into his forties. He referees both rugby and football and now lives in Canada where two of his children also live. His youngest son has lived in Japan, Korea and South America before settling in Majorca where he now lives.

None of the original Stevens family lives in the Rhondda any longer, but wherever we end our days, the Rhondda will always remain locked in our hearts as the home to which we always love to return. Our valley, green and beautiful once more, still acts as a magnet drawing us back time and again to celebrate our love for our home and the long departed loved ones that together forged us into the close family that we remain today. Our roots remain firmly, and proudly, planted here in the rich black soil of the valley that nurtured and sheltered us from birth.

# Further information about Roots in the Rhondda

Dear Reader, I hope you enjoyed reading my Memoir. If you would like more background information, and/or like to view more photos, videos etc., please visit the Facebook page:

www.facebook.com/Roots-in-the-Rhondda-110816796983434

# About the author

Patricia Luther Mellor, née Stevens, was born on 22 October 1934 in Ynyshir, Rhondda Valley, South Wales, the eldest of five children brought up in an impoverished coal mining community. Unlike the vast majority of their contemporaries, Pat and her siblings escaped the poverty into which they were born by the sheer determination and efforts of their parents to ensure that they all had a good education, something that had been denied to them. All five children seized this chance and carved a niche for themselves in the wider world.

Pat attained a place to study languages in Bristol University in 1953 and was sent to Paris where she obtained a Diplôme de Civilisation Française from the Sorbonne. Her honours degree in French with Latin in 1956 was followed by a Certificate of Education also at Bristol. Finally she was awarded an MEd from the University of Wales, Swansea in 1976. She began a career in education teaching in all types of schools before marrying Archie Jonathan Luther in 1959. They settled in Bristol where she had two children, Mark and Angie, before Archie died suddenly and Pat went to spend a year with his family in Pakistan. She later returned to South Wales to take up her teaching career once more, eventually retiring as Head of Languages in Treorchy Comprehensive School, Rhondda, in 1990.

While in Treorchy, she inaugurated French Exchange visits between The Rhondda and The Dordogne, France, which took place successfully for many years. In 1992, she established the first magazine for the Federation of Retired Members of the Teaching Union, NASUWT, called *FORMAT* and edited it for a number of years.

In 2015, she created a French Association "Les Amis du Festival de Musique" bringing a troop of young British opera singers, directed by her son Mark, to her village in France to establish cooperation between French and British musicians inaugurating an annual music festival in La Provence Verte.

Pat now lives mostly in Le Val in the South of France with her husband Raymond Mellor. She shares her time between her homes in Le Val and Penarth and her travels around the world, though she still retains strong ties with the Rhondda, the home of her heart.

Printed in Great Britain
by Amazon